THE CHALLENGE OF
BASIC
CHRISTIAN
COMMUNITIES

THE CHALLENGE OF BASIC CHRISTIAN COMMUNITIES

**Papers from the
International Ecumenical Congress of Theology,
February 20–March 2, 1980, São Paulo, Brazil**

*Edited by
Sergio Torres and John Eagleson*

Translated by John Drury

ORBIS BOOKS

Maryknoll, New York 10545

Second Printing, September 1982

The Catholic Foreign Mission Society of America (Maryknoll) recruits and trains people for overseas missionary service. Through Orbis Books Maryknoll aims to foster the international dialogue that is essential to mission. The books published, however, reflect the opinions of their authors and are not meant to represent the official position of the society.

Papers at the International Ecumenical Congress of Theology were delivered in Spanish, Portuguese, or English. Unless otherwise indicated, translations for this volume were made by John Drury.

Library of Congress Cataloging in Publication Data

International Ecumenical Congress of Theology
   (1980: São Paulo, Brazil)
   The challenge of basic Christian communities.

   Includes bibliographical references.
   1. Christian communities—Catholic Church—
Congresses. 2. Christian communities—Latin
America—Congresses. 3. Christian communities—
Congresses. I. Torres, Sergio. II. Eagleson,
John. III. Title.
BX2347.72.L37157   1980   261.8   81-38361
ISBN 0-88344-503-4 (pbk.)   AACR2

Contents

2311439

PART I
CHRISTIAN PRESENCE IN
SITUATIONS OF DOMINATION

PART II
REFLECTIONS ON
POPULAR CHRISTIAN COMMUNITIES

PART III
PERSONAL EXPERIENCES
AND LITURGIES

PART IV
FINAL DOCUMENTS

PART V
EVALUATION AND INTERPRETATION

To
Archbishop Oscar Arnulfo Romero,
Archbishop of San Salvador,
1917–1980

Preface

It is eminently fitting to dedicate this volume to the most prominent Christian martyr of recent church history, Oscar Arnulfo Romero, Archbishop of San Salvador, murdered while celebrating Mass on March 24, 1980.

Those of us who met in São Paulo February 20–March 2, 1980, from forty-two countries for the International Ecumenical Congress of Theology had him and his persecuted church very much in mind as we heard and discussed the papers here published. The reasons are not hard to figure out. Three days before our meeting he had read as part of his homily the now famous letter he wrote to President Carter. It was an urgent plea not to send U.S. military assistance to the Salvadoran junta because "instead of favoring greater justice and peace in El Salvador it will most surely intensify the injustice and repression of the common people who are organized to struggle for respect of their most basic human rights." That night, YSAX, the Catholic radio station over which his country heard him every Sunday, was dynamited into silence.

We frequently mentioned him in São Paulo because the Congress was an extended theological reflection of something to which he gave top pastoral priority, the so-called base-level communities, or more accurately, the Christian communities of the common people (CCPs). Perhaps he took more seriously than any other bishop the "preferential option for the poor," the official position of the Latin American Bishops' Conference both at Medellín (1968) and Puebla (1979). But as was repeatedly confirmed in São Paulo by bishops, theologians, and leaders of the CCPs, in today's Latin America the Christian defense and self-defense of the common people are inevitably accompanied by martyrdom. And we knew that was especially true of the church of El Salvador.

As a Presbyterian layman from Mexico, a naturalized U.S. citizen, and also a personal friend of Archbishop Romero, I was often gripped in São Paulo by the premonition of his own martyrdom. I could not help repeatedly recalling my last conversation with him three months before. I had traveled to San Salvador to carry one more message of solidarity to him and his church from the National Council of Churches of the U.S.A. for which I worked at the time. As he took me on his pastoral rounds, invariably someone would voice concern for his safety. At my prompting, he acknowledged with reticence the increasing frequency of the threats on his life. "I have no appetite for dying but for living," he told me. It was a springtime for his people, never before so faithful or courageous in the face of unprecedented persecution. He could not lay claim to a security his flock did not enjoy. "I must continue to be as vulnerable as they are."

In his last broadcast homily on March 23, 1980 (YSAX had just been rebuilt), he let go of what little security was left to him. He made an appeal to soldiers that was tantamount to a call for insubordination: "Do not kill! No soldier is obliged to obey an order counter to the law of God." And he fulminated against the government with the anguish of an indignant prophet: ". . . in the name of God and in the name of this long-suffering people, whose laments rise to heaven everyday more tumultuous, I beseech you, I beg you, I command you in the name of God: stop the repression!" His fate was sealed. The next day, while he stood at the altar of a hospital chapel preaching of death and resurrection, he was felled by an assassin's bullet.

The story is so well known by now that I fear for its misuse. It is the best news the Christian church has heard in a long time, and it is also an appalling crime that keeps on repeating itself in the fallen lives of more and more martyrs, most of them anonymous except to their friends and kin. "Stop the repression" is still the most valid demand of Archbishop Romero's legacy. Must Christ continue to be crucified over and over again in the person of the most vulnerable of his sisters and brothers?

The reading of these São Paulo papers should help especially Christians of the United States to understand the forces of death and life involved in the martyrdom and hope of the poor who have heard and believed the Good News. We need to hear the harsh truths and the redeeming prospects held out to us by fellow Christians in lands where the power of our nation is feared, and where the hope of our conversion is earnestly prayed for. Perhaps the most appropriate tribute to Archbishop Romero is our willingness to hear his voice as it echoes through the pages of this volume. The worst that can happen is that we will be offended. The best will be a new encounter with the Christ who, being rich, became poor for our sake.

JORGE LARA-BRAUD, *Director*
Council on Theology and Culture
Presbyterian Church in the U.S.

Messages of Greeting

LETTER OF GREETING
Cardinal Johannes Willebrands (Holland),
President of the Vatican Secretariat for Christian Unity

Secretariat for Christian Unity
Prot. N. 124/80
Vatican City
January 9, 1980

To: His Eminence
Cardinal Paulo Evaristo Arns, O.F.M.
Archbishop of São Paulo

Dear Cardinal:

You have been gracious enough to send me the program for an international convention of an ecumenical character that will take place in São Paulo in February 1980.

In Brazil, as in Latin America in general, the ecumenical movement has its own specific and distinctive problems that give it a character of its own.

Hoping that the Brazilian Episcopal Conference, and in a larger sense, CELAM, will be able to make a new effort from the Catholic side to promote the ecumenical movement in Latin America, I assure you that the Secretariat for Christian Unity stands ready to help with its advice and experience.

While wishing much success for the convention in São Paulo, I must indicate that the theme proposed seems to relate more to the jurisdiction of the Papal Commission for Justice and Peace.

On the occasion of the New Year I send you my best personal wishes for your own pastoral and apostolic work as well as my fraternal sentiments in the Lord.

Cardinal Johannes Willebrands
President

OPENING ADDRESS
Cardinal Paulo Evaristo Arns (Brazil), Archbishop of São Paulo

Beloved Brothers and Sisters in Jesus Christ:

Welcome to Brazil and to our archdiocese!

It was with great joy that, a year ago, during the Episcopal Conference in Puebla, we learned that the city of São Paulo had been chosen, by the Ecumenical Association of Theologians, as the place for this Congress. Others had been held in Africa and in Asia. In the Third World, there only remained Latin America. Our city is only a point on the map of this immense continent and we are only the hosts, without any power of decision over the themes that will orientate your work. This time, if you wish "to complain to the bishop"—as our people say—speak to our dear brother, Bishop Paulo Ayres Mattos, the person who is really responsible for this event. However, we are grateful for the invitation we received from the directors of the Association to be honorary president of the Congress.

"If it is not the Lord who builds the house, the work of the bricklayers is worthless," says the psalmist. We are certain that this Congress is one more brick that the Holy Spirit—Author of our unity—is placing on the work of ecumenism. In this line, we would like to remember the recognition given at Puebla to the "growing interest in ecumenism among us, especially since Vatican II. We find proof of this in joint efforts to promote knowledge, appreciation, and the spread of Sacred Scripture; in increasing frequent private and public prayers for unity, which find particular expression in the week dedicated to prayers for unity; in inter-confessional meetings and reflection groups; in joint efforts for the advancement of human beings, the defense of human rights, and the construction of justice and peace. In some places people have reached the stage of bilateral or multi-lateral church councils on various levels" (Puebla, no. 1107).

Our wishes are that the pastoral priorities of our archdiocese be present among your preoccupations during these days: the intransigent defense of human rights, chiefly of the prisoners, the tortured, and the minorities such as the indigenous peoples, the blacks, as well as women, in whose emancipation Pope John XXIII saw a "sign of the times"; a real commitment to the labor world, so that the urban and rural salaried workers can free themselves from the condition of being exploited; the incentive to multiply the basic Christian communities which, according to Puebla, "embody the Church's preferential love for the common people" (no. 643); the support of the periphery of the city, not only in the geographic sense but above all in the social sense, of those who are on the outskirts of the channels of participation and decision of the society. The gospel of Jesus obliges us to make all of these the center of our liberating *diakonia*.

We wish all of you to pay close attention to the fact that this is a congress of theology, and not of theologians. We came here to meet people from the grassroots, indigenous peoples, farmers, and workers who in their Christian communities, make theology in the measure that, in their theological life, they reflect the faith-commitment relation as a requirement of love. The theologians are those who capture and systematize this lived experience of the People of God. In this sense, this Congress should constitute a space in which the clamor of the oppressed can be heard. May the Christian communities of Asia, Africa, and Latin America mutually enrich themselves, so that "while preserving unity in essentials, . . . all members of the Church, according to the office entrusted to each, preserve a proper freedom in the various forms of spiritual life and discipline, in the variety of liturgical rites, and even in the theological elaborations of revealed truth. In all things let charity be exercised. If the faithful are true to this course of action, they will be giving ever richer expression to the authentic Catholicity of the Church, and, at the same time, to her apostolicity" (Vatican II, *Unitatis Redintegratio,* no. 4).

In our country and, especially, in our archdiocese, ecumenism, long before being a theme of encounters and conferences, has been the fruit of our struggle for justice. Orthodox, Protestants, Jews, and Catholics have met in the same evangelical challenge of the defense of the rights of the poor and oppressed (Luke 4). In this our common task, we verify that the Holy Father, Pope John Paul II, manifested in his allocution of last January 23 the objective of the Week of Prayer for Christian Unity: "The division between Christians is a happening contrary to the demands of the Kingdom of God, opposed to the very nature of the Church that is the beginning and the instrument of this Kingdom." The Holy Father says that the Kingdom of God is not a spiritualized rhetorical figure; on the contrary, "it is rooted in the concrete history of mankind. But how can it pass in silence that, in our times, the rights of man are violated?" (*L'Osservatore Romano*, January 27, 1980). We hope that, in the same way, this Congress will not be silent about the obligation of the Church of Christ to the oppressed multitudes of the Third World, because only in this way will humanity believe in the Church as the sacrament of the Kingdom of Justice and Love, realizing the appeal of unity in love that the Son of God left us (John 17).

We celebrate today, in the Church, the opening of the season of Lent. However, we do not want this Congress to be, for you, harsh penance but rather a sign and instrument of the Easter horizon, a happening of fraternal joy in the Spirit of the Lord, present where one or two are united in his name.

May the love of Christ be in your hearts.

—Translated by the EATWOT staff

MESSAGE TO THE CONFERENCE
J. R. Chandran (India),
President of the Ecumenical Association of Third World Theologians

It gives me great pleasure to greet you on behalf of the Ecumenical Association of Third World Theologians. This is a conference mainly of theologians from the Latin American region held under the auspices of the Ecumenical Association of Third World Theologians. The Ecumenical Association asked a group of church leaders and theologians related to the Association to organize the congress on our behalf. They met and organized a planning committee with the Methodist bishop from Rio de Janeiro, Paulo Ayres Mattos as the president.

In my capacity as president of EATWOT I welcome all the participants and express my gratitude to the Latin American organizing committee for the excellent work they have done to prepare for this meeting. Whenever we have a continental conference of Third World theologians we have observers or fraternal participants from the other continents. Accordingly we have at this meeting a few participants from Africa and Asia, and I extend a warm welcome to them. I am myself an Asian, and even though I am supposed to speak on behalf of the Ecumenical Association, you will pardon me if I begin by making a comment as an Asian Christian. This is not my first visit to Latin America. I have made some brief visits to Mexico, Paraguay, and Peru. But my knowledge of Latin America is still very limited and dependent on my reading of the present Latin American theologians and my personal acquaintance with several of them. One of the facts of the Asian reality is that Christians constitute a small minority and critics of Christianity continue to associate it with the history of colonial and imperialist expansion of the West. Latin America also has been seen as another example of colonial and imperialist domination, and the link between Christianity and the Latin American regimes has been seen as evidence of the use of Christianity for the legitimizing of unjust socio-economic structures all through the centuries. In this context the discovery of movements in Latin American countries to conscientize the people to oppose the status quo of injustice and oppression and the role played by church leaders like Bishop Helder Camara and liberation theologians, Catholic and Protestant, for the reinterpretation of the gospel of Jesus Christ as the power of God against dehumanizing structures was a tremendous encouragement to our Christian witness in Asia. Therefore as an Asian Christian I am grateful for this opportunity to dialogue and confer with Latin American theologians.

As president of EATWOT I would like to explain what EATWOT stands for. In some ways we do not know fully yet what this movement is. It has come into being as a new work of the Holy Spirit for the discernment of the reality of the presence and work of Christ today. We have yet to understand and experience where the Holy Spirit is leading us. There are, however, certain important insights of our understanding and commitment expressed in the name of the Association.

First it is an ecumenical association. Even though the original proposal for an association like this came from the African Roman Catholic theologians, because of their conviction that theology in Africa cannot simply be a repetition of the theology which had been formulated in Europe, a wider discussion of the proposal led to the organizing of an ecumenical association. This was because what the African Roman Catholics were concerned about was the

experience of Protestant theologians also in Africa and other regions where
the churches had inherited the theological formulations of the West. Therefore the Association consists of theologians from the Roman Catholic, Protestant, and Orthodox churches. The leadership is also ecumenical. I belong
to the Church of South India, a United Church with close links with the
churches of the Protestant tradition. The executive secretary, Father Sergio
Torres, is Roman Catholic. The program coordinator, Sister Virginia Fabella, from the Philippines, is also Roman Catholic. The Advisory Committee consists of an equal number of Protestants and Catholics from Asia,
Africa, and Latin America.

Secondly, it is an association of Third World theologians. The expression
"Third World" is not a happy one, but it was accepted as more adequately
descriptive of the main concern of the association than any other term. While
broadly it has the geographic connotation of the continental regions of
Africa, Asia, and Latin America, its main meaning is something deeper and
more radical than geographic. It is meant to include the section of humanity
subjected to the colonialist imperialist domination of the West or North
Atlantic nations, the so-called First World. The Association also includes
people in the First World who were originally from the Third World continents and are involved in struggle against different forms of exploitation and
oppression.

It is also important to bear in mind that the category of Third World
theologians does not represent simply professional theologians, but those
committed to the interpretation of the power of the gospel of Jesus Christ in
different ways, including active participation in groups or movements for the
transformation of socio-political structures. The goal of the Association is
certainly not to perpetuate a new association, however stimulating the fellowship in this new enterprise might be, but to work toward the overcoming
or the elimination of thirdworldness. Therefore we share the insights of our
discussions and conferences with the theologians of the First World. We have
also involved the First World representatives in our enterprise in the matter of
financial support. In addition we are planning to have a meeting in another
two years for dialogue between Third World theologians and First and Second World theologians. Our objective is the development of a theology which
will meaningfully serve the gospel of Jesus Christ and help in the evangelistic
task of making him known as the one who breaks down all walls of hostility
and oppression and unites all peoples in a single new humanity. This would
mean the removal of all vestiges of thirdworldness. Therefore, the Ecumenical Association of Third World Theologians has a built-in agenda for
working toward the time when the Association will no longer be necessary.

It should also be pointed out that while the Ecumenical Association of
Third World Theologians is not an association of professional theologians,
its basic concern is theological. However, our theological reflection in the
light of the Third World realities has compelled us to shift from the traditional epistemology to a praxis-oriented, inductive epistemology. Christo-

logy, ecclesiology, soteriology, etc., continue to be our major concerns of theological reflection. But instead of uncritically accepting the formulations of the past we seek to discern under the guidance and power of the Holy Spirit the reality of the presence and ministry of the crucified and risen Lord in contemporary situations and then reflect on our faith and action response to that reality. This was brought out quite forcefully in two meetings in Asia—the Conference on Theological Education held in Manila in February 1978, and the Asian Conference of Third World Theologians held in Colombo, January 1979. Both conferences affirmed the reality of the presence of the Holy and the presence of Christ where members of the believing community were involved in the struggles of people against injustice, oppression, torture, and other forms of dehumanization, struggles through which people were seeking the fullness of human dignity.

I am happy that the theme of this conference is the ecclesiology of basic Christian communities. In a real sense this is a theme relevant for theological reflection everywhere, particularly in all Third World regions. The outcome of this conference can make a significant contribution to Christian theology today. It is with great expectation therefore that I greet you.

May God accept our work and make it a blessing to the world we are called to serve as disciples of Jesus.

GREETINGS FROM THE WORLD COUNCIL OF CHURCHES
Emilio Castro (Uruguay),
Director, WCC World Missionary Committee

It is a pleasure and a privilege for me to convey to this conference the best wishes of the World Council of Churches and its secretary general, Philip Potter, himself a Third World theologian.

We have followed with sympathy and interest the various conferences of the Ecumenical Association of Third World Theologians which have been held in the past, and we have high hopes for the work of this particular conference. We have made use of the theological material from previous meetings. It has enriched worldwide ecumenical dialogue. Various committees of the World Council of Churches have utilized this material as a valuable contribution to our ongoing effort to maintain our missionary obedience as the Church of Jesus Christ today.

The Ecumenical Movement has become a real encounter between cultures. When it began, its main concern was rapprochement between various Christian confessions and denominations. Today it has been enriched by the reality of the church worldwide, of a church implanted in the many and varied cultures on our continents. Reflection on the church's responsibility vis-à-vis differing cultural contexts offers enrichment to its duty of obedience to the Lord of history in these new situations. It also adds complexity to ecumenical dialogue and debate on the international level.

The beautiful reality of the Church of Jesus Christ sinking its roots into different historical grounds allows for a more suitable and responsible fidelity on the local level. It also facilitates mutual inspiration, correction, and questioning of an ecumenical cast.

It should not surprise anyone that theological and intercultural dialogue within the church entails reciprocal questioning and produces conflicts, contradictions, and temporary misunderstandings.

The gospel of Jesus Christ is a perduring summons to repentance, a call to rethink our attitudes and seek out new forms of obedience. This summons comes to us within the ecclesial community through reciprocal correction motivated by love for the truth and the search for it.

This conference will not escape the law of conflictual elements and passionate feelings that are part of every sincere quest for the truth. Hence we do not ask a mild, peaceful atmosphere for your meetings. Instead we ask for the presence and inspiration of the Holy Spirit, who is able to use even our disagreements to lead us to unsuspected truths.

The gospel of Jesus Christ obliges us to introduce the totality of our people's lives into our intraecclesial debate. We are living in an age when relations between nations are marked with the brand of dependence on the international level. So in our theological reflection we must consider solutions for the global problems of justice that divide our world.

Debate within the church will be marked by conflict and passion. Taking its stand amid the conflicts of this world, it will look for concrete signs and invitations to greater and better obedience. Reflection and discussion are also conflictual in themselves because they embody a struggle with God, a search for the response of the Holy Spirit to the yearnings of the common people who are trying to live their faith and their fidelity to the gospel message amid oppressive circumstances.

We trust that the theme of this conference—"The Ecclesiology of Christian Communities of the Common People"—will make a solid contribution to discussions going on within the World Council of Churches. This coming May (1980) we will hold our own World Missionary Conference in Melbourne, Australia. Its theme will be "Thy Kingdom Come," and the proclamation of the Good News to the poor will be one of the basic poles of reflection. The conclusions of your conference will be passed along to the participants in our meeting as an aid and a stimulus for their own reflection.

I also want to let you know that the Central Committee of the World Council of Churches will meet in August of this year. It will receive the report of the Melbourne conference, and also a study on the church of the poor that has been under preparation for three years by our committee for the participation of the churches in development.

The delegates at our August meeting will formulate a declaration expressing the commitment of the gospel message to the poor. At that time I am sure that your documents, reflections, struggles, and prayers will serve as a help and an inspiration to all of us.

I want to greet and thank the executive committee of the Association and the organizers of this conference. We in the World Council of Churches have lent our support in the past, and will continue to lend our support in the future, to the efforts of various ecumenical organizations to elaborate theological perspectives that combine the universal and the local and that foster mutual challenging within the bosom of the universal church.

In the conviction that your conference is an integral part of this broader ecumenical movement, I greet you on behalf of the World Council of Churches. Our prayers go with you, and we look forward to the fruits of your labor as a gift from God to the universal church. God bless you.

WELCOMING ADDRESS AT THE OPENING SESSION
Beatriz Melano Couch (Argentina), President of the Conference

Dear Sisters and Brothers:

Before I open the first session of this conference, I would like to introduce myself. I am Beatriz Melano Couch from Argentina, and I am a professor of theology at ISEDET, the Institute for Theological Studies in Buenos Aires.

By way of introduction I would like to share three deep feelings with you. Those feelings fill my heart with emotion and gratitude as we begin the Fourth International Ecumenical Conference of Third World Theology.

First of all, it seems to me that this conference is taking place at a historic moment. Looking out over this assembly of delegates from all the countries of Latin America, and from many other countries on other continents, we cannot help but express our gratitude for the maturity of the Latin American church and for the progress achieved in recent years.

We have gotten here by overcoming many obstacles, and we are determined to move ahead with our work of evaluating and planning for the future. We do so with our trust placed in God and with a determination to move ahead with sureness and realism.

This assembly represents a step forward in Christian obedience for the Latin American church. We have gotten beyond the somewhat naive optimism and somewhat closed-minded dogmatism of earlier years. That is why I detect a new sense of joy, happiness, and peace in this conference.

Secondly, it seems to me that our hope is more realistic because it has been purified in suffering. It has been said that Latin America can be compared to a huge cross stretching from north to south and from east to west. All of us have gone through suffering. Right now I need not detail the *via crucis* traversed by many countries and by many of our brothers and sisters. In the course of the conference we surely will have an opportunity to tell our own stories and to reach out with hands and hearts for an embrace of solidarity and hope.

We know that the Resurrection comes after the Cross. We recall the biblical dictum: no redemption without the shedding of blood. It comforts us and impels us to continue our fight.

We are certain that each of us will leave this conference with our courage renewed, ready to carry on our task in our own country, our eyes fixed on the near or far-distant day of our liberation.

Finally, I would like to say a word of thanks to God, and to the organizers of this conference, for the presence of women and their integral participation at this meeting. I have never been at any conference, aside from ones for women only, at which there was such a significant proportion of women. And this fact is all the more important when we realize that this is a *theological* conference.

We women are tired of it all. We are not in a mood to keep on accepting the marginalization and discrimination practiced by society and our churches. Living in the context of the Third World, we feel a threefold oppression and discrimination: sex discrimination, because we are women; racial discrimination, when we are blacks or indigenous peoples; and class discrimination, when it comes to economics or relations with the affluent countries.

Our hope is that in this conference we will be able to move a step closer to overcoming these obstacles. In such moments as this we already detect signs that it is possible to look forward to the egalitarian integration of women into every level of life and reality.

May the canticle of Mary, the Magnificat, and the promises of Jesus guide us at this conference so that we, in a spirit of openness and love, will be wise enough to carry on the ministry to which the Lord has called us.

1

Introduction

Sergio Torres (Chile)

As we begin our work I feel the need to thank God and to proclaim Jesus as Lord and Savior. It is good to recall the words of the Second Letter to the Corinthians: "Indeed, as the sufferings of Christ overflow to us, so, through Christ, does our consolation overflow" (2 Cor. 1:5). This is the sign of Latin America at this hour: the confrontation between "suffering" and "hope," between "oppression" and "liberation."

This interpretation can be extended to the whole world. We can read theologically the situation at an international level as a dialectical relation between the "sufferings" of Christ and the power of his resurrection.

It is in the light of this sign of "suffering" and of "hope" that I wish to make my presentation: to discern, in the first place, this dialectic in the Third World, to help to define the theme and the spirit of our Congress, and finally, to celebrate the presence of representatives from so many countries.

THE "SUFFERINGS" AND THE "CONSOLATION"
OF CHRIST IN THE THIRD WORLD

We cannot forget that our life as believers and our theological efforts to formulate and communicate faith in Jesus Christ are worked at within a great historical contradiction: the growing division between the rich countries and the poor countries.

The poverty and the exploitation of the countries of the "periphery" constitute the greatest challenge for the disciples of Jesus Christ in the world today.

Our association does not want to fall into compromising alliances, as has happened in the past with slavery and colonialism. With vigor and humility we aspire to be a prophetic voice denouncing the structural causes of oppression. However, it is not enough to diagnose or to denounce. That is only the

This introduction is an edited version of the Opening Address of the Congress.

1

first step. We have to go further. Christians and theologians live in specific countries. We must participate in the profound movement of history, which under the guidance of the Spirit impels the poor and oppressed to struggle for their liberation. It is in this struggle that we Christians seek to express, communicate, and celebrate ecclesially our faith in Jesus, Our Lord. We must look carefully at what is happening in our lands, discern the transformations of history in this hour, interpret "the signs of the times" and read the "sufferings" and the "liberating power" of Christ on the faces and in the lives of the women and men of this continent.

We should recall two recent ecclesial events: the Conference of the Catholic Bishops (CELAM) held in Puebla, Mexico, in 1979, and the Assembly of the Protestant Churches at Oaxtepec, Mexico, in 1978.[1]

The Catholic bishops, citing John Paul II, said in Puebla: "Viewing it in the light of faith, we see the growing gap between the rich and poor as a scandal and a contradiction to Christian existence. The luxury of a few becomes an insult to the wretched poverty of the vast masses. This is contrary to the plan of the Creator and to the honor that is due Him" (Puebla, no. 28).[2]

THE SPIRIT AND THEME OF THE CONGRESS

To define the nature and spirit of the Congress, I invite you to hear the words of the Gospel: "At that time Jesus exclaimed, 'I bless you, Father, Lord of heaven and of earth, for hiding these things from the learned and the clever and revealing them to mere children. Yes, Father, for that is what you pleased to do!" (Matt. 11:25–26).

We must begin this Congress in this spirit. Let it not be just an academic discussion, but rather an interchange concerning the faith experience of our communities. We are not concerned so much about conclusions as with the perception of the presence and the voice of the Spirit of God in the sufferings and experiences that we will share.

The Congress is a meeting of theology and not a meeting of theologians. To do theology is to give reason for the common hope of the people of God. Let us listen to the wisdom of the people and let us work with the understanding of the oppressed, for it is they who are best prepared to listen to the Word of God. May the power of understanding of the "important" people and the "experts" not crush the creativity and the voice of our grassroots people.

This attitude demands a profound conversion. During these days, we will give a privileged place to the moments of common prayer to allow ourselves to be converted, to ask pardon for our sins, to encourage us in our search for God.

But we must define the spirit of this Congress more concretely. Our attitude is positive, one of openness and collaboration. Many of us were in Oaxtepec or Puebla. Those of us who were in Puebla were invited by our bishops as personal consultants. Some feared that this would become a protest group. Some even used the absurd term "anti-Puebla."

The facts gave the lie to such fantasies. The group of theologians made a positive contribution that was publicly recognized by the president of CELAM, Cardinal Alosio Lorscheider.

The same positive spirit inspires this assembly. We are a small group, without official representation, who have agreed to dialogue as Protestants and Catholics from different countries of the world about the common experiences of the Christian communities.

The Protestants of the continent consider the Oaxtepec Assembly as a new starting point in the history of efforts toward unity. Catholics find a wealth of inspiration in Puebla. For a year now we have worked to apply the recommendations found in the Presentation of the Final Document, signed by the co-presidents: "These guidelines are of profound interest for our pastoral activity. A process of assimilating and interiorizing their content must take place at every level, if they are to be implemented" (Puebla, "Presentation").

Participation in this Congress is one more step in this process of assimilation and interiorization.

On the other hand, acceptance of the invitation to this Congress appears to us as the exercise of an inalienable right, the right of freedom of assembly and of expression: Oaxtepec and Puebla criticized the violation of human rights. We are inspired by these statements, for we believe that liberty and justice must be lived out within our churches.

Nevertheless, we cannot deny that there are divisions within the church. One of the documents of Oaxtepec asserted: "Our starting point is an awareness of our division."[3] The bishops at Puebla, for their part, stated:

> Brothers and sisters, do not be impressed by reports that the episcopate is divided. There are differences of opinion and outlook, but the truth is that we live the principle of collegiality, complementing each other in accordance with our God-given capabilities. Only in this way will we be able to face up to the great challenge of evangelization in Latin America's present and future ["Message to the Peoples of Latin America," no. 4].

Once we have recognized our differences, we can dialogue and make progress in our discussion in a climate of liberating "communion and participation." Such is the intention of this Congress: to contribute to "communion and participation," as was recognized also at Puebla, from the standpoint of a preferential option for the poor.

GENERAL THEME

The general theme for the Congress is "Ecclesiology of the popular Christian communities." The theme has an international dimension; it is a dialogue concerning the experience of the life of the church among all the participants. As in our previous conferences, however (Accra, 1977; Sri Lanka, 1979), the discussions will be focused especially on the ecclesial experience of the continent on which the conference takes place, in this case, Latin America.

The non-Latin Americans are invited to share their own reality, to raise questions about our experience, and to help us to express ourselves better.

There will not be sharp divisions in the agenda.

In accord with our methodology, practice and theory, action and reflection, discussion and prayer, social analysis and theological reflection, form part of a single process.

But there will be different stages in the process. As the Congress begins I see five stages, at the same time allowing for later changes. Let me list them quickly.

Stage 1: Interchange of Experiences

Priority will be given to personal encounter, to a discovery of the existential richness of each other, to living a collective experience of solidarity, to a celebration of the life of the Spirit of the popular Christian communities of the Third World.

The first two days will be dedicated to this interchange of experiences and to an analysis of the life-giving and stagnating factors in the church on the Latin American continent.

On the basis of our experiences we will try to discover the objective, collective reality of our people, thus going beyond our subjective, individual perceptions. Our theology should take unto itself, in the light of faith and in the communion of the church, the historical memory and the theoretical creativity of our exploited people.

Stage 2: Analysis of Domination on the Continent

The second stage is a more specific analysis of reality in its economic, political, cultural, and racial aspects.

We want to discern more closely and very clearly "the sufferings of Christ" in Latin America. One day will be dedicated to an analysis of capitalism on the continent. We need to study with scientific rigor and within the tradition of the Latin American social sciences certain decisive factors of our present situation, for example, the current policies of imperialism, the program of the Trilateral Commission, the activities of the multinationals, new forms of exploitation of the workers, the exile of vast numbers of militants committed to the liberation of the people.

We must continue this analysis and learn from one another in our interchange concerning oppression on the continent and the efforts being made toward liberation.

The Congress will study a theme that is relatively new to our discussions, *concrete situations of domination*. We will analyze the oppression of women and cultural and racial discrimination against indigenous groups and blacks on the continent. We will hear reports from the three preparatory seminars that were held recently.

The *indigenous* and *black* cultures make up an integral part of our history. At Oaxtepec concern was expressed for the indigenous peoples: "The situation of the indigenous peoples," says the final statement, "presents a discouraging picture that shocks our Christian conscience."[4]

A positive element in theological developments of recent years has been a deeper understanding of the theme of *culture* in pastoral and theological reflection; unfortunately this had been previously overlooked.

Racism is a form of domination that has been present in oppression and discrimination against Indians and blacks down through our history from colonization to the present day. Perhaps because slavery was abolished shortly after independence in most of our countries and because those who suffered the discrimination—the Indians and the blacks—were voiceless and unable to express their oppression, racism has not been adequately analyzed or formulated in the theology of liberation.

The *oppression of women* in society and in the church confronts us with one of the countervalues most deeply rooted in our civilization and culture. Patriarchal interpretations give the man a prominent place and relegate the woman to a secondary one.

This attitude pervades every sphere of culture and society and affects the reading of revelation and the exercise of responsibility within the church.

We are confident that this discussion concerning the concrete situations of domination will awaken new energy, hidden until now, that can be incorporated into the struggle for liberation.

Stage 3: Popular Movements and the Presence of Christians

The poor and oppressed people of Latin America for centuries have suffered oppression and in recent years have experienced repression under national security states; but they have not passively accepted their situation.

Following a long tradition of struggle, which began with the indigenous peoples who resisted and continue to resist white domination, the people have a beautiful history of resistance and organization.

Although it is true that in the seventies there was an increase in the repression that attempted to dismantle the popular organizations, the people were able to resist, to keep their hope alive, to keep intact their power for liberation, and to prepare new forms of struggle. We will be able to see some of this vitality as we listen to testimony of the experiences of the organizations of workers, peasants, and indigenous peoples from the various countries. It will be of great interest to discern the presence of Christians in these experiences.

Stage 4: Ecclesiological Reflections on the Life of the Christian Communities

Here we want to reflect on the specifically Christian element in the communities. Our starting point is the common profession that the church is the sign and seed of the kingdom of God and that it has received the mission to announce and establish that kingdom (cf. *Lumen gentium,* no. 5).

Our reflections cannot include every theme in ecclesiology. In line with the general theme of the Congress we will study in a special way the church that is born of the people as a response of faith to the invitation of the Lord.

The church that is born of the people—or, in a word, the people's church *(la iglesia popular)*—will be an important theme in our discussions. The people's church, according to Puebla, should be understood as "a Church that is trying to incarnate itself in the ranks of the common people on our continent, and that therefore arises out of their response in faith to the Lord" (no. 263). Speaking of the church, one of the participants at Oaxtepec said that "its option for the poor is what guarantees its relevance in history. The very life and future of the church is at stake in this option."

The people's church is the vocation of the entire church, which is called to be constantly reborn from within the poor, who are the privileged of the kingdom. Thus we are not speaking of a church that is parallel to the institutional church, but rather one that responds to the most basic gospel demands. Like Jesus Christ, who became poor (Phil. 2:5-11), the entire community of the saved should be naturally rooted in the people.

As we share our ecclesial experiences we need to pay attention to several important points, including the following:

a. We must situate in its true perspective one of Puebla's basic conclusions: *"the preferential option for the poor."*

It was here that Puebla adopted the prophetic tradition of Medellín and "opened new horizons of hope" (no. 1165).

The "preferential option for the poor" calls the churches to a definition and to a conversion: to a definition within the harsh social conflict of the continent, and to a conversion to follow Jesus Christ unambiguously. The gospel concept of poverty, in its social, historical, ecclesial, and spiritual dimensions, is one of the richest sources of our theology and our spirituality.

b. The poor evangelize us. For some years now the themes of evangelization and liberation have been part of the daily life of the continent and of theological reflection. In Medellín it was clearly defined that the challenge to evangelizing activity comes from the situation of oppression and exploitation.

Puebla reaffirmed the Medellín tradition and took a step further. In a beautiful text it says: "Commitment to the poor and oppressed and the rise of grassroots communities have helped the Church to discover the evangelizing potential of the poor" (no. 1147). Thus the poor are not only the object of evangelization; they are also the active subject of this task of proclaiming the word.

c. Pastoral practice and political practice. For a long time now the cry for liberation has been heard in Latin America. Recalling Medellín, Puebla says that "the cry might well have seemed muted back then. Today it is loud and clear, increasing in volume and intensity, and at times full of menace" (no. 89).

The Christian communities, which in many countries began to be organized to serve the internal life of worship, catechesis, and preaching, quickly were confronted with "the social situation of sin" on the continent, as was said in Oaxtepec.[5]

Conflicts then arose between pastoral activity and political activity. Medellín provided very positive guidelines for a beginning to the resolution of this conflict.

An entire day will be dedicated to reflection on this theme; there will be interviews with people from various countries that will give us an idea of the variety and richness of the different situations.

d. Conversion and spirituality. This Congress would like to provide an opportunity of conversion for all.

It is perhaps necessary to repeat what the bishops at Puebla asked in their Message to the Peoples of Latin America: "In this pastoral colloquy our first question in the face of the collective conscience is the following: Are we really living the Gospel of Christ on our continent?" ("Message," no. 2).

The participants at Oaxtepec made the following assertion: "We confess," they said in their final statement, "that we have insulted God with our divisions, our pride, and our disobedience to him."[6]

We must say it again very clearly: what has traditionally been called spirituality has been and continues to be one of the most characteristic marks of Christians committed to the process of liberation and the theological reflection that arises from it. This commitment is a privileged place for spiritual experience, for encounter with the Lord, which is celebrated with vigor and joy in the people's Christian communities.

I want to recall with reverence and devotion the *martyrs* of Latin America: those thousands of men and women who "have been found worthy to suffer for the name of Christ" and have given their lives in the struggles for liberation. We want to proclaim aloud these brothers and sisters in the struggle, witnesses to the faith, whom the poor have begun to consider as their patron saints. In them the theology of liberation and the people's church are challenged to gospel authenticity and encouraged to develop it.

e. Elaboration of an ecclesiology that gives reason for the hope of the popular Christian communities. The bishops in Puebla said:

> In 1968 base-level ecclesial communities (CEBs: *comunidades eclesiales de base*) were just coming into being. Over the past ten years they have multiplied and matured, particularly in some countries, so that now they are one of the causes for joy and hope in the Church. In communion with their bishops, and in line with Medellín's request, they have become centers of evangelization and moving forces for liberation and development.
>
> The vitality of these CEBs is now beginning to bear fruit. They have been one of the sources for the increase in lay ministers, who are now acting as leaders and organizers of their communities, as catechists, and as missionaries [nos. 96-97].

We believe that our theological reflection on the church has not matured with the same speed and profundity that the Spirit of Christ has been abundantly poured out in our communities. The life of the churches has moved forward with its own theology. This ecclesiological delay has created no little confusion and some institutional tension within the church. We must create an ecclesiology that gives reason for this joy and this hope that the church is manifesting in the maturation and multiplication of the base-level Christian communities.

No one puts a piece of unshrunken cloth on an old cloak, because the patch pulls away from the cloak and the tear gets worse. Nor do people put new wine into old wineskins; if they do, the skins burst, the wine runs out and the skins are lost. No! They put new wine into fresh skins and both are preserved" [Matt. 9:16–17].

GREETINGS TO THE PARTICIPANTS

Now I want to say a word of greetings and of gratitude.

I greet the representatives of *Latin America.* I would like to name each of the countries, including my own. But I want to refer especially to the delegation from Nicaragua. That people's victory has enkindled a new light of hope on the continent. Every morning that light penetrates the prison cells of repression, it illuminates the pathway of the poor of the city and countryside, it makes the powerful tremble, and it is a forerunner of the victory of the poor and the oppressed of the continent. We appreciate the pastoral letter of the bishops, which carries the formulation of Christian commitment a step forward.

I welcome the delegates from *Africa* and *Asia.* Their number is limited, but their presence is rich and meaningful. They bring us not only the echo of their civilizations and religions that are thousands of years old, but also the example of their victorious liberation struggles. This Congress is an opportunity to get to know each other better and to deepen our friendship and solidarity.

With great joy we welcome the representatives from the *French- and English-speaking Caribbean.* There are social processes under way in that region that could transform the geopolitical power relationships in the Americas. Nevertheless, the Caribbean is unknown in Latin America, notwithstanding its geographical proximity. Let us make of this Congress a moment of unity and hope.

In the past few years I have learned to distinguish between *the people of the United States* and the ruling classes of that country. I greet the representatives of the people here with us. They are part of a growing minority who, in the heart of the system, are not in accord with the legitimating role of the churches, are struggling against capitalist oppression and every form of discrimination, and are in solidarity with the liberation causes of the peoples of the Third World.

A group of *observers* come from Europe, the United States, Canada, and other countries. Some represent the funding agencies that have supported the program of our Association. Others hold responsible positions in national or international ecumenical organizations. They are our friends and they deserve our welcome.

A WORD OF GRATITUDE

This is a difficult moment, because there is always the danger of forgetting someone. Thanks to all who have made this Congress possible: the national coordinators in Latin America, the funding agencies, Margaret Coakley of the New York office, and very especially the many Brazilians who have prepared the meeting. It is impossible to mention them all.

For justice' sake I should name certain people. First, Cardinal Dom Paulo Evaristo Arns, who, without taking part in the administration or organization of the Congress, has welcomed us to his archdiocese and as homage of our gratitude has received the title of honorary president of this Congress.

Thanks to the planning and organizing committees who accepted the request of the Ecumenical Association of Third World Theologians to organize this Congress.

In the name of the Association and all here present I want to thank the members of these two committees, represented by the executive president of the Congress, the Methodist bishop of Rio de Janeiro, Paulo Ayres Mattos.

I want to make particular mention of three people: Frei Betto, Regina Festa, and Silvio Pilon deserve our special thanks for their dedication, their sacrifices, and their efficiency.

Finally, allow me a personal word. Since October 1973, I have been outside my country, like many other Latin American exiles. Although I intend to return, the future is uncertain and there are clouds on the horizon.

During these years I have dedicated a part of my life to promoting understanding and dialogue among Christians of the Third World. As a faithful member of the church, I feel the urgency of the call of Jesus Christ to proclaim the gospel in the context of the cultures and the poverty and oppression of our countries. This Congress is for me a motive for gratitude to God and for hope.

In my work, I have had the understanding and assistance of many people, for example, the Maryknoll Fathers in New York, the two parishes I lived in, and my friends at the offices of the National Council of Churches of the United States. I recall the faces of friends from many countries, for whom I have affection and gratitude.

Among them I must mention Sister Virginia Fabella. She has been with the Association of Theologians from the beginning and we owe to her a great part of the success of our work.

I also thank the president of the Association, Dr. Russell Chandran. I have always respected his experience and wisdom, and I have appreciated his orientation and the trust that he has extended me. It is he who officially represents our Association and is the official spokesman for dialogue with other institutions or organizations.

I should end as I began. I recall Saint Paul: "As the sufferings of Christ overflow to us, so, through Christ, does our consolation overflow." This is our power, our hope.

NOTES

1. Representatives from 110 Latin American Protestant churches gathered in Oaxtepec, Mexico, from September 19 to 28, 1978. At the conclusion of this meeting the Latin American Council of Churches (Consejo Latino Americano de Iglesias—CLAI) was created. This provisional organization fulfills a role of coordination on a continental level and can be compared to CELAM.

2. For the official English translation of the Puebla documents, see John Eagleson and Philip Scharper, eds., *Puebla and Beyond: Documentation and Commentary* (Maryknoll, N.Y.: Orbis Books, 1979).

3. Emilio Castro, "En busca de la unidad," *Revista Pastoralia,* año 1, no. 2 (November 1978), p. 103.

4. "Carta a las iglesias cristianas," in ibid., p. 128.

5. Carmelo E. Alvarez S., "El papel de la Iglesia en América Latina," in ibid., p. 109.

6. "Carta a las iglesias cristianas," in ibid., p. 126.

PART I

CHRISTIAN PRESENCE IN SITUATIONS OF DOMINATION

2

Structures and Mechanisms
of Domination in Capitalism

Luis A. Gómez de Souza (Brazil)

At this Convention we have seen some specific mechanisms of domination, and we are very mindful of the personal experiences of struggle, suffering, and activity that we bring with us. Moreover, we have just come back from an encounter with the concrete experiences of communities on the periphery of São Paulo. There we heard comments about food prices, violations of human rights, the jailing of people, an exercising of democracy and participation in a country where democracy is such a relative thing, and so forth.

This is the material we must work over. Theologians and social scientists without concrete practices cannot move theory forward. By the same token, if personal or lived experiences are not situated in a broader context, they remain isolated; they do not acquire any meaning and they can disappear without leaving a trace.

I recall what our companion from Nicaragua put so clearly a few days ago. She said: "We must transcend concrete experience with an overall analysis, otherwise we fall into subjectivism. For that we need a method of scientific analysis, and Marxism is the scientific method that people's movements possess to understand their practices."

THE THEME IN CONTEXT

My theme here is the relationship between scientific analysis and concrete actions. Let me offer a few remarks that will enable us to place the theme in context.

From Concrete Experience to Practice

Experience is something subjective. Practice is an action, which means that it is an experience that is *definite and specified*; in other words, it is related to other actions in the broad structure of society and in a historical process.

So when we are talking about pastoral practice, it is not simply a matter of describing what is being done in a community, a concrete struggle; we must also integrate the concrete struggle into a historical process and a wider struggle in society. We must work on the level of practices, not simply on the level of narrating experiences.

To study a practice is to do more than describe what is being done; it is to give it some meaning and place it in context.

The Relationship between Theory and Practice

Some have said: "There is no revolution without revolutionary theory." On the contrary, there is no revolutionary theory or progress in it unless it is challenged by concrete practices. That is why we all are meeting here: pastoral agents, grassroots companions, theologians, and social scientists. It is a difficult dialogue but a fruitful one, perhaps the most fruitful kind of all.

It is very important because there is no theory that need only be applied, no finished theory; theory must be fashioned and re-fashioned continually.

We have talked about scientific method. The method of Marxist analysis arose out of the concrete European struggles of the nineteenth century. Marxism was rethought in the struggles of Czarist Russia, and that gave us the thinking of Lenin. It was rethought again in Germany, and we got the thinking of Rosa Luxemburg—an enormous contribution. It was rethought again, and we got a great contribution from the struggles in China and Mao Zedong. Then the struggles in Italy gave us the contribution of Gramsci. This means that there is always a link between concrete processes and practices of sociopolitical struggle and a scientific theory or method that is to keep on developing. The problem is that theory often remained locked up in the manuals or in school debate. University people even created a term to satisfy themselves, referring to "theoretical practice." They combine the two things, stay at the university doing "theoretical practice," and do not relate to the practices of the common people.

New problems keep cropping up: e.g., women's liberation, the racial problem, the rebellion of youth, and so forth. These problems pose serious theoretical questions that cannot be quickly integrated into an already existing framework. Instead we must rework the framework with these problems, and there is the challenge to the theoretician.

The theologians present here say—and I learned from them—that liberation theology is in the making, in process of transformation, on the basis of pastoral practice. I would say the same thing in my field of endeavor: a committed and involved social science is continually in the making on the basis of the people's practice.

If they are honest, social scientists are not going to bring in finished, ready-made scientific answers because they *don't have them*. Instead they will offer the *proposal* for a long journey with the forces of the people, their leaders, pastoral agents, and theologians.

Adding up the Total Situation

In the testimony presented in our meetings we have encountered concrete mechanisms of domination affecting women, indigenous peoples, and blacks; and we have listened to personal experiences of such domination. Some might think that we should now move from the concrete to the abstract, from the precise to the vague. That is a mistaken notion. Instead we must try to make things even more concrete.

When Marx talks about the scientific method for approaching reality, he talks about rising from the abstract to the concrete—what he calls a *specified concrete*. So when we analyze mechanisms of domination, we are not seeking to formulate some abstract scheme, some overall set of pigeonholes, that will take in everything. Instead we are committing ourselves to a lengthy common effort, not resolved in a debate, to specify, spell out, relate, and interconnect more satisfactorily the concrete practices on which we must work. Let me give an example. We cannot now decide that we are not going to say any more about women, indigenous peoples, workers, peasants, and so forth; that instead we are going to sum them all up in the more general category of the oppressed. To do that would simply be to move to a broader but vaguer expression. What we must do now is keep on working with the same groups, but in an even more concrete way. Those categories must be linked up even more clearly with other elements of the social structure. Here we come to a basic underlying issue which I am not going to discuss now; it goes by the name of a *concrete totality*.

The Historical Process

Mechanisms of domination are *historical* problems. Not only must I make them more concrete by relating them in space; I must also make them more concrete by relating them in time. The struggle of any of you—of a community of indigenous Mexicans in the state of Chiapas, for example—has a history. It is linked up with many of the Mexican peasant struggles going back to the decade of the twenties, and also with a liberation project for the future.

Theory for Whom and from Where?

Another point that I will analyze briefly is the fact that theoretical analysis is not neutral. It is affected by the standpoint from which it is made and by those for whom it is made. This is the problem of the social locus of theory. Reflection is one thing when it is made to advance the cause of the common people. It is something else again when it is being made by a group of sociologists to help maintain the mechanisms of domination or to serve as an academic exercise.

Now if we want to analyze mechanisms and structures of domination, we must do so by answering the problems raised by the people's struggle; our analysis must be in the service of their struggles. The point is obvious enough, but it is worth remembering. And those actually involved in the struggle should pose the problems that are to be examined on the level of analysis.

Analysis of Domination as Inseparable from Analysis of Liberation

We cannot talk about mechanisms of domination without talking about mechanisms and processes of liberation. For example, some mechanisms of government coercion cannot be understood unless we realize that they are designed to check the people's liberation process. Consider education as one instance. Historically speaking, we know that the educational structures have been mechanisms of domination. Through them certain values and conceptions of life have been transmitted, a certain attitude of passivity has been interiorized, and mechanisms of domination have been accepted. But education can be something very different, as instances of liberative or grassroots education prove. Among the common people educational experiences may have a very different result.

The same holds true for religion. At various times in history the churches were places that abetted the domestication and oppression of the people. They helped to legitimate a situation of domination. But now they are becoming locales of liberative practice, fostering a very different kind of action.

Thus places and institutions in civil society that once functioned as mechanisms of domination can be taken over by the common people and used for activity of a transforming sort.

AN ANALYSIS OF LATIN AMERICA'S DEPENDENT CAPITALISM

In this second section I would like to make a few points about the structures and mechanisms of domination in one general historical process, which also contains mechanisms and instruments of liberation. My focus is *Latin America's dependent capitalism*. I hope that our brothers and sisters from Asia, Africa, Europe, and the United States will excuse me for restricting my analysis to this particular subject.

One country, Cuba, falls outside my discussion because it is not situated in the trammels of dependent capitalism. But it should be noted that it is involved here because it represents one possible historical horizon in the overcoming of dependent capitalism.

A Situation of Bourgeois Domination in Permanent Crisis

First of all, we must realize the situation in Latin America. Bourgeois domination here did not suddenly enter a crisis a few years ago. There was no long period of undisturbed domination that is now entering the final crisis of capitalism. The history of bourgeois domination and its mechanisms in Latin

America is a history of constant, ongoing crisis for our dependent brand of capitalism. From the very beginning it has been challenged by emerging forces of the common people.

The process of domination was more tranquil around the turn of this century, when the large landlords ruled. The dominant classes exercised a much stronger leadership presence in society through two processes: *(a) legal coercion* (laws) and *direct coercion* through the government apparatus; and *(b)* the exercise of *hegemony* in civil society.

The second process deserves clarification. Domination was exercised through values, ideologies, lifestyles, and beliefs. This is the realm of hegemony, what Gramsci called the intellectual and moral management of society. This realm was to be found in civil society. There the schools, social organizations, the press, and the churches served as places where certain values, beliefs, and views of life were transmitted.

At the point in the historical process we are considering here, however, the bourgeoisie and the petty bourgeoisie began to appear in the cities. They sought to make their presence felt in civil society and to organize a new power bloc. Political and ideological power was not to remain wholly in the hands of upper-class landlords. There was to be a new pact that would include the presence of the bourgeoisie and, in some instances, the petty bourgeoisie. In many instances that is what happened. The old landholding class was not destroyed, but it was dragged into a new political and social pact. The alliances between liberals and conservatives in so many of our countries around the start of this century clearly point up the coexistence of the old ruling classes with the new ones. They made a pact and kept the same mechanisms of domination.

Take the case of Argentina and its old oligarchy of ranchers and cattlemen. For all the tension and struggle, it remains very much present in the political history of the country. Indeed it seems to be strong and healthy today in 1980 with Martínez de Noz in power. In Brazil we find subclasses arising within the landholding class: a coffee-growing bourgeoisie in the countryside and an industrial bourgeoisie in this area of São Paulo. The latter group often came from the coffee-growers or else grew up alongside that class and in alliance with them.

Insofar as the old dominant classes are concerned, they are pushed back into second place; but in many cases they manage to maintain their place in the new power arrangements alongside the newly emerging class. They make alliances with the bourgeoisie and the middle classes. Of course we must remember that some situations are more complicated: e.g., the situation in Mexico and all the violence in Colombia.

Now the point I want to call to your attention is this. The new emerging classes, the common people, were already present at precisely the time that the bourgeois classes were moving into a position of dominance in civil society and government. They were present as the bourgeois classes sought to take over social organizations, the press, the schools, the churches, and the coercive apparatus of the state. I don't mean simply that they existed as a class; obviously the mode of capitalist production always generates bourgeois classes and laboring classes. I mean that the common people had organized, highly operative class practices.

Let us take a quick look at a few examples. Starting around the decade of the twenties, the bourgeoisie began to come to power. Sometimes they made a pact with the old landholding classes, sometimes with sections of the petty bourgeoisie or the middle class. This happened in Argentina with Irigoyen, in Chile under Alessandri's government, in Brazil in 1930, in Mexico in the period between Calles and Cárdenas, and so forth. But the forces of the common people were also present and operative in the same years—not just as a class situation but with their class practices as well. Consider the labor movement in Brazil, for example. In the late twenties and early thirties there were strikes and big demonstrations even before the new classes came to power. In 1922 and 1923 Marxist revolutionary parties appeared all over Latin America. Bolivia is a most interesting case. There the bourgeoisie came to power in 1952 in conjunction with the people's movement. For several months in 1952 and 1953 there was a coalition government composed of the MNR and the COB. The MNR represented the interests of the rising new classes that sought domination; the COB (Bolivian Workers' Central) represented the emerging classes of the common people. It is as if Bolivia experienced a February 1917 without a later October 1917. The case of Bolivia is the most instructive one in Latin America, as far as I am concerned. The bourgeoisie and petty bourgeoisie began to organize politically around the end of the Chaco War (1937–38). They came to power in 1952. At the same time there existed a labor movement which possessed impressive clarity in its theory and strong organization. Consider the 1947 Pulacayo Theses of the miners. Those political theses represented one of the high points of class and political consciousness among the classes of the common people in Latin America.

My point is that we do not first have a period of domination when the bourgeoisie enjoys peaceful hegemony in civil society and government, and then move on to a crisis. Right from the start we have the various forms of populism that are efforts to fashion a broader alliance. They do not seek solely to reunite the petty bourgeoisie with the old landholding class and the industrial bourgeoisie. They also seek to coopt the new forces of the common people and bring them into the pact. Such was the effort of Cárdenas in Mexico and of Vargas in Brazil at the end of his first term (1943–45). What is evident is that the new class, the bourgeoisie, which is trying to take over the mechanisms of civil society and the apparatus of government, has need of permanent, ongoing alliances. And when alliances fail, it appeals to a government apparatus of coercion: the Armed Forces.

The matter is further complicated by the fact that there is no single, straight-line evolution. It would be very easy to analyze the situation if it went in neat stages: e.g., (1) an alliance between the bourgeoisie and the landholding class; (2) the bourgeoisie exercise domination in peace; (3) an expanded pact of a populist nature; (4) crisis leading to an authoritarian pact. But that is not the way it goes. There is a constant shifting back and forth. Otherwise we could not understand the case of Venezuela, where things went in the opposite direction: first an authoritarian pact and then a liberal, bourgeois experience. The case of Argentina is enormously rich as an example of this continual zig-zag and the crisis of hegemony. Radicalism came to power in the twenties, then came the infamous thirties, then Peronism, then a military coup, then Frondizi, then a military coup, then Illía, then a military coup, then the return of Perón, and then the military again. A permanent, ongoing state of crisis!

What I would like to stress here is that there is *a permanent crisis of hegemony* and *a permanent crisis of coercion*. But "crisis" does not mean that the system is on its death-bed. There are chronic crises, and this may be one. There is fragility, but also an enormous capacity to adapt once again and survive. When the dominant classes have less impact on the mechanisms of hegemony in civil society (e.g., the churches, the schools, social organizations, and parties), then they need to use more coercion; so we get military intervention to restore their tottering domination. It is a permanent state of tension, with periods of authoritarianism returning at regular intervals.

The emerging classes of the common people, too, are gradually infiltrating the mechanisms of civil society, which are not simply mechanisms of domination. They are taking possession of the church, for example. In one sense the church is a mechanism for domesticating the people; but it is also being transformed into a locale of liberation. The whole problem of the permanent crisis afflicting the structures of domination is a very complex one. That fact must be realized if we are to avoid Manichean analyses, placing mechanisms of domination over against mechanisms of liberation as if there were some neat dividing line between the two.

The historical process is a complicated one. The very same institutions of civil society mentioned above, which are in the hands of the dominant classes, are continually threatened by the emerging classes; indeed they are now being occupied by the latter classes. That is the history of Latin America's dependent capitalism in recent years.

The Internationalization of Bourgeois Domination

Now we must discuss a second point to complete the tableau given above. In the process of bourgeois domination we do not have an initial stage of national domination followed by a second stage of internationalized domination. At all times this capitalism of ours was dependent. Latin America was born with capitalism, grew up in it. International capital and its extractive enclaves were present from the start. So-called nationalist projects usually used the rhetoric of nationalism, but in practice they opened their arms to foreign capital. That is what one finds in Mexico when one closely examines the government of Cárdenas and those that followed. In Brazil there was the development project of J. Kubitschek; never was there more talk about nationalism, yet that is when the door was opened wide to foreign capital.

In other words, so-called nationalist projects were exercises in rhetoric on the ideological level rather than realities of economic policy. The whole period of bourgeois domination, then, was one which saw the internationalization of that domination. Sometimes people talk about the national bourgeoisie and an alliance with it. My question is: Where is the national bourgeoisie really?

I would like to make brief mention of the concrete phenomenon of multinational corporations. They represent a new type of monopoly capitalism based on the new resources of modern technology. One type, which is very important for the church's pastoral work but which I will merely mention here, is made up of the multinationals in rural agriculture. They are part of a process of modernization that will have enormous repercussions, expelling people from the fields and transforming land holding. In Brazil, for example, Volkswagen is becoming a major cattle business in the Amazon. With the oil crisis Volkswagen may soon be more interested in cattle than in cars. Countless examples of this sort could be mentioned.

Then we also have the problem of the Trilateral Commission, which I can mention only briefly. This commission exemplifies the political strategy of imperialism around the years 1972 and 1973. It was created after world capitalism began to enter a crisis stage in 1968, after rising tensions between Europe, the United States, and Japan. It was very important to point up and denounce the strategy of the Trilateral Commission as a club for the rich and a center for their strategy. When we hear talk today in Brazil and other countries about giving priority to agriculture and fostering relative or limited democracy, we must realize that such talk was already embodied in the texts of the Trilateral Commission. At one point the Commission was a decisive force, but every indication is that it has already lost some of its effectiveness. Behind it stands imperialism, which possesses economic structures of domination like the multinationals and centers of political strategy like the Trilateral.

The Church, a Social Locale of Domination and Liberation

A third subject is the church. It is central in the historical process of Latin America. Here many Marxist analyses fall short because they have been imported from Europe. Some even represent a poor adaptation of Gramsci's theory; they derive the problem of the church from Italy, where the church is often tied to surviving feudal structures. We must consider the church from two standpoints.

First of all, we must consider the church as a *social locale*, as a space in civil society. For a long time the church in this sense has been a place where the bourgeoisie and its allies have exercised their hegemony. For years the middle classes have occupied this locale. Consider the various liturgies suited to their sensibilities. But then we have the impact of grassroots communities of the common people (CCPs) as well. More and more the church is being occupied and taken over by the emerging popular classes. Thus the church can simultaneously be a mechanism of domination and a place for the exercise of liberation. It is not both in the same physical places, of course; but we are talking about the very same church with its inner tensions and contradictions.

Second, the church is not just a social locale. It is also an *institution* with its authorities, teachings, and doctrines. With its authority and its doctrine it has often been in the service of domination; it has served as a mechanism of legitimation. But at other times its magisterium and authority have served as instruments of liberation. We possess symbols of that fact: e.g., Archbishop Romero in El Salvador and all the struggles of local churches we have learned about here.

What sociologists would call social locale and institution is what theologians would refer to as community of the faithful and institution.

All this confirms what I tried to say before. The mechanisms of domination and the instruments or mechanisms of liberation can be the very same, depending on whether the force of the common people is operative in them or not.

The Complementarity of Actions on Behalf of Liberation

Mechanisms of domination exist on many different levels. There is economic domination of the land and of the means of production. There is cultural domination by the dominant classes. There is male domination of woman. There is domination over blacks, and domination over young people. There is domination over all sorts of oppressed minorities who are subjected to discrimination.

But we must spell out and articulate these mechanisms to see their reciprocal relations in a concrete totality. At a time when the emerging classes of the common people are struggling to take over civil society, labor unions, parties, block organizations, and so forth—a time which Gramsci called "the battle for positions"—all these struggles are of enormous importance. On the surface they seem to be unconnected. Union does not come through theory but through action, and especially through a decisive confrontation.

When it is no longer a matter of simply taking positions, when it comes to taking over political society and the government in what might be called the "battle of movements," then the Nicaraguan experience has something to tell us. As one of its representatives pointed out, it proves that all these seemingly isolated movements and processes of liberation come together in one and the same unified action. Thus black and indigenous movements of self-assertion are historically complementary to other processes of liberation, such as those of the common people in urban and rural areas.

The Differing Tempo of History in Different Countries

There are differing historical tempos in our countries. Twenty-one years ago, in 1959, we had a revolution leading to socialism in Cuba. In other countries we have had spates of progress or retreat. Now we have the victory in Nicaragua. It is most important as a sign and possibility of hope, as a concrete example of victory for the common people.

But tempos differ. When our companions in the southern part of South America consider their companions in Central America, or specifically their companions in Nicaragua, they realize that their own process is quite different. And I myself can remember back to 1971, when our companions in Nicaragua under Somoza looked to Chile as a sign of hope.

History is complex; it is not a straight-line business. Even in Central America, for example, the process in El Salvador is not an automatic repetition of what happened in Nicaragua. Remember the "domino theory" that was formulated for Southeast Asia. It maintained that the processes of political radicalization would move from country to country as a chain of revolutions. Something similar could happen in Central America, according to certain people. But things are not that simple. To analyze a situation of domination and how to overcome it, at least three elements must be considered:

—the level of awareness and practice attained by the forces of the common people;

—the strength of the domestic and international mechanisms of domination. That is to say, the possibility of the dominant classes being able to compromise in order to maintain themselves in power.

—the international factors. The fall of a people's government in Chile was not due solely to U.S. intervention. There were more important internal elements. But we still must take into account Kissinger's Latin American policy and its goal of destabilizing the situation. Consider the difference in the Dominican Republic, where a people's rebellion was crushed by the OAS, and Nicaragua, where the OAS was unwilling to intervene. The contradictions of Carter's policy made such intervention difficult.

In all these cases we can apply the points I made above about analyzing reality from the standpoint of the common people. We must consider the strategy of the dominant international sectors. For example, they may be behind certain political openings. But besides considering the aims of such policies, the forces of the people also want to know if it is possible for them to take advantage of them. Thus it is not enough to analyze the strength and power of international mechanisms of domination. We must also examine their contradictions and weaknesses, which may enable us to create new spaces.

Finally, our analyses must show us that there are no ready-made political recipes. Everything depends on the movements of the common people as well as on the mechanisms of domination.

At the end of the Spanish Civil War, just before he went into exile, Antonio Machado wrote down his melancholic observations. His basic point was that history does not follow the rhythm of our expectations. Sometimes it proceeds more slowly and hesitantly, even though domination is in permanent crisis. Its mechanisms manage to reinforce themselves through alliances.

But we must also remember what Salvador Allende said two hours before he died. In his moment of defeat he bade farewell to the people of Chile with these words: "History is ours; the people make it."

That says everything. There is a history that the people make. There is hope. But we also need historical patience in this work. To analyze the mechanisms of domination is at the same time to discover their strengths and their weaknesses. It is to see the long-term rise of spaces and mechanisms belonging to the common people. In Latin America the church is a locale and institution of the greatest importance in this whole process of liberation.

3

The Latin American Woman:
The Praxis and Theology of Liberation

Cora Ferro (Costa Rica)

The Ecumenical Association of Third World Theologians asked the Mexican organization, Women for Dialogue (Mujeres para el Diálogo), to organize a meeting of women from all over Latin America to reflect on the issues and problems confronting women. The seminar was held in Mexico from October 1 to October 5, 1979. The participants were twenty women and four men, who came from eight American countries.

The theme of the seminar was "The Latin American Woman: The Praxis and Theology of Liberation." Surprising as it may sound, it was the first time that Christian women had gotten together to reflect systematically on the situation of women in Latin America. The women participants were people who are working on this issue both in theory and in practice, and who are trying to formulate the problem systematically.

We worked intensively on the theme for a week, using a methodology that I shall now briefly describe. On the basis of the grassroots experience provided by each participant and its systematic organization, the seminar formulated the theory that was presented in its final document. That document is recapitulated in the pages that follow.

Reflection at the seminar centered on the structural causes of social oppression, wherein we found that women were exploited in a twofold way. All the contributions in support of the theoretical framework were made by women participants at the seminar. They had ten minutes to offer clarifying or complementary remarks on the draft paper, which they already had in mimeographed form.

There were no basic contradictions, so our work was able to proceed smoothly and productively. But I should point out that the final document is meant to be merely a point of departure. It has weaknesses, particularly insofar as its conclusions are concerned.

In the pages that follow here, you will find the final document of the seminar. The only thing omitted is an early section on the reality of people's movements in Latin America, which is discussed in other sections of this book.

THE FINAL DOCUMENT OF THE WOMEN'S SEMINAR

1. In October 1979 we, a group of women involved in people's movements, have met for the first time to reflect on the situation of oppression confronting women and their contribution to the revolutionary struggle. Our reflections are made in the light of faith, and our aim is to organize them theologically in ecumenical terms.

2. Our seminar is being held near Tepeyac, the sacred hillside of Tonantzin, "the mother-goddess who consoled the oppressed of the Aztec empire," and the place where people now venerate Our Lady of Guadalupe. She was the banner of Hidalgo in the last century, of Zapata and the peasants in the abortive revolution of the twentieth century, and also of César Chavez and the Chicanos in the United States.

3. We, the participants at this seminar, come from Brazil, Colombia, Costa Rica, Peru, Argentina, Cuba, the United States, and Mexico.

4. The seminar was a profound experience of community for us all. It ended with an ecumenical service led by one of our members, who is an ordained minister of the Presbyterian Church and comes from Cuba.

5. A service held in Tepeyac, presided over by an ordained woman, who comes from a socialist country in Latin America: three signs heralding a new world in which women will more completely express their creative capability that is still repressed.

6. We also wish to point out that our seminar coincided with the visit of the pope to the United States, where he manifested the position of the ecclesiastical hierarchy against women. It symbolizes the historic struggle that we women have to wage within the church.

PART I
THE COMMON WOMAN IN LATIN AMERICA

7. The common woman in Latin America (*mujer popular*) is one who belongs to the exploited class either by birth or personal choice. In other words, we are talking about the majority of Latin American women.

8. The oppression of women, which has existed under all socio-economic systems, takes on a specific character under capitalism. Capitalism gives women a role in the family, and it uses the family to reproduce and maintain itself as a system of domination.

9. In the family the woman has for her responsibility the task of daily restoring the strength of the laborer, reproducing sons as the labor-power of the future, transmitting an ideology of submission to the system, and channeling the consumption needs of the family. All this is to be done in the service of capital.

10. As a result, the role assigned to women in the family leads to a set of conditionings that are profoundly oppressive for women.

Economic Conditioning Factors

11. The woman is dependent on a masculine economy. The domestic labor of women has an economic value that is not acknowledged.

12. In the factory she does the cheaper manual labor at a more inhuman pace and rhythm. While her production is equal to that of a man, she always gets a lower salary.

13. In field work she is the backbone of the family economy, yet she does not have control over production.

14. She is the generator of wealth because she sustains the economy, which is then absorbed by the capitalist structure. She reproduces the labor force, particularly in fieldwork where many hands are needed. From early childhood on, peasant women have a heavy workload. They have many important responsibilities and little time to rest.

15. There is discrimination against women in production work. Her participation in heavy industry is obstructed. Unemployment and instability in her jobs, due to the fact she is a wife and mother, is a known fact. The laws protecting women are a vicious circle favoring discrimination.

16. Women constitute a reserve force. The doors are opened or shut to women as it suits capitalism. Women are doubly exploited because of their work both in the production process and in the home. This makes it impossible for them to organize to demand their rights.

17. The native Indian woman, the *mestiza* woman, and the black woman suffer even greater discrimination because of their race. This only adds to the exploitation of these social groups.

18. The working woman could achieve economic independence vis-à-vis her husband, but she does not win such independence under the capitalist system.

Political Conditioning Factors

19. Women are also marginalized in the political sphere. They are excluded from executive posts even when they have been the organizing force behind the creation of some group. No account is taken of them in making decisions. Women are not given any political education because they are not considered active political protagonists. Here again the double work-day (on the job and at home) prevents them from organizing and forming syndicalist unions.

20. The attitude and behavior of right-wing parties, insofar as women are concerned, is to use them as a demagogic tool. Left-wing parties proclaim sex equality in theory, but in most instances their attitude is one of *machismo* in practice. This prevents women from gaining access to leadership posts and executive responsibilities. Furthermore, they do not know how to spell out the role of women in the practice and strategy of their movements.

21. Women frequently decline in militancy once they marry. This is due to the *macho* ideology, which justifies an unjust distribution of roles within the family and assigns political responsibility only to the male.

22. Social laws are discriminatory. When laws about equality are on the books, they are not observed.

23. When a woman discovers the importance of her role in the struggle, she is forced to confront a life-crisis because she gets no understanding from her family, her male comrade, or society. This crisis affects her inner emotional life, her family relationships, and her social relationships. She does not always manage to resolve the crisis in positive terms.

Ideological and Cultural Conditioning Factors

24. In the bourgeois ideology woman is considered an object, a decoration, a frivolous pleasure. There is the myth of woman as the "weaker sex" and the "second sex." There is also the myth of the "ideal woman" reigning as "queen" in the home.

25. Bourgeois, capitalist ideology works to make sure that the exploited class does not become conscious of its real situation. It makes every effort to keep women confined to the lifestyle that the system assigns them: i.e., subjects and objects of consumption.

26. The mass media of social communication, tools which the bourgeois class employs to impose its values on the exploited class, are especially utilized to maintain women in a situation of marginalization, alienation, and dependence.

27. Some movements for women's liberation, with a bourgeois ideology, are out looking for their own selves; they have no class consciousness.

28. The whole sociocultural framework is male. A *macho* ideology uses the existing structure as a vehicle for the submission of women, who are trodden underfoot by men at every level. *Macho* ideology, which says that a man should have many women, leads to serious consequences: a great deal of irresponsibility and abandonment.

29. On field and farm the women live an isolated life—no communication. Her pregnancy and maternity is a perpetual perplexity, for she fears she will bear females instead of the males her husband wants.

30. In the home the father and male children exercise authority and make decisions. This means that the spouses are not a real "couple" because there is no relationship of equality between two free subjects.

31. Even though woman suffers from *machismo*, she fosters it insofar as she is not permitted to take cognizance of her dignity as a person and insofar as she does not work out the mechanisms needed to confront this reality.

32. In the field of education discrimination intensifies. In rural farm areas she has no access to education, and in urban areas she is wont to remain at the second-class level of intermediate professions. Rare is the woman who attains the scientific level. Normally the humanist professions are left to women while the scientific professions go to men. Women are rejected for top-level executive posts in educational establishments.

33. The sexual oppression of women is linked up with their economic, ideological, and political oppression in a capitalist society. It cannot be dissociated from a sociocultural concept.

34. The family also serves to foster the woman's subjugation and submissiveness. It affects every level of her relationship with her companions and with her surroundings, imposing on her a restrictive sexual role that does not allow her voluntary maternity.

35. The ecclesiastical structure has reinforced this oppression by imposing moral norms that sacralize male domination of women.

36. The left-wing view of sexuality as a woman's private affair is a curb on her political participation.

Ecclesial Conditioning Factors

37. The church is a patriarchal structure allied to those who wield power. Women do not participate at the level of church decision-making. The ecclesial structure, which is hierarchical and masculine, is a model of the oppressive man-woman relationship. At the level of conscience and faith the male dictates what a woman is supposed to believe and practice.

38. From the religious standpoint it is the woman who participates most assiduously in everything organized by the church: worship, social assistance, and catechesis. She transmits religious values and beliefs, but in the fatalistic vein in which she herself accepted them. They only help to confirm her in her attitude of passivity and resignation.

39. Women are really the operative manual laborers in the pastoral infrastructure. In the church she can move without too much control. So when she does encounter consciousness-raising groups, they may well become the starting point for opening up to liberation.

40. Not only does the church not support movements for women's liberation, it actually opposes them.

41. The hierarchy uses the bourgeois woman in the religious sphere to maintain the existing social classes.

42. Mariology presents a submissive, hidden virgin. This image does not abet women's liberation, and it does not fit in with Mary's canticle of liberation.

43. In the area of theology the participation of women as active subjects of systematic work has been denied. By male standards the worth of a person is judged in terms of what that person knows in male terms.

APPROACHES AND REQUIREMENTS IN THE STRUGGLE

Theoretical Contributions

44. The revolution and societal changes cannot move ahead without the participation of women on all fronts.

45. The various levels of woman's awareness, organization, and struggle make it necessary to distinguish and respect the specific character of people's fronts, grassroots organizations, and political parties in which women participate.

46. One cannot talk about the Left from outside, just as one cannot talk about the faith without community participation. One must be present in the party, the organization, or the front of the masses.

47. The witness of militant women is a living benchmark for reflection.

48. Through the involvement of women in the prerevolutionary and revolutionary struggle we get the dialectical concept that their liberation does not begin only when political power is won. It is an ongoing dialectical relationship between space, advance, and struggle.

49. Women's participation should be a basic element in articulating the anticapitalist and antipatriarchal fight. The revolutionary struggle must be reformulated on the basis of the reality facing women, on the basis of their twofold oppression and their progress toward liberation.

51. Women must face up to the tasks of women's organizations that are connected with organizations of the common people and the higher echelons of the proletariat.

52. In the struggle women cannot limit themselves to the industrial sector. They must reach out to all the sectors of the common people.

Practical Contributions

53. In Vietnam, China, Cuba, and Nicaragua the contribution of women to the struggle has been decisive. Innumerable forms of aid tactically framed in the strategy were effective contributions to victory.

54. The lower-bourgeoisie woman, won over to the people's struggle, notably helps the liberation process. She is a potential liberator when she takes the side of the exploited.

55. In general, the contribution of women enables people to see more clearly the inhuman aspects of oppression. Women bring with them elements of humanization for the struggle, as well as cultural and artistic values in the process of liberation.

56. The capacity for enduring suffering and displaying courage and constancy, which characterizes women, is a decisive element in the revolutionary struggle. Women participate fully in the struggle without generally nurturing aspirations for power.

57. Women have lent their presence and support to the people's cause in the various forms of organization and, in particular, in the various tasks of the people's war. That in itself is a concrete experience indicating the revolutionary potential of women when they organize and fight.

58. For all this to be possible, women must develop a clear-eyed political awareness with regard to their participation in the people's cause. This will enable them to evade any and all manipulation, while at the same time working out their own specific contribution to political action.

REVOLUTIONARY STRUGGLE, PATHWAY TO HOLINESS

59. A Christian community is identified as such by its incorporation into the liberation process. Only in this process can one recover the way in which a human being is to find fulfillment as the image of God (male and female).

60. Christian communities must account for their faith and for the historical project they are fighting for. The Christian woman is playing a significant role in this area.

61. In revolutionary praxis we find a new pathway of holiness for the committed woman. Hundreds of women have been imprisoned, tortured, and persecuted for the cause of liberation.

62. In Latin America a special challenge faces Christians because they are a real force on the continent and must live out their Christian praxis. A church that risks itself for the people's movement creates the conditions for authentic militancy within the revolutionary movement by Christian women.

63. Because she is both female and Christian, a woman must pay double duty to legitimate her status as a believer in militant revolutionary activity. She is viewed with mistrust because she is a woman and because she is a Christian.

64. It is important to stress the contribution of Christians, and of women in particular, to the Nicaraguan revolution. Their faith in the spiritual mystique of victory helped them to bring about the triumph of the revolution. Believing in the resurrection, they believed that victory was certain and they fought with generosity to the end.

PART II
WOMEN IN THE BUILDING OF THE PEOPLE'S CHURCH

The People-Oriented Vocation of the Church

65. The people-oriented basis of the church goes back to its very source and foundation: Christ the poor person. God became human by becoming poor. The humanity of Christ, in which we have been saved, is the humanity of the poor.

66. The message of the kingdom is a promise and a fulfillment announced to the poor. They will announce it to all humanity and the church until the end of time.

67. To be faithful to its origin, the church today must return to being the church of the poor. It must elaborate its people-oriented vocation.

68. The Latin American movement of the common people is a sacrament of the Holy Spirit who renews the face of the earth, and of God's power and wisdom. It is also a historical mediation, in and through which the church undergoes conversion and grows in its service to the kingdom. The people's movement is the church's vocation and mission.

The People's Church: Vocation or Alternative?

69. We consider that the option for the poor and oppressed is the way that Jesus preferred to have his church take to be faithful to the kingdom. The church is not free to choose not to opt for the poor. Seen in this light, the people's church is not an optional alternative but the vocation of the whole community.

70. The institutionality of the church finds definition in its fidelity to Jesus Christ and concrete embodiment in its vocation and mission to the common people. This institutionality—i.e., its origin, message, and function in the kingdom—is inextricably bound up with its fidelity to the poor, who are a true sacrament of the risen Christ.

71. The people's church as a course, which is now in full gestation, is not an alternative to any other church. It is absolutely senseless to set up an opposition between institutional church on the one hand and people's church on the other. Hence a "parallel church" is any and every sort of church that seeks to develop from a perspective that denies the people-oriented vocation and mission of Jesus' church.

72. We see and acknowledge various tendencies and tensions within the church. Such things as liberation theology, liberating evangelization, and base-level communities represent an alternative to theologies, pastoral approaches, and structures that are domineering and hegemonic within the church. The majority of the latter are traditional in character or limited to progressive, modernizing measures.

73. The people's church is not an alternative to the people's movement. What is more, this church is the vocation of the people's movement insofar as in its life it seeks to express the deepest yearning and motivation of the common classes: universal love. The people's church strives to be the sacrament of Christ and of the people's movement with ever growing authenticity.

74. Precisely by virtue of its option for the classes of the common people, the people's church effectively regains its universal evangelical vocation. It is from that vantage point that it summons all the communities of faith to unity, and it is in its service to the poor that it makes concrete the following of Jesus. The pathway of solidarity and fidelity in the people's movement is a pathway to holiness when it is lived out in the light of faith in Jesus Christ.

The People's Movement: A Theological Datum

75. The people fighting for its liberation is thereby constituted as a historical subject. Here we are dealing with a collective subject made up of individuals who are related to one another by virtue of the vision they share about their own condition and class interests. These interests are antagonistic to those of the dominant class.

76. The people's movement—by virtue of its awareness, its fighting spirit, its confidence in the future, its courage, generosity, mystique, and joy—reveals the power of the risen Lord and speaks of God. So for us the people's movement in Latin America can be considered a theological datum.

Christian Communities: A Collective Theological Subject

77. Christian communities are originated by the Spirit on the basis of the people's movement and its dynamism. By virtue of their specific Christian nature, they perceive, live, and proclaim the power of the Lord in the people's movement. By their solidarity they contribute profound values to the struggle: e.g., gratuitousness, mystical elements of spirituality, confidence in victory, and opening-out to universal love. These are decisive factors in the construction of the new society.

78. Theological production arises out of the life of Christian communities. They constitute the subject of theological activity. This production arises spontaneously out of the celebration of the faith, or out of broader events in which people share sufferings and struggles, life and joy, study and reflection.

79. Theological production is the fruit of struggle and prophetic reflection, of living as a community in the spirit of God. Theological production is the fruit of the pastoral creativity of communities, of their own conversion to Christ, the poor man and fighter.

80. Within the communities we find efforts to systematize this experience of God. There is a plethora of pamphlets, bulletins, songs, poetic pieces, and plays. Here people with specialties add their contribution. They bring together the living experience of the community, work it up, and then return it to the community. In so doing, they carry on the process of production. Hence the individual theologian, in order to fulfill his or her task, will have to be organically linked up with the Christian community and the movement of the common people.

WOMEN IN CHRISTIAN COMMUNITIES
OF THE COMMON PEOPLE

Presence and Absence

81. In the church the woman is present *en masse*, but she is absent in the orientation and management of the institution.

82. The image and role assigned to women by bourgeois society has found its reflection in the presence and absence of women in the church. Moreover, thanks to the dominant currents of biblical interpretation and theological tradition, the church has helped to reinforce the ideology of the ruling classes concerning women. At the same time it has elaborated a brand of charity that is meant to offer assistance and protection to women.

83. On the basis of the way in which the church has viewed its relationship to the political authorities, it has read and interpreted biblical and theological tradition and elaborated a pastoral approach with these characteristics:

—Permanent absence of the women's question as a specific focus for community pastoral work and theological reflection.

—Uninterrupted presence of the women's problem as a preoccupation with morals and charitable assistance.

—Women's presence in the construction of Christian communities of the common people, but the absence of any theological reflection that incorporates the women's question.

84. The people's church adopts a class-based perspective and incorporates the woman into the life and evangelical work of base-level communities. Its development remains limited, however, insofar as it has not explicitly posed the issue of women as a specific challenge with regard to the buildup of the church, its ministries, its organic setup, and so forth. It is not elaborating or systematizing any theological reflection that has been reformulated on the basis of the alternatives posed by feminism.

Women and Theological Activity

85. The woman who belongs to the classes of the common people by extraction or choice is part of the collective subject that transforms history, a true theological happening.

86. The woman believer, as a member of a Christian community, is also a subject of day-to-day theological work. She shares its experience of God and participates in the celebration of the faith by study groups. She takes part in the preparation of pamphlets, bulletins, and so forth.

87. Even though women participate in Christian communities, up to now we do not see any specific contribution based on the whole woman's problem in the theological production of such communities.

88. If the people's church is to make progress and if liberation theology is to mature, we simply must adopt the rule of making every effort to incorporate elements specifically rooted in the situation of women into any and all theological articulations.

89. At various levels there are a few women who do contribute to the systematization and communication of the theology arising out of communities of the common people. Since their participation has had very little significance, however, we must push for the specialization of our female comrades in theological tasks; the aim would be for them to become organic intellectuals within the people's process.

Possibilities for a Biblical Theology from a Woman's Standpoint

90. We would like to point out that every reading of the word of the Lord, if it is to be a summons to conversion and an act of contemplation, must be read from the standpoint of the poor. When he read and explained the Scriptures, Jesus offered a rereading of them (Luke 4:16f.). In other words, he read them from the standpoint of his own poverty and his struggle for justice. Rereading the Bible—i.e., going back and reading it from the standpoint from which it was written—entails an effort to discover its central message, with the aim of living it and communicating it in the day-to-day struggle.

91. Our concern is to see how the Bible might be a source for elaborating a theology from a woman's standpoint. We can say that the Bible brings together only a few facets of the people's life and God's revelation. Hence it is a fact that woman does not constitute a direct preoccupation of the biblical redactors. The central focus is the saving activity of God, who fulfills the covenant despite the people's infidelity. And God does this from the standpoint of the poor, be they male or female.

92. But above and beyond the cultural and anthropological mediation through which the Bible speaks to us of women, its message is clear and enlightening. For example, it tells us:

—That no form of oppressing women can find legitimation on the basis of the Law or in the name of Yahweh;

—That fidelity to Yahweh means subverting the cultural patterns imposed on women, and even the lines of conduct among God's people;

—That the representative women who could not be passed over in silence by the Bible play a role that, in general, is linked with politico-religious events of importance to the people;

—That the "women witnesses" of the Bible are a prototype of the new people. They are pedagogical figures linked with broader groups of men and women who brought prophecy and the promise of the kingdom to life and effect.

93. In its reading of the Bible, church tradition has injected antifemale prejudices. These prejudices have not only obscured the wealth of women's witness but also stripped the whole reading of the Lord's word of its spiritual force and undermined its historical effectiveness.

94. A militant reading of the Bible enables us today to recover and elaborate the collective experience of women who have staked their lives on the liberation of the people and the proclamation of this good news both in the present and the past.

Christology and Women

95. The key to a coherent exegesis that will facilitate the formulation of a theology based on a women's perspective is to take the prophetic practice of

Jesus as the starting point. Jesus himself continues, concretizes, and revitalizes the prophetic practice of the Old Testament.

96. This christology will find its historical context and development insofar as we contemplate Jesus in terms of the situation of oppression, injustice, and exploitation that dominates the countries of Latin America. Its characteristic stress will be on the historical Jesus—his practice, his status as a poor person, and his fight for justice. The experience of Christ's resurrection will be emphasized as a gift to the people and a collective achievement to be won.

97. The behavior of Jesus toward women is consistent with his mission and message of justice. It is to be understood and articulated in the light of his commitment to the cause of the poor and oppressed.

98. The imitation and following of Jesus by his disciples entails the obligation for them to overcome and get beyond the cultural and ideological obstacles that foster discrimination against women. It is not possible to embrace Jesus' cause if one maintains attitudes that oppress and marginalize women.

99. For a theology based on the reality of women, we think it is important to remember that the incarnation of God's Son took place in the humanity of the poor, and that his resurrection is the victory of the new humanity over death. Jesus' specific preoccupation with women is inscribed in this dynamism. It is the dynamics of a God who became poor first and foremost, rather than male or female, and who overcomes death to create a new humanity devoid of divisions by class, race, or sex (Gal. 3).

100. The christological perspective just outlined above enables us to recapture the role of Mary as an element in a theology from a women's perspective. By way of example, we might cite the following points:

—Mary commits herself to the cause of the kingdom, disregarding her own reputation as a woman. She gets pregnant even though it causes great pain to Joseph and much scandal to her neighbors.

—The *Magnificat*, a prophetic canticle, summarizes in advance women's role in the liberation of the people.

—Mary offers her witness of fidelity, resistance, and self-surrender during the trial of Jesus, his death on the cross, and his victory over death.

—Mary displays her fortitude during the difficult times when the early community faces persecution. She opened new pathways in the foundation of the church.

—In Mary we see the unique, authentic sense that maternity can have. It is the generation and creation of the new humanity. It has a communitarian sense insofar as Mary hands over her son to humanity. Thus her life has a social dimension that she contributes to humanity. In the generosity of her commitment and surrender we can appreciate the community-oriented reality of the woman as a sacrament.

CONCLUSIONS AND PROPOSALS

101. We have sought to examine and analyze the oppressed situation of women in Latin America, and also their participation in Christian communities and the revolutionary struggle. Our examination prompts us to make the following proposals.

102. We should reformulate the whole issue of a revolutionary Christian morality. It should be framed in terms of oppression versus liberation, and its theological implications should be worked out. For the transformation of relationships, we would offer the following suggestions:

—The false values that have impeded a commitment to liberation, particularly among women, should be called into question.

—There should be a socialization of relationships in order to destroy private property and power-plays in every aspect of human life: in the production and labor process and in the process of reproduction, so that there can really be voluntary maternity serving the community rather than only the family nucleus.

—Sex relationships and relations of friendship should be enriched so that they are not exclusivist and oppressive. Instead they should help to foster personal growth and participation in the revolutionary struggle.

103. We would like to see the organization of a women's collective. Such a collective would reflect on the faith and elaborate its theology on the basis of actual practice in the revolutionary struggle and among Christian communities.

104. Women should be encouraged to participate in grassroots communities engaging in Christian reflection. This is urgently needed. Women should also be trained to undertake the work of educating, systematizing, and leading.

105. Every theologian of liberation should be urged to reformulate his or her theological categories from a women's standpoint, and to explore revelation more deeply from that same standpoint.

APPENDIX
Testimony of María Etty C.   T.I. 493,368
Cali, Colombia, June 17, 1979

To the Christians of Colombia: From the women's prison of Palmira I am sending this letter to the Christian people of Colombia, and to those entrusted with the task of bringing Christ's message of justice and love to all humanity. The present letter is human testimony to the abuses committed against my physical, moral, and psychological integrity by the military authorities.

I was picked up in Cali on May 10 of this year. Four men whom I had never seen before took me by force and hoisted me into a white jeep. They blindfolded me and tied me up, pointing a gun in my face.

They took me to an area known as the *remonta*, belonging to the Pichincha batallion of Cali. The place is *hell itself*. They left me standing in the rain, and they beat me with sticks, guns, and kicks. (The men said they were from B2 Intelligence.)

They pressured me to say that I possessed arms. I could not because it was not true. Since I refused to admit to accusations and things of which I was not guilty, they took me to a lake and held me under several times. When I was on the verge of drowning, they would drag my head above water. Seeing that I was pretty well suffocated, they pulled me out and made me vomit out the water inside me. Then they brought me to an anthill and stuck ants into my genital organs. They beat my breasts, saying that I would never be able to nurse a baby if I had one. Each man in turn raped me, causing a hemorrhage. The hemorrhaging lasted for two days. I got no medical help, no food, not even a drop of water. All this physical torture was nothing compared to the *psychological torture*. They showed me girls who had been beaten and raped. They said they were going to bring my sister there and do the same thing to her.

The pressured me by taking advantage of the great affection that exists in my family. They said they would beat up my mother. I was at the batallion headquarters almost thirty days without being able to see my family. Toward the end of that time I was permitted to see a lawyer only.

When I became ill, I was taken to their infirmary. There they applied ointments and remedies to the wounds. They gave me tablets for my vaginal infection. I still was suffering from hemorrhages, a sore knee that could not bend, a backache along my spine, and constant nightmares. My stomach also was burning because I had been without food for five days.

I beg all people of good will, all Christians of Colombia, to show concern for their brothers and sisters in Christ. I beg them not to overlook or forget the situation of people like me, who have been beaten and maltreated by men who have forgotten that we deserve respect as human beings.

To the ecclesiastical authorities, whose concern is to turn the message of Christ into a reality, I offer this testimony of martyrdom and calvary through which I was forced to go by the authorities mentioned at the start of this letter.

I thank you for the help and attention you may deign to give my letter, and I invite anyone to verify my words and share my anguish.

Signed: María Etty C.
T.I. 493,368, Cali

4

Indigenous Mobilization and the Theology of Liberation

Juanita Vásquez (Guatemala), Manuel Amboya (Ecuador), and Gregorio Vásquez (Mexico)

There are many and varied experiences of indigenous liberation on the continent. They are not all of equal importance, nor do we have a sufficient knowledge of the reflection about them. The theology of liberation has made little contribution to these indigenous processes. Nevertheless, they have advanced.

Within this context, and in response to requests from distinct countries, a meeting on Indigenous Mobilization and the Theology of Liberation was prepared. This meeting was held in San Cristóbal de las Casas, Mexico, from September 3 to 7, 1979. Eight countries were represented: Brazil, Ecuador, Guatemala, Nicaragua, Mexico, Peru, Panama, and El Salvador. A total of sixty persons participated.

PARTICIPANTS AND OBJECTIVE

The meeting was carried on in an ecumenical climate. It was open to indigenous and non-indigenous delegates. A majority of those who participated were indigenous lay persons from the base, although there were also several indigenous priests and religious women. The rest were lay experts in the social sciences, anthropologists, theologians, priests, bishops, and religious.

The objective of the meeting is expressed in its very title. The idea was (*a*) to get to know the struggles and the mobilization of the indigenous nations in their process of liberation; (*b*) to spell out the vital faith content within these liberating experiences; and (*c*) to arrive at concrete commitments.

This document is a synthesis of the responses of the working groups to questions regarding the three themes of the seminar. The direct conversational style is maintained for it better expresses the indigenous culture and the authenticity of the reflection.

NATURE OF THESE CONCLUSIONS

The conclusions have neither the structure, the language, nor the internal cohesiveness of a theoretical exposition. But beyond the heterogeneous description of situations and experiences, including some personal interpretations, there exists an enormous convergence of certain fundamental political conclusions. These political conclusions are not necessarily based on an analysis of the existing socio-economic system, nor of the actual political situation in Latin America or in the world. The theoretical framework of contemporary social sciences and of the theology of liberation were not used in its elaboration. In fact, contemporary social sciences as well as the theology of liberation are found to be trailing behind the development of the farmworkers' mobilization and the ethnic problem of the indigenous peoples.

There was no opportunity to allow a theoretical elaboration within the theology of liberation or the contemporary social sciences. *Rather, the conclusions flowed quite naturally from the very experience of the indigenous struggle:* the struggle for land; its importance as a fundamental element in the process of conscientization and identification; its limitations within the broader struggle of indigenous people and farmworkers, its more tactical than stategic characteristics; the forms of ownership and organization of the means of production; and the necessity of popular organizations that have broad regional bases; the politics of alliances and the unity of the exploited; the problem of the ethnic dimension as the starting point within the struggle, but also as a limiting factor as well as the object of manipulation by external interests; the necessity to include the ethnic dimension in a class perspective. In processing this data, it was thought better to show how the people, by their own experience, arrive at the conclusion that they are exploited not only, and not principally, because they are indigenous, but fundamentally because they are of the working classes, that is, farmworkers.

LAND AND INDIGENOUS ORGANIZATION

Questions:
  —What does the land really mean to you?
  —What kinds of organization help and hinder us in our struggle for liberation?

Group 1

—Those who possess land feel secure, feel that they have life. But some, egotistically, reserve it only for themselves. It is better when the land is possessed by the community. The possession of land *helps* the struggle, although at times this is not true, because it is not sufficient to maintain the people.

—At times the land is a way of exploiting, by means of taxes and other things. We have very little land, only the bare minimum with which to survive; the large landowners and cattle-raisers exploit us; we are forced to leave our land and rent somewhere else. Those who expel us from the land strip us of our identity as a people.

—We see the possibility of having our own indigenous popular organizations. But we should be united to other non-indigenous organizations. There are certain organizations that do not help us, but rather promote the oppressors. We have learned by experience that when we organize, we are killed or put in prison.

Group 2

—When we have land we are happy because we have food. We feel committed to its production. We feel that we are persons.

—The land is not an end in itself, but rather the force necessary to get out from under the domination of the petty chiefs (local leaders of economic, political, and cultural exploitation).

—Within the existing system, to possess the land does not really give security, but it does give us the possibility of struggling. The fruits of the land belong to the exploiters. We have to begin by discovering how they rob us of our land and its fruits. The struggle for the land does not end when the land is won, but rather in the taking over of power.

—Organization is necessary, because without it we cannot struggle against the system that kills us, nor achieve the right to live. The struggle has to lead to a collective work system, different from the present one.

—Experience has shown us that political parties are proselytizing, have their own selfish interests, and do not concern themselves with the interests of the people. They divide us to defend their own interests. It is necessary to form parties that really represent the farmworkers. If not, they will always manipulate us. There are already small organized groups, cooperatives, that are a first step.

Group 3

—The land is our life; it is the source and protection of our life. It is like a mother. On it we stand, we walk, we rest. From it God drew life.

—Some covet it for themselves (even some Indians): it becomes a source of conflicts, even conflicts within the family. There are indigenous farmworkers who labor up to twelve hours a day, just like animals. The land must be redistributed.

—The agrarian reforms have not benefited the Indian who works the land. Often the land remains in the hands of the old traditional landowners. At the present time, even the women are inciting their husbands to fight for the land, because their salaries are insufficient.

—The land belongs to everyone, because its only owner is God.

—The farmworkers who are most politically aware claim the land not only for themselves, but for all their fellow workers. Divided as it is, the land does not produce. To possess land is to possess power for everyone. We have to find ways to make it produce more. The populist governments make certain concessions simply to win electoral bases. What they really do is divide the farmworkers.

—The land is a means of exploitation used by the intermediate sectors of society. It produces food, but our situation is a sad one, full of injustices. Those who leave the land in order to study want to work only with their minds, while we work with our sufferings. The large landowner does not live on the land but only sees it from time to time.

—Organization leads to unity provided that tactically one is organized starting from and with the people. The problem is in how to maintain unity despite the repression. We regret the fact that there have been betrayals of Indians by other Indians as well as acts of violence against committed pastoral agents. Some, however, became traitors by reason of necessity.

—Traditional forms of organization are not enough. At the present time we have new enemies. New organizations are demanded to face up to new projects, many of which come from outside the country. These will be made by being aware of the indigenous community spirit.

—The parties, always interested in gaining votes, promise, deceive, divide, but do nothing for the people. We should not exalt the party but rather the popular farmworkers' organization. Participation in the party depends on its objectives, on our objectives, and on the intensity of the struggle. Some new popular movements think that the political parties can be used.

—We perceive the charismatic movements as enemies of the farmworkers' progress, likewise the branches of Protestantism of evangelical origin. The majority of the ecclesiastical hierarchy does not support us.

Group 4

—The land is a mother for us. It is our inheritance as a homeland. It includes the water, the trees, the mountains, all those things that make it function as the earth. The land is the farmworkers' sustenance, as it is for the whole of society. It is the heart of the nation.

—Behind the notion of the land there are profound truths. It represents three themes in our struggle. First, to win the land—even though we know that it is not sufficient to conquer it in order to secure it. The powerful can always avenge themselves for what we have won by selling goods to us dearly while buying from us cheaply what we produce. Second, in order to sustain our struggle for the land it is necessary to take control of power; only in this way can we assure that justice be done. Third, it is necessary to change the system of working the land; community work should prevail over a more individualistic system.

—For this reason we need a great deal of organization, much strength; we need to join the indigenous forces with those of the farmworkers and the other workers. In this way we will be a great force. Education is also demanded to work with the head and the heart to insure that things may be from everyone and for everyone. Furthermore, organization to win the land is a great step forward; but there are groups who do not organize to gain the land, since for them the struggle is tremendous. So we have to create small organizations to achieve little things; we have to leave the women freer so they can collaborate.

Group 5

—The land is the mother who gives us everything; without it we would die. It is our blood. With it we live; without it the others suck our blood. God is the heart of heaven and earth; if the land is offended, we offend God.

—When it is planting time, some of us do not have relations with our wives because it is time to fecundate the land.

—The land calls the community together to sow, to reap, and to celebrate the fiesta.

—Other communities see the land related to the water; without water the land does not bring forth life.

—We have had to organize ourselves to defend our land. Otherwise they leave us with nothing and we die. We need to be organized, with organizations born from the people themselves and from their needs. The political parties cause divisions among us. The most viable type of organization would seem to be one which comes from the people and is for the people.

CULTURE, ETHNIC ROOTS, CLASS

Questions:
      —Is the indigenous culture an obstacle or a liberating element?
      —What should be used for the liberation of the indigenous peoples?
      —Are there any historical projects that begin from the indigenous culture itself?
      —Does class analysis help or hinder the liberation of the indigenous peoples?
      —Do cultural analysis and class analysis oppose one another? If not, how are they integrated with one another?

Group 1

—Culture itself can be taken as a starting point.

—The value of culture depends on the concrete struggle. It is useful in function of the objectives of liberation. It provides a moment of identity, the point of departure; it provides an opportunity for linkages when the struggle is broadened.

—It will be necessary to create new customs and values of liberation from the perspective of one's own culture. Given the fact that culture implies an economic base, it will also be necessary to create work bases and means of production proper to each indigenous nation.

—Those who do not belong to the indigenous culture (anthropologists, sociologists, theologians) have a role in the process of liberation, provided they participate in it and incarnate themselves in the culture.

—The dominant culture has made the indigenous cultures into folklore.

Group 2

—In an abstract way, culture can be either a help or a hindrance to liberation. But in its historical context of oppression, we have discovered it as an instrument of liberation, inasmuch as it is a historical element.

—Culture is an instrument and serves specific interests. For example, in the liturgy the minister expresses himself in the language of the indigenous group. But whom does this serve? With what interests is it used?

—In the process of liberation every culture has value, and specifically as it expresses the interests of the poorer classes as opposed to the interests of the dominating classes.

—It is necessary to use class analysis, especially with indigenous cultures, given the fact that the indigenous peoples have an isolated and limited perspective. Thus they have confused things and have lived out oppositions between indigenous people and those who side with the landowners, even though the latter have been just as exploited as the former. Class analysis helps to clarify the real causes, thus helping to advance the process of liberation, which we express in terms of power or as the kingdom of God.

—We believe that the indigenous cultures do contain in some way historical projects, as expressed in their values of dignity, solidarity, and fraternity.

Group 3

—The indigenous cultures are of great importance. Without them the people could not survive. Just look at what happens when the Indians lose their native culture. The native languages are an important factor in communication. But our cultures have both positive and negative aspects. We are trying to purify them by giving emphasis to the positive aspects. Thus we hope to find our identity.

—There is no one culture that is better for liberation than another. What is important is that the people consciously use their own values, and especially that of unity.

—As indigenous peoples we have to unite ourselves to other poor people

who are in equal or similar circumstances, those who suffer exploitation as
we do. The power does not reside simply in the culture but in the forms of
organization that our ancestors have handed over to us. If we exist today, it is
because there is something in our traditions that has helped us continue living.

Group 4

—When it was asked if culture helped or not, we responded that it did, but
that it was important to create solidarity with other groups and peoples
engaged in the same struggle, based not so much on a given culture or words,
but on what lies behind the words in a given culture.
   —We arrived at the following conclusions:
      —to encourage more ties with other indigenous groups on an interna-
tional level.
      —to stress such values as equality, unity, community, which are the
essentials of our cultures.
      —to study and decide how to support other indigenous nations in the
same country and in other countries.
      —more than simply recognize the values of each culture, we should
prove that they really exist and are lived.
      —clearly we have to forge more links with other groups, indigenous
or not; but the indigenous people have to affirm their own identity so as
not to lose it in these new alliances.

Group 5

—Culture can be an instrument of liberation.
—Our culture is the soul, the heart of all that we do. We have to see our
own culture as an element that unites us. But there are difficulties, because
our cultures exist within the broader culture of our countries, which dominate us and impede the living out of our cultural values.

THE CHURCH AND LIBERATION

Question:
   —Have the faith, the church, and religion served to help or stimulate
   your process of liberation?

Résumé of the replies:
   —The Protestant sects only serve to divide and to impede our union. They
preach a great deal that we should serve the boss and participate in the official
farmworkers' cooperatives. There are many of these sects out there where
petroleum is being discovered or where large agricultural or electification

programs are being established. These sects, in order to win entry into the communities, say that they are coming in the name of the priest.

—Many Catholic priests and religious are on the side of the exploiters and at times even turn us in to them. They defend the large landowners and the rich. However, there are also priests, bishops, and religious committed to the cause of the Indians. Some indigenous priests are with their people. They commit themselves, and struggle to defend the people. There are priests who have died together with some of our communities.

—In some places the church is the strongest political supporter of the Indians, when it says what it should say. Catholic priests and bishops have supported our social struggles; some were killed because of their commitment.

—Our religious "fiestas" have been moments of self-questioning for us and sources of community.

—The Word of God has allowed us to understand things even though we did not know how to read or write. The Epistle of St. James, Chapter 2, throws much light on our situation and struggle. For this reason we do not ignore it; we are distinctly spoken of in that epistle. We do not separate what is Christian from what is political in the struggle. In this manner one's conscience is more profoundly touched. We recognize the fact that the motives behind our struggle are not a question of revenge. It is a question of fighting for our rights.

5

The Situation of the Black Race in Latin America and the Caribbean

Lloyd Stennette, Mauro Batista, Barry Chavannes

In analyzing the existence of domination on the Latin American continent, the Conference set aside time for the specific issue of the oppression of the black race. This particular analysis was a continuation of the preparatory seminar held in Jamaica from December 27 to December 31, 1979.

At the São Paulo Conference two papers on the subject were presented, and they are included here. Also included is one of the papers presented at the earlier seminar in Jamaica.

THE SITUATION OF BLACKS IN COSTA RICA
Lloyd Stennette   (Costa Rica)

First of all, I would like to introduce myself. I am a black priest from Costa Rica, and I am a member of the Episcopal church. I carry out my ministry in the major port city of Limón along the Atlantic coast, where the largest concentration of blacks in Costa Rica is to be found.

My task this morning is twofold. I am to present a brief report on the Jamaica Seminar, which dealt with "Race, Class, and Liberation Theology." And I am to talk about the situation of blacks in Costa Rica.

The Jamaica Seminar

From December 27 to 31, 1979, a Seminar was held in Kingston, Jamaica, on the general theme of "Race, Class, and Liberation Theology." The Seminar was organized by the Ecumenical Association of Third World

Theologians (EATWOT) as part of the preparation for this São Paulo Conference.

The participants included representatives of black theology from the United States such as Professor James Cone, black representatives from the Caribbean and Central America, and a few liberation theologians from South American countries.

The central aim of the seminar was to explore the topics indicated in the title: i.e., to examine the difficulties existing in the practice and the conceptualization of racial and class oppression as the starting point for theological reflection and a struggle for liberation.

As we know, Latin American liberation theology has elaborated its central themes around the contrast between oppression and liberation. But it has not given sufficient consideration to the particular forms of oppression suffered by the indigenous peoples and the black race living on the Latin American continent. Thus the Jamaica Seminar was very important as a preliminary probing of the topic.

Unfortunately the results were not what had been hoped for. Various reasons precluded the participation of all those who had been invited. There was an interesting and fruitful exchange of valuable experiences, but we did not get down to writing a document that could have been presented here at the São Paulo Conference. I see that such documents have been presented by indigenous peoples and women.

The Jamaica initiative must be judged positively, however, and we hope that this conference will help to make people more aware of the importance of the racial issue on our continent and stimulate theological reflection among their communities and their theologians.

The presence of us blacks here, a small number of blacks from Central America, the Caribbean, and Brazil, is one result of this new interest in the realities and problems surrounding race and color. The unanimous decision of the Jamaica Seminar was to ask this conference to place the black problem on the agenda. In other words, we want it to be viewed as an important reality in the theological reflection of liberation theology.

Blacks In Costa Rica

Having heard about the problem of indigenous peoples, I believe that the problem of blacks in Latin America is practically the same. Often people simply try to evade the issue. It seems as if we, as members of the black race, don't even exist on the continent. But there are millions of blacks in Latin America, in Brazil especially but also in the Caribbean, the countries of Central America, Venezuela, and Colombia.

I can't speak about the whole continent, nor about blacks in the United States. I can speak more authoritatively about the situation of blacks in Costa Rica. My confrere from Brazil will speak about the situation of blacks in this country.

I would like to begin by telling a story. When I talk to people who have visited Costa Rica and ask them if they saw any black people there, they always answer that they didn't see any. In the eyes of many people, Costa Rica is reduced to its capital, San José. They have never visited the port city of Limón, where I live amid a huge concentration of blacks.

The History of Blacks in Costa Rica. To become acquainted with our history, we must go back to the last century. In 1871 blacks were brought over from Jamaica to engage in forced labor. It was around that time that banana-growing began in Central America. Foreign corporations discovered that the soil of Costa Rica was suitable for bananas, but the native population was of no use because it could not resist various diseases. So blacks were brought over from Jamaica because they had a resistance to those diseases and could adapt better to this type of work.

They came to Costa Rica because they were promised that they would earn a lot of money and be there for only a short time. But the majority of them stayed in Costa Rica, and they have suffered a profound identity-crisis. In Costa Rica we blacks are not considered to be Costa Ricans. When we go to Jamaica, we are not Jamaicans either. And those who might go to Africa are not Africans. Frankly, I don't know what we are. In my country we have an expression that sums it all up. We are "neither *chicha* (a liquor drink) nor lemonade."

From my own limited experience and reading, I would say that this seems to be a reality affecting blacks all over the world. It seems that blacks have no home country and no clear awareness of their history or their identity. Throughout the world blacks have had to struggle to survive.

The situation of blacks in Costa Rica and in Latin America is worse than it is in the United States, it seems to me. In the course of time, and particularly in the decade of the sixties, blacks in the United States made great progress in the fight for civil rights.

We are still fighting to gain recognition and to win respect for our identity, our history, and our culture.

The 1948 Law and the Present Situation. In 1948 a law was passed which stipulated that all those living in Costa Rica were to be considered Costa Ricans. The initiative did not come from blacks. It came from José Figueres, a political leader of European descent, who would later be president of the republic. So after almost a century of possessing no nationality, blacks came to be considered Costa Ricans.

It is hard to know how many blacks there are in Costa Rica. The census gives no clear idea because many mulattoes do not consider themselves blacks. But on the whole I think that about 10 percent of the total population of two million is black.

There still exists a profound crisis of cultural and psychological identity among the blacks of Costa Rica. For one hundred years we have been geared to feel that we cannot go on being blacks. I don't know how we can change our color. If we want to be part of the national society of Costa Rica, the first thing we must do is learn Spanish. But our mother tongue is English, and that is what we speak to our families at home.

Many blacks are ashamed to be blacks. They would like to be white because they cannot get anywhere as blacks. Since they cannot return to Jamaica or head for Africa, they try to ape white society. That, too, is impossible. The result is frustration and resentment, which makes us marginalized and left behind.

The economic situation of Costa Rica has deteriorated in recent years. We are suffering from a socio-economic problem, and pay is very low. This affects black workers in particular.

Indulging in the myth that Costa Rica is the Switzerland of Latin America, the government says that there is nothing wrong in the country. All the problems are to be found in neighboring countries: e.g., Nicaragua, El Salvador, and Guatemala.

Reality gives the lie to such a view. Working people, and blacks in particular, are suffering from the rigors of the economic crisis that afflicts our region.

Culture, Religion, and the Churches. Another aspect of our oppression is the whole story of efforts made to strip us of our traditions, which are part of our culture. That is what has happened to many black customs and organizations in Limón. Let me give you a couple of examples.

Lodges have traditionally been a fraternity or a brotherhood where blacks have found help and solidarity. But they have suffered persecution and have almost disappeared, because they are viewed as secret or clandestine organizations with evil aims. The same thing has happened to the Jamaica Burial Scheme and the U.N.I.A., which were mutual-aid societies. The opposition and harassment by whites has undermined their prestige, so these organizations are disintegrating.

The majority of Costa Rican blacks belong to Protestant churches. They are Baptists, Methodists, or Episcopalians like me. In Costa Rica there are only two black priests in the Catholic church. The same is true in the other countries of Central America. My confrere from Nicaragua tells me that he is the only black Catholic priest in his country. The Catholic church has not taken any interest in the blacks of Costa Rica.

We blacks have suffered discrimination and segregation within our own churches. Moreover, a prevalent interpretation of the Bible in popular circles condemns blacks as evil people. For example, sin is black; purity is a virtue as white as the lily. These symbols, used in preaching and catechetics, reinforce the latent racism in whites. And this is true even though they may be as poor as we are.

That is why the task of theology must include a serious study of racism. It must be seen as one specific form of oppression within the oppressive capitalist system prevailing in Latin America and the Caribbean.

I would like to speak to this conference on behalf of all the blacks on our continent and all over the world, not just on behalf of Costa Rican blacks. I urge this conference not to try to avoid the black question. We must face up to it because the black race is suffering from discrimination and other ills. And I pray that this reflection, begun here, will continue to go deeper in the years ahead.

BLACK AND CHRISTIAN IN BRAZIL
Mauro Batista (Brazil)

The following remarks are the fruit of a series of meetings and reflections presently being undertaken in Brazil by some black Christian bishops, priests, nuns, and other pastoral agents. The basic problem under discussion has been that of blacks as Christians within the Catholic church. And the basic question being raised is this: What place *should* the black Brazilian Christian occupy in the church? What, in other words, is the place of blackness or negritude in the Brazilian Catholic church? Once we give up the destructive ideology of the "black person with a white soul," how will black Brazilians be able to broaden and deepen the qualitative catholicity of the church by affirming their black identity within the ecclesial community?

I will try to present some of the considerations that have been brought up. In particular, I will pose some of the questions that are presently being raised.

Remembering History

Traffic in black slaves to Brazil began around 1530 and continued to 1850. Some four to six million Africans came to Brazilian territory, and millions more died on the journey from Africa to Brazil. They were used on plantations—farming, stock-raising, and mining. Most of them came from West Africa, the region around the Gulf of Guinea (Nigeria, Dahomey, Ghana, etc.) and the old Portuguese colonies in Africa (Angola, the two former Congo regions, and Mozambique). They were settled mainly in the Northeast states and Bahia, Rio de Janeiro and the adjacent states, and the mining areas in the state of Minas Gerais. Brazil was the last country in the world to legally abolish black slavery (May 13, 1888). One of the myths given widest circulation in our official history is that slavery in Brazil was mild, almost a fraternal and family-like relationship. The myth of the Black Mama and the Black Old Man—kindly, humble, and ready to serve—still goes on today, glossing over the truth of real oppression and the crushing of black cultures and black people. Is it possible for there to be such a thing as mild, benign slavery? That sort of ideologically manipulated historiography tries in every way to camouflage slave uprisings and slave revolts. Here we have an important truth that remains to be unveiled and brought out into the light.

For a long time the black population constituted the majority in Brazil. The 1872 census, twenty-two years after the suppression of the slave trade and sixteen years before the abolition of slavery, gave these figures: 3,854,000 whites; 4,862,000 mulattoes (Indian mestizoes were included in this figure); and 1,996,000 blacks. With the proclamation of the Republic (November 15, 1889) and the arrival of various waves of immigrants (chiefly settling in the southern states), the population picture changed.

It is certainly true that Brazilian statistics, particularly with regard to the item of "color," are not entirely trustworthy. Indeed, given our famous picture of "racial democracy," that item does not even show up in our 1970 census. But surely we can state that the black population of Brazil (including blacks and mulattoes) is around forty to fifty million. Thus, Brazil has the second largest black population of any country in the world, coming behind Nigeria. And in certain areas of Brazil (e.g., Bahia) the black concentration is very great.

The "Place" of the Brazilian Black

After 1888 blacks were more or less driven out of the centers of production. They had to rest content with peripheral positions in society. The abolition of slavery favored the Brazilian economy far more than it favored the Brazilian blacks who, with their slave labor, had built that economy up to then. Coming out of slavery, blacks possessed no primitive accumulation on either the intellectual or material level. They have not managed to forge their identity even up to today. It has been said that it is not true that Brazilian blacks know their place. They *simply don't know any other place.*

And there is nothing wondrous about the "place" of the black person in Brazil. Leaving rural areas, where their density drops, the ex-slaves and their descendants become members of the proletariat. They enter into the savage competition that is part of Brazil's urban, industrial system. There they must compete with other elements in society: other Brazilians who are not ex-slaves, immigrants, and their descendants. Legally speaking, society is no longer divided up into "masters" and "slaves," as it was in the earlier period. Instead, it is divided up into economic classes fighting to get ahead within the capitalist system of production. Exploitation of manual labor is blatantly a part of that system and its methods.

We are in a certain sense still very close to the era of enslavement. So the vast majority of the ex-slaves and their descendants will find their "place" at the most critical point on graphs, at the most mediocre level in statistics, in the most gloomy paragraphs of reports, and on the lowest rungs of the socio-economic and cultural ladder. The "place" of the black shapes the map of an underdeveloped Brazil.

This is due to various factors. To mention a few, there is their lack of preparation and training; there are also color prejudices that are more or less veiled but nevertheless real and operative. Officially speaking, such prejudices do not exist in our country; but in fact they have accumulated over four centuries of black bondage. So blacks are rejected and forced to occupy the lowest social strata. We need not resort to specific studies or investigations by social scientists to prove this. The painful day-to-day experience of blacks living in Brazil is more than sufficient proof.

One result of this unfavorable social situation finds expression in the living situation of blacks. They live in various types of slums where family life crumbles and disintegrates, where the mortality rate is high, and where physical and mental diseases take their toll. Lacking educational training and living in this unwholesome atmosphere, many blacks turn to crime, alcohol, promiscuity, or an unreal dream world. In these things they hope to find refuge from a hard and often cruel reality.

The Ideology of Making Blacks White

Now let us say that it is true that racial discrimination does not exist in Brazil. After all, there is even a federal law prohibiting that type of discrimination (Afonso Arinos Act). And if we compare the situation in Brazil with that in the United States or South Africa, we can say that their sort of racial discrimination does not exist in Brazil. On the other hand we do see something in Brazil that is even more serious, insidious, and poisonous. It is the ideology that seeks to make black people white, the ideology of *branqueamento*. It is present and powerfully operative in our multiracial society.

How might we describe this ideology? Basically it is profoundly dualistic and Manichean in its view of reality. It says that white is good, black bad. Being black means embodying everything that is worthy of discredit and hate and that should be discarded rather than given recognition. The human ideal is being white, or being human and being white are completely equated. This ideology is not just to be found in the white population. It has penetrated every level of society and struck deep roots in blacks as well. As a result, blacks reject their own blackness, their selfhood, and their real identity as black human beings.

It is easy to see the consequences—personal, social, cultural, and so forth—of this ideology, which is still being upheld in our country. Black human beings are being affected at the very core of their being because this ideology suggests that being Brazilian essentially means being white; and Brazil does not want to give up the idea that it is a white country. This stance, hidden under the myth of "racial democracy," is responsible for all the distortions, prejudices, and inauthentic aspects to be found in our interracial relationships.

The Catholic Church and the Black Brazilian

Without going into great detail, we can certainly say that in the course of time the Catholic church was permeated by this ideology of *branqueamento*. Its pastoral activity was deeply marked by this way of looking at reality. This is particularly evident in the church's relationship with what are called Afro-

Brazilian cults. There we find the vision of the white European, the ideology of dominating white classes, and stubborn refusal to dialogue with those who are different. Such was the church's relationship with the black community during and after the period of slavery.

In broad terms we can say that the attitude of the church may be delineated in three stages:

1. From 1530 to 1950: Complete contempt for Afro-Brazilian cults. They are superstitious, crude, and savage. They are for ignorant people, who will abandon them as they become more civilized. Sometimes the cults are described and approached as works of the devil.

2. From 1950 to 1968: The Afro-Brazilian cults begin to grow and to penetrate the most varied sectors of the Brazilian population. It is the era of violent attacks and of apologetics that often fail to show respect for persons, races, and social groups. This attitude begins to undergo change around the time of Vatican II, and particularly after the Medellín Conference.

3. From 1968 on: After the Medellín Conference the church slowly begins to take sides with the poor. A goodly portion of the church drops its traditional alliances with the dominant classes and moves to the side of the marginalized and the oppressed. There is where the blacks are to be found for the most part. There is a growing interest in the religiosity of the common people, in religious practice that is black in origin. We see the beginnings of sympathy and dialogue. It is still an interest in religious matters *qua* religious, but some small groups are beginning to raise questions that are basically anthropological, or even racial and ethnic.

The First Stirrings of a New Stage

In Brazil's civil society some blacks with a university education are displaying ever increasing concern over the problems of color, race, and ethnicity. In 1977 these people began to organize in various parts of Brazil. The Unified Black Movement Against Racial Discrimination arose. Gradually more and more blacks are joining this movement. There is a certain amount of eclecticism in it, but the most radical wing of the movement is displaying three tendencies at least: *(a)* a strong Marxist influence; *(b)* a steadily intensifying anti-white attitude; *(c)* an attitude of distrust toward, if not outright rejection of, the Catholic church, based on historical reasons. They do not wish to be *re-baptized.* Hence they are restoring and upgrading the value of religions that are African in origin.

Starting in 1978, some black priests, religious, and committed lay people in the Catholic church have also begun to raise questions. They feel that in the Catholic church there is no room for the black person to be a black Christian. They are beginning to question the ideology that poisoned Catholic pastoral work in the past, that sought to make them black Christians with white souls. The preferential option for the poor, which was solemnly proclaimed by the recent Puebla Conference, makes this problem all the more urgent. Black

Christians of Brazil are seeking their authentic "places" within the catholicity of the church. It is a difficult task, and it has only just begun. It is a challenge, with countless obstacles both inside and outside the church. Much of the ground remains to be broken on the road ahead.

Where are we headed? This is the question we black Brazilians are asking ourselves.

DIALECTIC RELATIONS OF RACE, CLASS, AND CULTURE
Barry Chavannes (Jamaica)

Race and color have historically been part of social and cultural relations in Jamaica, as well as the rest of the English-speaking Caribbean. Race and color tend to emerge as problems at times when the national struggles reach a peak.

We need to ask ourselves why is there a race/color question 140 years after slavery and years after political independence from colonialism. The answer lies in the fact that there tends to be convergence between class and color. This also explains the failure to develop a vibrant national culture, as well as the ambivalence toward color that is apparent in times of relative calm.

Capitalism emerged in the west as a national force against feudalism and the aristocracy. The slaves in the colonies at first found a natural ally in the British national bourgeoisie. Emancipation along bourgeois lines would have meant the liquidating of the power of the oligarchy and the rise of a local national bourgeoisie, which in turn would have given rise to the subordination of British goods and capital. Faced with this contradiction the British bourgeoisie struck a compromise with the oligarchy. Slavery was abolished but plantation society continued.

Nevertheless, the new situation gave rise to a new alignment of social forces: the Jewish-mulatto-merchant capitalists involved in light manufacture and trading; the middle and rich peasants, a small but energetic stratum comprised of that section of the slaves closest to the slave masters; and the poor peasants, essentially landless squatters and tenants. All these social forces stood in opposition to the oligarchy and formed the main elements of the national movement during the nineteenth century.

With the rise of imperialism, British capital became subordinated to American capital. One result of the competition was the merging of the Jewish-mulatto elite and the oligarchy into an alliance with British imperialism. The national bourgeoisie, the middle strata, and the petty bourgeoisie (mainly artisans and peasants) found themselves in sharp opposition to foreign and local reaction, an opposition defined by color.

The emergence of a small working class, beginning at the turn of the cen-

This paper was presented at the Seminar "Racism and the Theology of Liberation," Jamaica, December 1979.

tury, completed the constellation of social forces that took shape in the modern period in Jamacia.

The same processes were at work throughout the other colonies, resulting in the 1930s (and in the case of the smallest territories in the late 1940s-1950s) in the assertion by the working class of its increasing political maturity. This new component to the national movement—plus the increasing strength of the international working-class movement embodied in socialism and communist and workers parties—led to independence. The gradual nature of independence, however, preserved the essential features of the class structure with its apparent color biases.

The dominant ideas of society are those of the ruling classes. These ideas permeate all other social classes as well. Hence, it is not suprising to find even at the present time among the most politically backward sections of the working people negative sentiments toward the race and the culture of the African peoples. For example, woolly hair is "bad," soft hair is "good"; "pretty" referring to a baby indicates brown color; "black people" are said to be the ones who sold out Marcus Garvey for rice and peas; etc.

No greater testimony exists at the present time of the persistence of the racial and color question than the growth of the Rastafari movement among sections of all the main social classes that stand in dialectical opposition to imperialism and the local oligarachy. And as further proof that the same social processes at work in Jamaica, where the movement originated, are also at work in the rest of the Caribbean, the Rastafari have also taken root throughout the region.

Beginning in 1932 as a religious movement of the urban poor in Jamaica, the Rastafari hold to the belief in the divinity of the former emperor of Ethiopia, Haile Selassie, look to the "repatriation" of all Africans in the new world, and at the present time cultivate unshorn locks, which they refer to as their "crown."

Thus, the ideology and practices of the Rastafari may be said to be an inversion of the ruling ideas of the society. Africa, they proclaim, is the same as Zion, or heaven, written about in the Bible: black, and all the attributes of the black race, is comely, and thus the defining of the hair as sacred; God is black—a counterposition to the white God image.

The Rastafari, using biblical imagery, cast the members of the ruling class and the state apparatus into the role of "Babylon," whose opposition to the "children of God" they argue is being played out in modern times in Jamaican society. But they go even further in actively seeking to revive and develop explicit cultural forms which have for hundreds of years been the object of suppression and contempt by the ruling class. Some of these are exotic imitations of traditional African forms made popular with the rise of nationalism in Africa itself. Others, however, have their roots in the experiences of the Caribbean peoples from slavery to the present and may be said to form bases for the development of our national culture.

For example, taking up from where the Jamaican peasantry left off, so to speak, the Rastafari have consciously striven to make a lasting contribution to the plastic arts. They have brought about a revival of popular forms of wood-carving and painting. They not only are an integral part of popular music throughout the region, especially in Jamaica, but also exercise a great influence on the direction this music is taking.

Nationalism not based upon class consciousness inevitably leads to chauvinism and isolation. Class consciousness, on the other hand, rooted in national experience elevates the national liberation struggles and gives them an international and hence a powerful moral character.

The national liberation movement today is confronted with a historic choice: which road, capitalism or socialism? This question is at the heart of all liberation struggles.

The growth of a socialist movement in the Caribbean has been faciliated by the presence in the region of the Cuban revolution. In the first place, Cuba has exerted a positive moral influence over the oppressed peoples of the region. The solution of the racial question as well as the practical gains made on behalf of the Cuban people have not gone unnoticed. In the second place, the practical demonstration of socialist assistance to the progressive regimes that have defied North American dictates and established friendly relations has had a positive effect.

For this reason the main strategic question for U.S. imperialism is Cuba. Unable to reverse the Cuban revolution, American imperialism seeks to isolate it from the rest of the region and to discredit its foreign policy.

It is fairly obvious that the church cannot come to grips with national liberation today without also coming to grips with the main contingents of the national movement. The struggles at the present time are being fought against a background of a hardening of the line of U.S. foreign policy toward the region and unprecedented heights of anticommunist propaganda.

Caught in the web of anticommunism and injected with massive doses of propaganda against Cuba and the Soviet Union, important sections of the church have become paralyzed by fear and, in Jamaica for one, are in danger of playing into the hands of neofascist elements.

At the same time, there are signs of vigor, for example the role of the church in exposing the neofascist Gairy regime in Grenada. These need to be encouraged in the hope that progressive Christians will not be afraid of struggling alongside the movement for national sovereignty and economic independence.

6

Interpreting Situations of Domination: The Poor, Ethnic Groups, and Classes Made Up of the Common People

Miguel Concha (Mexico)

When people talk about ethnicity or ethnic groups in Latin America, they usually are referring to indigenous peoples and blacks. At present they usually start off from such notions as "nation" or "the poor." Thus, for example, the indigenous peoples as a nation are contrasted with society as a whole or the national society; or the indigenous peoples as poor may be contrasted with the non-indigenous as affluent people.

The problem here lies in the fact that while such terms as "nation" or "poor person" are frequently used and are common-sense notions, they are not analytical or scientific categories.

If one does not go in for deeper analysis, then one falls into the contradiction of opposing indigenous society to the national society. Moreover, one fails to link the liberation process of the indigenous peoples with the liberation of other oppressed groups.

The same thing happens with the notion of "poor" people, which is also a common-sense notion. Poor people are people who are below certain income levels and who belong to specific cultural systems. We would do better to talk about socio-economic classes, groups, or strata that have differing relations with the production system and the income earned. If we do that, then we can distinguish various categories of poor people. They take on differing historical status because they have their own specific characteristics. In short, we will talk about specific types of poor people: a peasant, a peasant who is indigenous, a marginalized city dweller, a factory worker, and so forth.

Operating in this context, we can comprehend the role of the indigenous peoples and their relationship with other groups that are part of the national society when it comes to the common struggle for their liberation.

From the anthropological standpoint there has been an exaggerated emphasis on ethnicity insofar as it has been applied exclusively to certain societies labelled indigenous or black. In fact, ethnicity is a sum total of various phenomena having to do with cultural, ideological, social, and economic processes. In the tradition of Third World social science, this notion of ethnicity would correspond to the superstructure.

Now if we start from this concept, it is a contradiction to talk about indigenous groups as if they were the only ones that possessed ethnic characteristics. For we can also talk about the ethnicity of peasant groups or, in even more general terms, about the ethnicity of Western civilization. And within Western civilization we can distinguish various ethnic groups. Hence we can conclude that there is ethnicity in every human group because it is a characteristic of social groups.

There is no sense, then, in raising the banner of ethnicity solely and exclusively in the defense of indigenous groups. Instead we should talk about defending ethnic pluralism because other groups also have an ethnicity to defend. We can talk about saving and protecting the ethnicity of laborers. We can talk about the ethnicity of the oppressed vis-à-vis the ethnicity of the oppressors. In this focus the process of liberation is not reduced solely to the indigenous group. It is broadened to take in all the masses of the common people and all oppressed groups.

ETHNICITY AND CLASS ANALYSIS

Though it should be common knowledge, it is worth recalling that Marx did not invent class struggle. He analyzed production systems and explored in depth the reality of social classes. This led him to introduce three new ideas: (1) the history of humanity is a history of class struggle; (2) this struggle will lead to what Marx called the dictatorship of the proletariat; by that he meant a society in which the majority would assume control over the means of production; (3) after capitalism, society will evolve toward the ultimate disappearance of social classes.

We must demythologize the tendency to identify the notion of social class solely with the economic realm. In fact, the notion of class is a sociological, scientific, and historical concept of great profundity and richness. When we talk about social class, we are not talking merely about the economic nature of groups. Neither should the economic realm be presented as something isolated and exclusive. Marx himself insisted that the economic level is the starting point for an analysis of society as a whole.

Seen in this light, there is no contradiction between an analysis of class and an analysis of the ethnic issue. Ethnicity must be understood within the more general framework of social classes.

In the social sciences theoretical concepts have various dimensions. When we talk about "social status," for example, we are talking about many factors: income, prestige, social role, and so forth. The same holds true for the concept of class. It has economic, social, political, and ethnic dimensions. All of these, including the ethnic dimension, must be considered.

A case can be made that social scientists usually talk about class oppression and forget the ethnic dimension. So it is necessary to engage in a systematic effort to make the ethnic question an integral part of our overall analysis of society, without reducing ethnicity to mere economics.

The notion of social class gives a historical perspective to the reality of ethnicity. And the notion of à mode of production, in turn, gives a historical perspective to the notion of class. The mode of production historifies class relations, and it also enables us to historify the very nature of the ethnic factor.

If we do not frame ethnicity in a historical perspective, then it looks like an atemporal notion floating beyond and above historical phenomena. The diversity of the antagonistic groups enables us to view ethnicity as something that arises at a specific moment and that follows the rhythm of transformations in the social system as a whole.

Ethnicity is a historical phenomenon, undergoing change in accordance with historical conditions. What we understand today by the ethnic nature of indigenous groups is not the same thing that existed before the colonial period, during the colonial period, or right after independence was won. Ethnicity must be viewed in terms of the transformations experienced by the production system and by the cultures of the social classes.

We must have an adequate understanding of the nature of ethnicity if we wish to transform the present situation, develop the richness and capacity of indigenous groups, and promote their ethnic liberation.

ANTHROPOLOGICAL INTERPRETATIONS OF ETHNICITY

There are three basic currents in the anthropological interpretation of ethnicity and in attempts to solve the ethnic question.

Traditional Indigenism

This approach arose at the Inter-American Indigenist Congress which was held in Pátzcuaro, Mexico, in 1940 under the sponsorship of General Lázaro Cárdenas, the president of Mexico.

This view holds that indigenous society has taken refuge in certain geographical and sociological zones where pre-capitalist social relations exist. Discrimination against the indigenous people and their distinctive identity is determined by relations of a sociocultural sort rather than by economic relations. The societies or socio-economic spaces inhabited by the indigenous people are stratified in terms of castes rather than in terms of social classes.

In this view liberation of the indigenous people means that they must go through a stage of proletarianization first. Proponents admit that the transition from caste relationships to class relationships will not annul the exploitative relationship. But they maintain that this shift will put the indigenous people in a better position to hasten their own definitive liberation. So this traditional indigenism offers proletarianization within the framework of capitalist exploitation now, with the hope of future liberation later through socialism. Needless to say, this solution is not acceptable.

Critical Anthropology

Proponents of this approach began by criticizing the first view, that of traditional indigenism. It found its inspiration in movements of a populist cast that upheld the specific originality of certain production systems and the permanent existence of these groups on the fringe of the general laws governing the system.

This theoretical view proposes the model of a peasant economy that has its own rationale and that is independent of the rationale of capitalism. Starting out with an incomplete analysis, it reaches conclusions that do not correspond with reality. For example, its proponents say that the peasant does not produce for the market, does not seek to make a profit, and works only to maintain the family group. Hence they deduce that peasants have their own rationale.

Something similar is said of indigenous groups. Proponents of this view maintain that indigenous society has its own cultural rationale. It is different from the Western cultural system, and it has its roots in pre-Hispanic cultures.

The most extreme proponents of this view maintain that indigenous culture does not just have its roots in the past but actually constitutes a pre-historic culture. Others would say that the roots are pre-Hispanic but that they have been modified by the colonial system.

The fact is that there is no coherence or consistency in this view. For if indigenous groups are the result of the development of capitalism, then one must conclude that their destiny is bound up with the destiny of the capitalist system of production that has had an impact on indigenous and peasant groups.

Proponents of critical anthropology maintain that the indigenous people have their own specific character and identity, that the destiny of such groups is not bound up with the general destiny of workers.

This view has been characterized as romantic, not in the sense that it is utopian but in the sense that it is fictitious; for it is a denial of the objective tendencies of history.

Third World Social Science

A more recent anthropological approach has appeared to take issue with the two preceding approaches. It stems from the reflection of social scientists working in the dialectical tradition evident in Latin America. It is of very recent formulation because the most progressive sectors have been more concerned with worker and peasant movements than with ethnic problems and movements.

According to this view, the indigenous problem is not an original problem even though it has its own specific nature. Since indigenous groups have been constantly created and re-created by the development of capitalism, the liberative solution to the indigenous problem is intimately bound up with the solution to the basic problem facing humanity; i.e., the destruction of the oppressor system.

The liberation of the indigenous groups cannot be simply an ethnic liberation. It must also entail economic and political liberation. It is not possible to attain ethnic liberation within a context of oppression.

If we really want the indigenous groups to develop their own cultural resources, we must realize that such a development depends on the destruction of the existing system. For that system does not accept cultural pluralism, just as it does not accept economic, political, and social pluralism.

The capitalist system is destroying the economic system of the rural peasant just as it has destroyed every other noncapitalist economic system. It is true that in Latin America we still find large pockets in which a traditional, non-capitalist economic system prevails; but the future of these pockets is very uncertain. There is general agreement that capitalism will come to dominate those pockets just as it came to dominate the continent's political and social systems.

If we want to uphold ethnic liberation, say the proponents of this third view, then we must take part in the project aimed at destroying the capitalist system. Efforts and struggles by indigenous groups that are isolated from the struggles of other laborers are doomed to failure.

7

The Experience of Nicaragua's Revolutionary Christians

Juan Hernández Pico (Nicaragua)

This presentation is meant to reflect upon an experience that people have actually lived through. I want to talk about the relationship between revolutionary Christians and non-believing revolutionaries. The experience in question is both a political experience and a faith-experience. It has to do with the problem of constructing the revolutionary process as viewed from those two aspects. On the one hand the construction of the revolutionary process can be seen as an attempt to move closer to a more just society; that is the political aspect. On the other hand it can be seen as a closer approach to the kingdom of God; that is the theological aspect. I suggest here that a joint effort along these lines is possible. In Latin America the proposal is that the effort take the form of an alliance between two convergent forces. Perhaps we can go even further than that.

The backdrop for this experience is the reality to be found in Guatemala, El Salvador, and Nicaragua; here, however, I focus on Nicaragua. In Nicaragua we are discovering the possibility of living Christianity in a new way. It is the joy of a people who have accepted the good news of their liberation and of their entry into history as active forgers of it. It is the same joy that other peoples in Central America and Latin America are beginning to share, which is offering nourishment to their hopes.

The experience in question has to do with committed revolutionaries and committed Christians who see the revolution and the faith summoning them to an increasingly better history. From time to time this might seem to be a mere "ideal," something that has to do solely with what ought to be. But in fact it goes hand in hand with actual practice. Formulating it is part of the task involved in trying to make sure that reality will move ever more substantially toward this sort of practice.

STARTING POINT: SOLIDARY PRACTICE
IN THE REVOLUTIONARY PROCESS

For the majority of revolutionary Christians, the relationship between non-believing revolutionaries and revolutionary Christians is not just a topic or problem for rational discussion; it is also an experience that has been lived through. In their concrete practice both sides have met in an embrace of total solidarity.

In the revolutionary practice of Nicaragua, Christian comrades have not been questioned about their baptismal faith in order to expel them from the ranks of the Front as counter-revolutionaries or to subject them to a process of re-education. By the same token Christians, upon entering the Front, have not sought to get the designation "Christian" added to its name or emblem. All are simply judged in terms of the quality and depth of their revolutionary commitment. Revolutionary commitment and a correct objective analysis of reality were the only criteria used to identify true militants and collaborators in the struggle for Nicaragua's liberation.

The Political Rationality of This Solidary Practice

From the political standpoint this revolutionary practice involves a step toward greater rationality. The revolutionary strategy consists in shouldering the interests of the exploited classes, getting involved in their fight, and transforming the system that continually reproduces the exploitation of the common majorities.

This struggle is illumined by a theory of history based on the scientific systemization of previous experiences and the further enrichment resulting from its application to new conditions.

Within the framework of this strategy it is necessary to investigate how religion serves as a spur or a brake to the revolutionary process. But there is no room in such a strategy for saying that revolutionary politics and religion are incompatible. In this revolutionary practice there must be an ideological struggle against those elements of religion that impede the revolutionary process in a new Nicaragua; but it does not give rise to any anti-religious legal statute or to any overall anti-religious practice.

In political terms the experience of Sandinista revolutionary practice does not include the atheism and the anti-religious outlook that have been traditional hallmarks and dogmatic components of other revolutionary movements. To that extent Sandinista practice acquires more rationality and has, in fact, de-ideologized itself.

The Religious Truth of This Solidary Practice

In theological terms this practice implies a move toward a greater religious truth. The Christian religious strategy consists in expressing love for the invisible God by means of visible love for humanity (1 John 4:11–12; 4:14–20). Closer approach to the kingdom of God finds concrete expression in universal love for human beings. To build up the kingdom is to shoulder the interests of the exploited multitudes in a love that is partisan and committed. This partisan, committed love, built up in a fight against forces that are implacably hostile, impels Christians to identify personal and structural sinfulness with those hostile powers.

Within the framework of this Christian strategy it is important for Christians to denounce religious attitudes that block commitment to the exploited multitudes and hence undermine professed acknowledgment of the true God. There is no place in this Christian strategy for saying that religion and revolutionary politics are incompatible. From the revolutionary practice of the Sandinista movement there arises a duty to purify those religious elements that impede a loving commitment to the exploited multitude. But that practice does not give rise to any denial of the faith-based motivation prompting revolutionary commitment, even as it does not justify any mistrust of a revolutionary commitment based on motives of unbelief.

Theologically, the revolutionary experience tends to be an encounter with God, and a fraternal encounter with those who have embraced the cause of the oppressed above any and all personal interests. Seeing people die for others, and not hearing any talk from them about faith in God being the motivating factor, liberates Christians from the prejudice of trying to encounter true love solely and exclusively within the boundaries of the faith. It also helps to free them from the temptation of not considering a revolutionary process authentic unless it bears the label "Christian." And it frees them from the temptation of finding support for religion in the new revolutionary power, of mixing up something that is the autonomous creation of history with the freedom of God in history. Sandinista revolutionary practice offers better conditions for a more authentic religion.

THE REVOLUTIONARY PROCESS
AS AN EVIDENT EXPRESSION OF ETHICAL GOOD

In this revolutionary practice one grasps a basic ethical intuition, an intuition that regards the revolutionary process as an evident expression of what is good.

The Ethical Decision from the Political Standpoint:
From Non-Awareness to Awareness

Commander Luis Carrión has said: "Human beings define themselves by their commitment, . . . by their decision for or against the interests of our people."[1] Behind this statement lies a whole process that began years ago. Carlos Fonseca, the founder of the Front, described the Sandinista movement as a kind of pathway or journey.[2] In the decade of the fifties the process meant seeing the other side of the coin, the back side of history as presented by official channels. Behind the image of the bandit affixed to Sandino, one now began to see a person who had given up his life for Nicaragua. And he had begun by awakening a sense of dignity in the workers and peasants who formed part of his troops.[3]

This meant giving up a comfortable future in the privileged university setting of the dominant classes. It meant associating one's own life with the cause of a person who had been relegated to the shadows, who had been removed from the heroic history of Nicaragua by the dominant classes.[4] In so doing, the dominant classes sought to effect a fundamental change in the awareness of the common people. They wanted to twist good into evil, justice into injustice, and a symbol of hope into a symbol of domination. By slandering the memory of Sandino, they sought to kill the hopes of the people and even make them ashamed of such hopes.

The revolutionary process undertaken by young people in 1961 began with a feeling of shame for what was going on. They felt shame for such a twisted perversion of history and the defilement it entailed. Somoza's dictatorship was not just an exploitative, oppressing government inside Nicaragua; not just an imperialist government of occupation disguised as a nationalist government; and not just a regime of accusations, torture, and genocide. It was also a philosophy trying to undermine and corrupt the whole of life by destroying culture, morality, and the most elemental loyalty.

Shame over the humiliation of one's homeland was followed by love for the people. The bloody reality of their lives[5] began to show up in the newspaper *El Universitario,* thus initiating the trek from shame to conscientious awareness.[6]

The revolution is a process designed to restore the dignity of the nation and its political independence, and to construct a new economy of social accumulation. It seeks to create history on the basis of the people's power and authority. It is a journey toward a new culture and a new human being whose worth is measured in terms of social, fraternal sharing rather than personal accumulation. As a work prompted by love for the multitude, the revolution is something evidently good that forced itself on the conscience of generous-hearted Nicaraguans and gradually became feasible through the efforts of an aroused and combative people.

So in every revolutionary commitment we find an ethical decision that gives definitive configuration to life. Commander Tomás Borge indicated this when talking about the founders and first recruits of the Front: "Only once in life is it possible to love the people with the irrevocable love that those people had."[7]

Loving the people and joining a revolutionary process that will create the structural prerequisites for a social management of production, government, and culture, is something justified in and of itself. The revolution stands on its own ethically as the greatest conceivable good in the temporal city. It is capable of constituting the maximum value for the new human being who emerges in this process. As a movement toward the new society and the new human being, the revolutionary process is the cause that gives meaning to a life dedicated to others.

The Ethical Decision from the Religious Standpoint: From the Poor to the Exploited Classes

For revolutionary Christians, too, people define themselves by the stand they take with regard to the vast majority of the common people. Christians expect the Front to display a revolutionary love. This love should characterize the whole process, and it should find concrete embodiment in the weakest especially—i.e., in those brothers and sisters who have the greatest difficulty in understanding the revolutionary process.

A long road lies behind the above statement. It is the road that has led many bourgeois and petty bourgeois Christians to change their class identification and to incarnate themselves in the plight of the exploited classes. Even more importantly, it is the long road that has to be traversed by the masses in order to recover the subversive memory of Jesus of Nazareth.

Because of their illiteracy, the life and concrete trajectory of Jesus of Nazareth had remained hidden from the awareness of the common people. In its place they had been offered a sublimated version of his death, which found expression in countless images of the crucified Christ. The life of Jesus was reduced inexorably to a peace based on submission and resignation. The people knew nothing about Jesus' life as a story of opposition to injustice, inequality, and the accumulation of possessions and despotic authority. The story of Jesus' efforts to give value to the dignity of all those excluded from the banquet-table of life was no part of the orthodox catechism lesson. The Son of God obscured the laboring man and the prophet of Nazareth.

The oral religious tradition offered no account of the subversive death of an authentic human being who had demonstrated an identification with God. The story told had to do with the crime of having crucified God. That crime, being so superhumanly shocking, hid the ongoing crime of every day: i.e., of robbing the means of life and even life itself, from the poor, ignorant multitude who stand as the visible presence of the crucified God. The death of God, separated from his human life and the historical causes of his death, was turned into a myth designed to dampen down the latent struggles of a class-based society.

The epic of a people driven by God to forge their own history in a fight for liberation—i.e., the epic of the Exodus—formed no part of the historical creed of Christians in our land. The God circulated for the consumption of our oppressed masses was the God of the philosophers and the God of the bourgeois ideologues—a combination of some omnipotent God outside history and a God mysteriously responsible for the established order.

The God preached by the churches was not a God familiar with the fight for justice on earth, a fight that varies in accordance with the different phases of human history. It was not the God who speaks to us in the Bible about those who truly know him: "Did not your father eat and drink, and do justice and righteousness? Then it was well with him. He judged the cause of the poor and needy; then it was well. Is not this to know me?" (Jer. 22:15-16). The God preached was a God confined to temple and church and dissociated from the historical construction of justice and fidelity in society. People supposedly learned who God was in the static repetition of a doctrinaire liturgy. There was no liturgy of liberation and new creation where they could celebrate the God of history and the values discovered by men and women in the fight for justice.

The result was a terrible confusion and mixup. The churches failed to recognize or disavowed the God hidden in the history of the struggle for justice. That God was turned into a God who was manipulated to serve the interests of the established order. The anticipatory memorial of a new earth in which the poor sit down at the same table with God was degraded into a spiritualized "Mass." In that spiritualized Mass the dictatorship of the rich "brethren" over the poor "brethren" was sublimated, as if it had already been abolished. Finally, the subversive memory of the death of Jesus, who died because of his fidelity to the God of the poor, was turned into a back-breaking reminder that all human beings, rich and poor alike, were equally responsible for the death of God.

When the total gospel message was rescued from Latin and handed over to the base-level communities, when the history of this country challenged Christians because of the revolutionary theory and practice of non-believing Nicaraguans, then shame crept into Christians and gave rise to their revolutionary commitment. They felt ashamed of the distortion of the Christian religion. For their religion obligated them to attend catechism classes, receive the sacraments, and give alms, while overlooking the most serious matters of the faith: justice, mercy, and loyalty (Matt. 23:23). They also felt ashamed over the fact that it was the members of the Front, not those who called themselves Christians, who had begun to bind up the wounds of robbed and assaulted people in the midst of their history (Luke 10:25-37).

Feelings of shame gave way to contact with the impoverished and oppressed people. And closer contact led to love. This love encountered the violated dignity of the people, their lack of awareness, and their submissiveness. But it also encountered their protest and rebelliousness, their solidarity and hospitality, their joy and their hope.

Encountering the poor as a people, they made a definitive ethical decision that shaped their whole lives. They would be either with the poor or against them. They had rediscovered the place of encounter with the face of God, the only one before whom life itself is at stake. This "place" was the concrete faces of Nicaragua's exploited and oppressed classes.

In this way the religion of Jesus became once again the religion of the marginalized, as it had been at the start of church history (1 Cor. 1:26-29). Once again it became the religion of laborers, uneducated people, and those rich people who turned their backs on exploitative wealth (the Simon Peters, Andrews, Matthews, and Zaccheuses in today's Nicaragua). Once again the religion of Jesus became what it had been in the world of the Roman Empire: the religion of "atheists," of those who refused to worship the emperor as a god. So twisted had the ancient hope become that some applied the label "anti-Christian" to those who were willing to fight for the life of the masses. One example is the assertion now making the rounds: "They are not Christians. They are agents of international Communist subversion against Western, Christian civilization."

To these revolutionary Christians it became quite clear that the exigencies of the Christian faith had little likelihood of being realized in the exploitative, oppressive structures of the Somoza regime. Poor, revolutionary Christians found no contradiction between their faith in Jesus Christ and their revolutionary fight.

Other Christians, who came from various levels of the bourgeoisie or whose religious culture was of a more official stamp, had to fight against other religious distortions. They were greatly helped by the conversion process through which the Latin American church had been going ever since the Medellín Conference.

To many observers of the religious process, this conversion was little more than an indication of the church's adaptiveness and opportunism. To those who lived it, it marked a return to a more traditional attitude. It was a return to the tradition of Bartolomé de Las Casas, Valdivieso, Francis of Assisi, Ambrose, Chrysostom, Basil, and, first and foremost, Jesus Christ himself.

Gradually the revolutionary process surfaced as the effective embodiment of Christian love for the multitude. To fight for the life of the least of Jesus' brothers and sisters (see Matt. 25:40) was to fight for the God of life. As a work of love, the revolution no longer needed any theological justification. On the basis of a Christian intuition of what conversion meant, the revolution was justified in and of itself. As the concrete mediation of love for the multitude, the revolution was able to become the highest value for authentic Christians. They could willingly lose their lives for the sake of others. They could see a better guarantee of liberty in the social appropriation of the product of collective labor because it offered a greater guarantee of fraternity.

The revolutionary process could now become the maximum Christian value because it represented the one and only approximation to the maximum, absolute value of the kingdom. In a word, the revolution was the historical version of the food given to the hungry person and the cup of water given to the thirsty person. So the revolution, as the high road to the new human being and the new society, became a cause that gave meaning to life.

GOING BEYOND A STRATEGIC ALLIANCE

Having come this far, we can now broach a question that has stuck with the revolutionary consciousness of Latin America ever since it was enunciated by

Ernesto Che Guevara and Fidel Castro. It has to do with the presence of revolutionary Christians as strategic allies in Latin America's revolutionary process. Here are the now famous words of Che Guevara:

> When Christians are bold enough to bear integral revolutionary wit- ness, the Latin American revolution will be invincible; for up to now Christians have allowed their doctrine to be used as a tool by the reac- tionaries.[8]

Speaking to church representatives in Jamaica in 1977, Fidel Castro made the same point he had made publicly in 1971 in Chile. In 1977 he said: "No contradictions exist between the aims of religion and the aims of Socialism." In 1971 he had said the following to a Christian audience in Chile: "We must make an alliance, but not simply a tactical alliance. I would say: a strategic alliance between religion and socialism, between religion and revolution."[9]

Mistrust of a Strategic Alliance

However, mistrust of these words spoken by Che Guevara and Fidel Castro exists among Christians. Among those Christians who have arrived at a revo- lutionary conviction, the mistrust takes the form of a vague fear. They feel that the revolution will not oppose religion so long as it needs the latter to consolidate itself politically, but that it will cast religion aside without scruple afterwards. Revolutionary Christians are afraid that they are considered second-class revolutionaries because it is hard for the modern revolutionary tradition to deal with the Marxist critique of religion as its legacy. The prob- lem is further complicated by the fact that many non-believing revolutiona- ries refuse to accept the notion of a strategic alliance between non-believing revolutionaries and revolutionary Christians. In their eyes such an alliance can only be tactical and temporary.

This question is very important for many Christians. They trust that the Front will do all that has to be done to effect a strategic alliance between non-believing revolutionaries and revolutionary Christians. They trust that the Front will never see an enemy in the God of the poor, the God who sus- tains their aspirations for liberation. If such a strategic alliance is worked out in Nicaragua, they feel it will be an original and novel thing, a sign of hope for all of Latin America.

Underlying all this is another hope, having to do with the Marxist critique of religion. Nicaraguan Christians hope that the Sandinista Front will re- move itself from all dogmatism in that area, even as it has done in other areas of revolutionary practice. But they know that past history makes this dif- ficult. Religion has been used so often as a tool by counter-revolution- ary forces, and revolutionary movements have consistently evinced scorn and deep hostility toward religion. It is difficult to imagine a different his- tory.

Going Beyond the Old Formulations

In the face of this old formulation, Commander Luis Carrión has insisted that it does not suffice to talk about a strategic alliance between revolutionary Christians and non-believing revolutionaries: "If we all are revolutionaries, then we all form one band. We are brothers and comrades, and that means much more than allies."[10]

This statement is a historical novelty in Latin America, and we must reflect on it.

The possibility of revolutionary alliances is a political problem. To achieve the objectives of a revolutionary process, it is necessary to create alliances with all those classes or fractions of social classes that have an interest in the success of the process. Revolutionary alliances are strategic alliances when they unite in one single historical bloc various organizations of the emerging classes—whether the latter be organizations of the common people or vanguard elements of the exploited and oppressed classes. Sometimes, as was the case in Nicaragua, individuals or broader segments of the dominant classes renounce their class situation and adopt the interests and the cause of the aforementioned historical bloc. Achieving a strategic alliance of classes entails getting inside, and linking up with, the various modes of production to be found within a given social formation. Such penetration is achieved by participating in the lives and struggles of the various social classes that are being exploited. In so doing, however, one must be equipped with a correct revolutionary theory and with a political option that is adequate over the long term.[11]

Christians are not a social class. Citizens of every social class adhere to the Christian religion. So even though the statement by Luis Carrión does not broach the issue of revolutionary alliances from the standpoint I have suggested in this paper, it is perfectly correct. Since Christians are not a social class, they should not be participants in a class alliance insofar as they represent a social group. That is why all types of Christian parties and organizations produce confusion within the realm of the revolutionary process.

So when one talks about a "strategic alliance" between revolutionary Christians and non-believing revolutionaries, one is not talking about the way things should be. One is talking about what has happened in the past, and what may continue along the same lines for now. One is talking about a reality of great social import in Latin America: i.e., the political weight that the Christian churches have exercised in Latin America. And sometimes one is also alluding to the statutory clause that prohibits the admission of Christians into the Cuban Communist party.

To clarify this whole problem, we must consider the relationship existing between the economic structure of society, the political field, and the ideological side. The reality is that religion has been utilized as a legitimating ideological tool and a moral authority in support of political consensus; it has been used to sustain an exploitative system.

On the one hand the capitalist system has held up certain Christian values as its ideals: e.g., personal freedom, brotherly love, the transcendence of history and the person. But on the other hand the logic of its own exploitative mechanisms has negated those same values. Moreover, political authority has been turned into an agent designed to provide and protect a certain area of autonomy and civil power for religion—or rather, for the churches.

Another result of no less importance has been the fact that political authority, even if it be a revolutionary one, finds it very difficult to free itself from legitimating religious overtones. One example is the atheism that is part and parcel of many revolutionary parties in history. Extrapolating the functions of the revolutionary theory, this atheism views religion as the illusory happiness of the people; it regards the fight against religion as a necessity so that the real-life happiness of the people may be attained.

We must free ourselves in a revolutionary way from this historical residue. We must do this on the political plane because religious legitimations make politics fanatical and strip it of rationality. We must do so on the theological plane because the favors granted religion by political authorities undermine the vocation of religion to serve and lend utopian support to the work of constructing the city of the future.

This process of liberation entails a hard effort by Christians to prevent the counter-revolutionary use of religion. It also entails their efforts to free their churches from the yearning to use political authority for the benefit of religion. But by the same token the process of liberation demands an equal effort from non-believing revolutionaries. They must strive to exercise political power within the humble limits of political rationality rather than trying to sacralize such power under some mystique of the party or the state.

When the problem is viewed in the above terms, the formulations of Che Guevara and Fidel Castro turn out to be strikingly accurate. We must look at them a bit more closely. Castro talks about a strategic alliance between socialism and religion. In today's Latin America there is no doubt whatsoever that both socialism and religion not only constitute a social system and a religious profession but also are cultural symbols of the boundless hopes of the exploited people. On this symbolic level both are strategic allies, since their aims are convergent rather than contradictory. If socialism is regarded as a concrete historical project for society, on the other hand, then the Christian religion is not on the same level; for the latter aims at the overcoming of history in the kingdom of God. At the level of symbolic motivation, religion is an ally of the concrete historical project because its task is to anticipate the kingdom of God in and through partial, approximate realizations—which continually inspire us to fashion an increasingly better society and humanity.[12]

Che Guevara said that with the participation of Christians "the Latin American revolution will be invincible." In his mind the Latin American revolution was not simply the effort to implement it in each country; it was also the anticipatory realization of the new human being—filled with love, dedicated to service, and generous to the point of death. Every Christian who realizes this new human being in an anticipatory way is contributing to the victory of the process. And that process often begins in places as politically devoid of rationality as the Bolivian forest.

A GOD HIDDEN IN HISTORY
AND AN EARTH HIDDEN IN HISTORY

This, then, is my thesis: In Nicaragua we must go beyond a strategic alliance between non-believing revolutionaries and revolutionary Christians. But we must proceed with modesty. We must not be so idealistic as to ignore the realities that still surround us: i.e., the "political" atavisms of the churches and the "mystical" atavisms of the revolution.

If religion is regarded as a faith journeying toward the divine surpassing of history in and through the struggle to construct a better human history, then it can form revolutionary Christians united in a unique commitment with non-believing revolutionaries. But a religion that sees itself as the doctrine of an ahistorical God, and that finds its institutional support in privileged areas of authority, is not the religion of the incarnate God. This God did not cling to divinity, but became one human being among many in history, serving others even unto death (Phil. 2:6-8).

Only a revolutionary process that is mobilized by the class struggle, and that takes institutional form as a lay, secular state, can heed the voice of the cultural symbolic forces that drive it forward. If a revolutionary process is erected into some doctrinal dogma or into a new religion, then it will tend historically to become fanatical and completely bureaucratic. And these seemingly contradictory tendencies come together in every ideologization of politics.

Sergio Ramírez Mercado, a member of the Government Junta for the National Reconstruction of Nicaragua, was commenting on a recent pastoral letter issued by the bishops of Nicaragua. At one point he was asked: "Do you think there is any compatibility between socialism and Christianity, seeing that Marx defined religion as the opiate of the people?" His reply was: "Marxism is an analysis of the dynamics of historical events. What I read in this letter, far from being an opiate, is a spur to this revolution."[13]

The God of revolutionary Christians is a God hidden in history (Isa. 45:15). We come to know God by following the footsteps of Jesus, who explained the God that no one has ever seen (John 1:18). Jesus did not explain God solely with his words, but with words that were consistent with his way of living. The life of Jesus banished from religion another image of God, one which pictured God as sending "twelve legions of angels" to substitute for humanity's difficult struggle to reach the kingdom (Matt. 26:52-53). The God of Jesus, hidden in history, cannot be discovered by anyone who does not engage in the practice of justice, a practice looking forward to a new society and a new human being. The God of Jesus will be present in history until its very end, accompanying the struggles of the poor with the impulse of the Spirit. The practice of revolutionary love fulfills an essential theological function. That is to say, it makes possible our liberating encounter with God. God is certainly there at the beginning. But in the future, when humanity and society are better, then God will be greater also.

The earth of non-believing revolutionaries is also an earth hidden in history. It is a society without exploiters or exploited, a society where dignity has been realized in equality. With the progressive disappearance of the state and unheard-of degrees of participation and liberty, it will give rise to a new humanity that will be "many new human beings." We come to know that earth only to the extent that we fashion it in the struggle, resolving contradictions politically. The struggle can never be dissociated from those who have not yet achieved liberation from exploitation and oppression. Complacency over liberations that have been achieved already is the thing that can undermine the process. The new earth ceases to be a real-life goal. It is turned into a "secular heaven" and used to justify all stagnation in the revolutionary process. The revolution, the power of the emerging classes, is certainly there at the start when they begin the effort to take over power in the state. But in the future, when the earth to be created and the humanity to be made new are better and greater, then the revolution will be greater too.

In the meantime, the face of our exploited brethren journeying toward their liberation is the horizon of the revolutionary process—both for non-believing revolutionaries and revolutionary Christians. The goal is to see joyous festivity and celebration grow on that face as fraternity grows; and that face is really "many faces."

Here we have something that we call gratuitousness and love. It is of that love that Che Guevara was speaking when he said: "Every day we must fight for this love of living humanity."

NOTES

1. Final panel discussion of a seminar on "Christians and the Sandinista Front for National Liberation," Managua, November 1979, mimeograph, p. 7.

2. Tomás Borge, *Carlos, el amanecer ya no es una tentación* (Managua: Ministry of Education, 1979), p. 16.

3. Sergio Ramírez Mercado, *El pensamiento vivo de Sandino* (San José: Ministry of Culture, 1978), p. 209.

4. Tomás Borge, *Carlos,* p. 23.

5. Ibid., p. 14.

6. Ibid., p. 23. See also *El pensamiento vivo de Ricardo Morales Avilez,* UNAN, Association of Psychology Students, p. 65.

7. Talk at the seminar on "Political Education" sponsored by UCA, August 1979.

8. Sergio Arce Martínez, *Cristo vivo en Cuba* (San José: DEI, 1978), p. 27.

9. Ibid., p. 170.

10. Final panel discussion, "Christians and the Sandinista Front," p. 11.

11. Pierre Filippe Rey, *Las alianzas de clase* (Mexico City: Siglo XXI, 1976), pp. 201–59.

12. Vatican II, *Gaudium et spes,* no. 39.

13. Final panel discussion, "Christians and the Sandinista Front," p. 15.

PART II

REFLECTIONS ON
POPULAR CHRISTIAN COMMUNITIES

8

Current Events
in Latin America (1972–1980)

Enrique Dussel (Mexico)

"We must call by its correct name injustice, human exploitation of human beings, and the exploitation of human beings by the state, institutions, and the mechanisms of systems and regimes."
—*Pope John Paul II (Weekly General Audience, February 21, 1979)*

In the same address to a General Audience Pope John Paul II said that "liberation, in the social sense too, begins with real knowledge of the truth." We must take cognizance of the historical moment through which we are living. Now if that is correct, then we would do well to devote our attention, however cursorily,[1] to the recent past. Hopefully we may discover the *meaning* of what has been happening in recent Latin American history, which is filled with key events.

INTRODUCTORY CONSIDERATIONS

Stages in the History of the Latin American Church

The history of the Latin American church has three main stages, which I shall briefly describe here:

a. Colonial Christendom (1492–1808). The life of the church was framed within a social structure in which the mode of capitalist production, dependent on Spain and Portugal, exercised hegemony over the other means of production.

b. Christendom in crisis (1808–1950). Latin America was dependent on Anglo-Saxon capitalism, on an industrial revolution taking place at the "center."

During this period the church sought a replacement for the "colonial" model. The search crystallized in the concrete model of New Christendom between 1930 and 1950.

c. The church of the common people, or "people's church" *(Iglesia popular)*. This emerged into prominence gradually after 1950.

This third major stage has had four phases. The first phase ran from 1954–59 (the fall of Vargas in Brazil, Castro's entry into Havana, the announcement and meeting of Vatican II) to 1968 (the Medellín Conference). The second phase ran from the time of the Medellín Conference to the fourteenth regular assembly of CELAM in Sucre, i.e., from 1968 to 1972. The third phase ran from the Sucre Conference to the Puebla Conference (1973 to 1979). Now we are in the fourth phase, which includes the CELAM elections of March 1979, the changes in the officials of the NCBB (National Conference of Brazilian Bishops) and, in particular, the success of the Nicaraguan revolution on July 19.

The Old Christendom in Crisis and the Search for New "Models"

Christendom was one "model" of the *relationship* that might exist between the church on the one hand and political society (essentially the state or government) and civil society on the other.[2] In this model the church defined its pastoral relations with the people in civil society through the state. The best example of this model was provided by the *Laws of the Indies* (1681) promulgated for Spanish America. The Portuguese system of *patroado* functioned in much the same way. The church made use of the state to build its churches, send out its missionaries, protect its holdings, publish its books, educate its agents, and so forth. In turn, the state received from the church legitimation for its coercive domination of civil society (the creoles, Indians, black slaves, etc.). This model came into crisis in the process of winning emancipation from Spain and Portugal.

It was not until the crisis of 1930, when the dependent, liberalist, mercantile oligarchy was seriously undermined, that the church was able to reinstate a model of positive relations with the populist state. It was an imperfect model compared with the old colonial one, and now the domestic or national bourgeoisie exercised hegemony. The newer imperfect model also made use of the state (to promote religious instruction in the public schools, for example) and in turn legitimated the government by helping to create a consensus. We may call this later model "New Christendom." The church broadened its base because it was able to make contact with groups of workers and marginal people, who were necessary allies of populism.

The crisis of this New Christendom model came with the crisis of populism itself, which entailed an effort to achieve an autonomous national capitalism. This was the objective of Irigoyen, Vargas, Cárdenas, Perón, and many others like them. Around that time (1954) a brief period of developmentalism began. In Brazil, for example, it ran from 1954 to 1964. But then it necessarily gave way to the National Security State and an economy in which the multinationals exercised hegemony. Faced with the crisis of capitalism around 1967, contradictions sharpened and the authoritarian state shifted to direct repression of the people. But on the other side something strategically more important had been taking place since 1959: i.e., the socialist revolution in Cuba. This, too, resulted from the crisis of populism, exemplified by Batista in the case of Cuba. Both the National Security State and the socialist state placed obstacles in the way of the New Christendom model.

Compelled by the critical circumstances, some churches (e.g., those of Brazil, El Salvador, and Nicaragua) undertook the search for another model. In the new model the church abandoned the illusion of trying to carry out the process of evangelization through the state. It gave definitive definition to its place in civil society and now established an alliance with the oppressed classes. It could no longer expect help from the state in carrying out its pastoral tasks; it therefore had to create new institutions, such as the base-level ecclesial communities (CCBs). By the same token, however, it no longer gave legitimation to the state's repressive actions. This break with the practice of legitimating the existing political society opened up new room for winning credibility among the oppressed people. This new model is already being lived by prophetic groups, and a majority of some episcopates have already adopted it. It is what has come to be known as the *Iglesia popular* (People's church, church of the common people, and equivalent terms). It is not a different church or a new church; it is simply a new model of the age-old church.

THE SUCRE PHASE (1972)

Sociopolitical Context

The model of dependent capitalism under a National Security State spread through Latin America. Here are the key dates:

March 31, 1964: Coup d'état in Brazil.
August 21, 1971: Coup d'état in Bolivia.
June 27, 1973: Dissolution of the Uruguayan Congress.
September 11, 1973: Coup d'état in Chile.
August 28, 1975: Francisco Morales Bermúdez in Peru.
January 13, 1976: Fall of the nationalist military government in
    Ecuador.
March 24, 1976: Fall of Isabel Perón in Argentina.

To these events we can add the continuing rule of Stroessner in Paraguay, Duvalier in Haiti, Balaguer in Santo Domingo, military dictatorships masked as democracies in Guatemala, Honduras, and El Salvador, and Somoza in Nicaragua. The reality of Latin America had indeed taken on a somber aspect. It was the counter-insurgency model, the National-Security model, proposed by Henry Kissinger to Richard Nixon and Gerald Ford.

From the economic standpoint the crisis that began in 1967 would ameliorate in 1972–73, then turn into the worst crisis faced by the capitalist system since 1929. Inflation combined with recession to produce "stagflation" in 1974–75. The doctrine of the Chicago School, led by Milton Friedman, was implemented by the various neo-fascist dictatorships. Multinationals gained complete hegemony over national economies. The monetary position of the IMF raised national debts to astronomical levels.

In addition, the center-versus-periphery relationship was now duplicated insofar as certain peripheral countries (e.g., Brazil, Mexico, India, and Iran) were defined as centers of development enjoying hegemony over other underdeveloped countries that were poorer still.

The expansion of international capital and the new technological domination called for a state or a government with a coherent ideology. This fact was voiced by Augusto Pinochet at the sixth Assembly of the OAS in Santiago (1976):

> Western and Christian civilization, of which we form a non-renounceable part, is internally debilitated and under attack from outside. The ideological war, which jeopardizes the sovereignty of free governments and the essential dignity of the human being, leaves no room for comfortable forms of neutralism. Meanwhile, in the domestic political life of various countries we are experiencing the ideological and social aggression of a doctrine that conceals its objective of imposing communist tyranny under the cloak of a pretended proletarian redemption.

This alleged situation gave rise to an integral doctrine of Total War at every level, including political strategy, economic policy, psychosocial factors, and military activity. The doctrine of National Security, which appeared in the United States after World War II, was now used by military leaders in Latin America to pave the way politically and structurally for capitalist expansion from the center.

The political aim was the systematic repression of the people. The economic aim was to maintain the profit rate of foreign capital investments.

Ecclesial Context

The most important papal document in this phase was the Apostolic Exhortation *Evangelii nuntiandi,* issued December 8, 1975, as the conclusion of many ecclesial events relating to this theme.

It appears that the crisis of capitalism during this period caused an atmosphere of pessimism to prevail in Italy. Simultaneously the emergence of Euro-communism and the progress of the Communist Party in Italy created fear among certain ecclesiastical groups. In any case Pope Paul VI expressed himself clearly:

> We all know very well in what terms many bishops from every continent, particularly those of the Third World, spoke during the recent (1974) Synod of Bishops. . . . As we now know, those [Third World] peoples are investing all their energy in the effort and the fight to overcome all those things that condemn them to live on the perimeter of life. . . . The church has the duty to proclaim liberation to millions of human beings . . . to help bring this liberation about (*Evangelii nuntiandi*, no. 30).

At the 1974 Synod, the bishops of Latin America were no longer talking in the terms they had used at the previous Synod, but neither did they come to any conclusion. They simply drafted a message of commitment. At the fifth Synod of Bishops in 1977, however, it was clear that the line adopted at their Sucre Conference had borne its fruits. It marked the start of a reaction whose effects would be seen at the Puebla Conference. One bishop from El Salvador remarked at the Synod that "in his country priests were becoming Communists or Maoists."[3] "One Spanish prelate remarked that the positions of the Latin American church marked an open retreat from those of the Medellín Conference."[4] Archbishop Alfonso López Trujillo repeatedly stressed that "Christian liberation need not necessarily be a politicizing liberation."[5]

Meanwhile the Jesuits had held their thirty-second Extraordinary Congregation in Rome (1973). Their conclusion was that they should place "the Company at the service of the church in this period of rapid world change and respond to the challenge posed to us by that world." An option for justice was one of their firmly chosen priorities.

Changes had also taken place in the Pontifical Commission Justice and Peace. "The officials of the Commission have decided to do without the services of forty international experts."[6] The curial Congregations had triumphed in determining what basic direction the postconciliar church would take.

In Germany the periodical *Publik*, under the sponsorship of progressive, critical-minded lay people, was closed down. In the United States Father Louis Colonnese was relieved of his job. He had done a brilliant job of running the Catholic Interamerican Cooperation Program (CICOP) and helping Latin America by showing North Americans the situation of poverty that they were creating in Latin America. The very emergence of Archbishop Lefebvre embodied an ecclesial reaction, a backlash opposed to the underlying reforms proposed by Vatican II.

This whole atmosphere reached Latin America toward the end of 1972.

Sucre (November 15-23, 1972)

The fourteenth ordinary conference of CELAM met in Sucre in 1972. Four principal matters were on the agenda: "The overall restructuring of CELAM, the replacement of its officers, the future of the specialized institutes and the financing of their activities, and the chief guidelines governing pastoral work on the continent."[7] Press reports at the time indicated that "CELAM, from Sucre on, will be an organism moving in the most conservative channels. This prediction is based on the fact that various Latin American episcopates have called into question the activities and pastoral approaches pursued by some departments of CELAM. Bishops from Colombia and our own country [i.e., Argentina], among others, have not concealed their displeasure over some of the undertakings sponsored by the organism."[8]

A similar comment came from Hector Borrat, a Christian journalist and intellectual: "The most recent attacks against Segundo Galilea, IPLA, and CEHILA were bound to reach a crescendo in one final assault. It came at Sucre, where CELAM met from November 15 to 23. It was not a reunion. It was the long-awaited and planned-for occasion when the Right hoped to topple the Medellín men. Would they manage, through the election of different officials, to finally effect the change of direction they sought, to derail the Latin American episcopate from the track they had laid in 1968 and followed since then?"[9]

These various commentaries written before and during the Sucre sessions give a good indication of the spirit that prevailed at the Sucre Conference. Elected Secretary General of CELAM was Archbishop Alfonso López Trujillo. Bishop Luciano Duarte became President of the Department of Social Action, and Bishop Antonio Quarricino took over the Department of the Laity.

Some ten or more German theologians later issued a *Memorandum* in which they spoke about a campaign against liberation theology. The campaign actually formed part of the backdrop for the Sucre Conference. Said the German theologians: "Insofar as the Latin American episcopate is concerned, some bishops support the campaign against liberation theology. . . . On the German side, the Bishop of Essen is a main figure in this campaign."[10] Theologians such as Professors Weber, Rauscher, and Bossler, well-known in their own countries for their conservative stances, formed a group known as "Church and Liberation," to attack Latin American liberation theology. One of the group went so far as to describe liberation theology as "irrational obscurantism."

There is only one point that might be added here. At the very least these criticisms of the ecclesial course that emerged at the Medellín Conference, of liberation theology and the church's option for the poor, certainly helped along the National Security States and the repressive plans of the U.S. State

Department. The physiognomy of our continent would be altered by violent coup d'états directed against processes of liberation. The church was left without a critical voice, looking on silently at the countless horrors perpetrated in the name of "Western and Christian civilization."

The theological backdrop for the reaction against Medellín and the ensuing debate found expression in the following text:

> It is clear that we cannot confuse or equate material poverty with spiritual poverty. People can be poor in economic wealth without being poor in spirit. This is true of those who deify money and covet the riches they don't possess. On the opposite side of the coin, we cannot neglect the cases where people rich in material things are in fact authentic *anawim*, or, people poor in spirit.[11]

So when poor people demand more pay, or when peasants demand their own land to farm—because the plantation owner is robbing them—they are to be classed among those poor people who covet weath; and hence they are lost. On the other hand, a landowning millionaire who "feels" or "thinks" that he is independent of his wealth, is now one of the poor in spirit. The inversion is complete. The gospel message has been emptied of all content so that it can be filled up with the ideology of dependent capitalism. Since 1972 the issue at stake in the Latin American church was whether the capitalist project for the continent should be criticized or legitimated. The Sucre Conference criticized liberation theology, the Latin American Pastoral Institute (IPLA), and the church's option for the poor. Thus the church was left without a critical voice on the continental level, though not on local or national levels.

ECCLESIAL EVENTS FROM SUCRE TO PUEBLA: 1973–1979

During this period a wave of terror broke over the Latin American church. During these five years the holy bride of Christ, the church, would offer more martyrs to Christian communities and the heavenly Jerusalem than it had in almost five centuries of existence on this continent. In and through those groups that united as a people, as the authentic people of God, the church has borne witness to the gospel message in a way that marks deep and profound growth. It can be truly said that this period, steeped in pain, bloodshed, and killing, marks a glorious epoch for Christianity in Latin America.

Here I shall present a typology of the various situations in which the Latin American church finds itself. My aim is to enable people to see the distinct moments and the differing challenges facing Christians, which in turn are due to changing political and economic conditions. For lack of space I shall content myself with quick brushstrokes and schematic descriptions.

The Church in Authoritarian, Repressive Regimes
(Chile, Argentina, Uruguay, Haiti, Paraguay)

Since it stands as a Latin American hallmark of the situation created by our repressive governments, we cannot overlook the seizure and confinement of seventeen Latin American bishops (including four Chicano bishops from the United States) in Riobamba, Ecuador, on August 12, 1976. The bishops had come from a meeting in Brazil dealing with base-level ecclesial communities, and they were planning to discuss the situation of the church on the Latin American continent. Said one of the bishops: "If this is what happens to us, who are people of note, what will happen to peasants, workers, or native Indians when they are captured?"[12]

Here I shall consider only two of the five countries indicated. In Uruguay the situation is much like that in Argentina. In Haiti and Paraguay the present situation is much like that which has existed in the ruling government for more than twenty-five years (as was the case with Somoza in Nicaragua until he was overthrown), but it does not specifically match the National Security model of Brazil.

In *Chile* the bloody coup of September 11, 1973, marked the violent end of the only form of socialism established by the electoral process. This type of repression has no parallel in Latin America. A real "theology of massacre" inspired the military men, who made much of being Christians.[13] Even more regrettable was the fact that two days later, on September 13, the Chilean episcopate published a document condemning the Christians for Socialism movement. The document was entitled "Christian Faith and Political Activity."[14] In it one can clearly ascertain the type of political project envisioned by most of the church hierarchy: i.e., that of the Christian Democratic Party. It was necessary to make it clear and obvious that the Popular Unity Front and Marxism were to be condemned, so that the church could establish some sort of autonomy vis-à-vis the new dictatorial government.

Some bishops came out in favor of the Junta: e.g., Tagle of Valparaiso, Fresno of La Serena, Vicuña of Puerto Montt, and Valdés of Osorno. Others expressed reservations: e.g., Camus, the new secretary of the episcopate, Hourton, Ariztía, González, and Piñera. The cardinal held to a middle position, much to the disgust of the new government, which wanted his support; but he was not explicitly critical either. What irritated the government the most was the Committee of Cooperation for Peace, presided over by Bishop Ariztía in the name of the episcopate. The organization was managed jointly by the Lutheran bishop, Helmut Frenz, and Father Salas, a Jesuit. After enormous pressure had been exerted, the organism was dissolved. A more ecclesiastical institution was then organized, the Vicariate of Solidarity. This sort of institution exemplifies a church maintaining some degree of relative autonomy vis-à-vis the totalitarian state. But the Chilean church is not maintaining this autonomy solely in the interests of a commitment to the poor, as could be said of the church in Brazil, El Salvador, and Bolivia now and then. The Chilean church is also holding on to the New Christendom model as something to be implemented in the future, when the present dictatorship gives away to the Christian Democrat party. It cannot be said that the Chilean church has gotten beyond that model, though it has become a national institution providing a certain amount of space for critical thinking. This explains why members of the Popular Unity front have changed their judgment regarding the historical function of the church in Latin American social formations.

In *Argentina* the situation grew increasingly tense and anxious around 1973. This atmosphere was quickly heightened with the death of Juan D. Perón in 1974. The military coup of March 26, 1976, did not produce any fundamental change, since López Rega had been fomenting dependence and repression already under the rule of Isabel Perón.

If anything will stand out in the history of the church during this period, the violent, bloody repression of the people certainly is it. Numerous Christians suffered the same fate: e.g., Father Carlos Mugica, assassinated at the door of his little neighborhood church on May 11, 1974; and the Bishop of Rioja, Enrique Angelelli, assassinated on August 4, 1976.

The cause of so much martyrdom must be sought in an economic model favoring dependence on North American capitalism. In this most recent phase the policy was directed by Martinez de Hoz, the government minister, who defined the country as an agricultural producer and exporter. The purchasing power of wages was diminished to ensure greater profitability for foreign multinational capital. The result was that increasing social pressure was exerted by a class-conscious working class. The ongoing mobilization is immediately repressed by institutional violence. The saddest part of it all is the fact that the hierarchical church still accepts the New Christendom model. It remains allied to the government and the dominent classes, even though the national bourgeoisie is in a state of crisis along with the petty bourgeoisie, its staunchest membership. Thus the hierarchical church condemns the guerrilla movement as the source of all evils, failing to see that it is merely the product of earlier injustice in both historical and structural terms. It was not hard to guess what the position of the episcopal delegation from Argentina would be at the Puebla Conference, and all the participants and observers at the Conference regarded the Argentinian bishops as the most conservative group there.

The Church and the Relative "Opening Up" in Peru, Brazil, Panama, Bolivia, Ecuador, and Santo Domingo

The "open" stance of the Carter government has fostered a certain policy of "opening up" *(apertura)* since 1976. This was not foreseeable in 1972. So I have grouped together here the various countries that represent a situation of relatively greater freedom in 1980. I will deal specifically with only two countries, although the situation in the other countries is most interesting, particularly in Bolivia and Santo Domingo.

In *Peru* the situation never went so far as it did in Chile or El Salvador. Nevertheless, since 1975 the government has been increasingly inclined to adopt the authoritarianism of dependent fascism. The forty-second assembly of bishops, held in 1973, gave indications of adopting the model of the people's church, though incompletely and indecisively:

> The liberative mission of the church, which is effective proclamation of the gospel message, signifies a hope-filled option for all human beings, but especially for those who suffer from injustice—for the poor and oppressed.[15]

Peru is suffering in a special way from the rigors of the economic crisis of capitalism. One need only allude to the rigorist monetary policy of the IMF, which is in the service of international finance capital. The modernizing, reformist revolution of Velasco Alvarado ended in frank retreat and forced submission to North American demands. The people suffered the consequences, mobilized, and were repressed. The people-oriented church is fighting alongside the oppressed classes; but it is still a minority faction, even though a representative one. The church is feeling pressure from the state, but the bishops have said: "We renew this loyalty and fidelity precisely at a time when there is danger that the orientations of the Medellín Conference will be forgotten."[16]

Some Peruvian bishops, theologians, and lay people would play a relevant role in Puebla, thanks to their experience and adopted course.

In *Brazil* the crisis of capitalism at the center and, in particular, the oil shortage had serious repercussions. The "Brazilian model" entered into contradictions in its country of origin precisely at the time when the model was becoming generalized throughout Latin America. Brazil's foreign debt rose by 3.5 million dollars in 1974. The Geisel government needed a certain degree of consensus and so it created room for greater freedom. The church moved with determination into this newly created room, courageously exercising leadership in the service of the people.

The many martyrs have not been rejected by the church, but rather accepted and put forward as witnesses to the gospel message. By their deaths Fathers Henrique Pereira Neto, Rodolfo Lunkenbeim, João Bosco Penido Burnier and many others bore witness to the church's break with the New Christendom model.

There is Cardinal Paulo Evaristo Arns of São Paulo on the urban, university, and laboring front; Bishop Pedro Casaldáliga in the backlands, supporting the peasant front; Bishop Tomás Balduino, President of CIMI (Indigenous Missionary Council), encouraging the native Indian front. It is a church standing tall against the militarist National Security State. Bishop Luis Fernández is coordinating thousands of base-level ecclesial communities. Archbishop Helder Camara continues to be the prophet of denunciation.

There is Aloisio Lorscheider, the President of CELAM; and Ivo Lorscheiter, leading the CNBB toward a new model of church relations with the state and the dominant classes. Great personalities in a revitalized and revitalizing church!

The new model (not a new church) of a people's church found eloquent expression in the document issued by the bishops of the Northeast on May 6, 1973. It was entitled: "I Have Heard the Cries of My People." An equally impressive message was issued on the same date by the bishops of the Central West. It was entitled: "Marginalization of the People, Cry of the Churches." In it we read:

> Only the people of the backlands and the cities, in union and work, in faith and hope, can be the church of Christ that invites and works for liberation. It is only to the extent that we immerse ourselves in the waters of the gospel that we become church, church-people, people of God.[17]

In Latin America it is the Brazilian church—its decision-making institutional members at least—that has displayed the greatest autonomy vis-à-vis political society and the National Security State, and the closest rapprochement with the oppressed classes. Their option dovetails with the model of the people's church, but it is not devoid of ambiguity. For example, it gets support from the middle and lower bourgeoisie, as well as from the national bourgeoisie. This enables the church to talk about "national" liberation, but still within the context of capitalism. Does it ultimately come down to some form of Latin American populism?

The Church in a Regressive Situation (Colombia)

Only one Latin American country, Colombia, finds itself in a situation of "Uruguayanization": i.e., a military dictatorship wearing the cloak of a civil government, as happened under Bordaberry in Uruguay. Formal democracy is less and less in control of the situation, and the institutional corruption of the regime is staggering. The church cannot abandon its traditional alliance, and it finds itself in crisis.

The "National Pact" of conservatives and liberals was passed on from Misael Pastrana to Alfonso López in 1974, and then to Julio Turbay in 1978. Applying the New Christendom model to perfection, the church has continued to be the legitimation of the system; but since 1978 it has adopted a certain critical distance.

The polarization of the church intensifies. On the one side Father Domingo Laín died as a guerrilla member of ELN on February 20, 1974. On the other side the cardinal formally received the Army's Order of Antonio Nariño on June 26, 1975, when a state of siege was declared; then, in June 1976, he was made a general of the Colombian army.

The most damnatory document of the decade in Latin America also came from the Colombian episcopate. On November 21, 1976, it issued the document entitled: "Christian Identity in Action for Justice." This lengthy work, which undertook to judge and condemn by name individuals, periodicals, and movements, was viewed by some as a preliminary draft for what would be the initial consultative draft for the Puebla Conference. The Colombian document said that the causes behind so many ills in the Colombian church "were due mostly to outside influences."[18]

Are the priests and theologians of Colombia that incompetent, or are they foreigners in their own country perhaps? How can they choose not to see that the cause of all the people's mobilization and the committed involvement of priests and Christians is the structural injustice of the capitalist system?

In the Colombian church the two models of the church are clearly present and in conflict with each other. Most of the bishops uphold the New Christendom model. Some of the clergy and religious are coming to a theoretical understanding of the people's church model and trying to put it into practice. In any case a crisis would seem to be facing the old alliance with the dominant classes, and there is much uncertainty. This might lead to a military dictatorship of the National Security type, which would suit many members of the church. Or it might lead to a social democracy more grounded in the common people, though this seems difficult to achieve. The church does not face an easy future, and it does not seem that the people are getting any witness to poverty or ecclesial commitment to their interests.

The Church vis-à-vis Formal Bourgeois Democracies (Mexico, Venezuela, Puerto Rico, Costa Rica)

The church's situation in these countries is stable. There is no persecution because a conservative stance dominates its top men. There are no conflicts because no prophetism is to be found. I shall focus solely on the example of Mexico.

In *Mexico* the situation is very varied. On October 18, 1973, the episcopate issued an interesting document on "Christian Commitment vis-à-vis Social and Political Options."[19] It had no impact on the lack of Christian commitment at the level of worker and peasant life. Indeed the only conflicts of any significance between church and state were in the area of education. Private schooling is desired by the upper, middle, and lower bourgeoisie—the core of the parish membership. The obligatory and free textbooks that the government distributes to all schools, even Catholic ones, raised much discussion. A settlement was reached peacefully. The textbooks need not be used in the private schools, or at least some of them need not be.

The rapid construction of the Basilica of Our Lady of Guadalupe, with the intervention of the government and the support of Mexico's major banks, was another event. Some interpreted it as a reconciliation between church and state; others saw it as the expropriation of the common people's Virgin by the dominant classes. There have been many clashes between priests and religious on the one hand and bishops on the other. These intramural conflicts again testify to the existence of two ecclesial models. The New Christendom model is legally impossible in Mexico but possible in fact. For though the understanding between church and state is extra-legal, it could hardly be better. But the model of the people's church is growing among countless groups, communities, and parishes. They are involving themselves with the interests of the common people as embodied in marginal colonies, peasants, and labor groups.

The assassination of Rodolfo Aguilar on March 21, 1977, pointed up the different ways of conceiving Christian witness that are now present in Mexico. Some hope to effect it some day through government power and authority. Others are already at work alongside the poor and oppressed, proclaiming the gospel message in poverty and simplicity.

The Church in Pre-Revolutionary Situations
(El Salvador, Guatemala, Honduras)

Central America has become the most critical juncture for Latin American capitalism. After centuries of oppression, the peasant population has begun to mobilize. The murder of Archbishop Oscar Arnulfo Romero (March 24, 1980) and the general strike called in his name three months later (June 24) have given El Salvador an opportunity to clarify the underlying positions. The Christian Democracy party met recently in Washington with representatives of Rightist groups and the State Department. It gives its support to a repressive regime that hopes to use modernizing reforms to forestall a thorough revolution of the Nicaraguan type. Here, even more clearly than in Chile and Venezuela, the Christian Democratic Party has made clear the role that it is playing in the present situation. But even in Chile and Venezuela it has been pro-developmentalism, pro-reformism, pro-capitalism, and pro-dependence on North American and European capitalism.

In *El Salvador,* as in Guatemala and Honduras, the situation of the peasantry grows increasingly terrible. There is growing confrontation between the military dictatorships and the oppressed people. The SEDAC board, headed by Archbishop Miguel Obando y Bravo, who was absent from Puebla, had this to say on June 24, 1977:

> We deplore deeply the fact that in order to silence those who are working committedly in the social arena out of fidelity to Christ, people brand them as Communists, subversives, and proponents of wild doctrines, . . . all this being done in flagrant violation of human rights.[20]

In El Salvador, peasant people were assassinated in 1974 in such places as San Francisco Chinameguita, La Cayetana, Tres Calles, Santa Barbara, Plaza de la Libertad in the capital, and so forth. Archbishop Chávez complained: "Here coffee is devouring human beings." He was alluding to the fact that the plantation owners were exploiting their peons.

One person who symbolizes the whole period is Father Rutilio Grande, who was assassinated on March 12, 1977. This parish priest of Aguilares was not the only priest-martyr. On May 11 of the same year Father Alfonso Navarro fell; on November 28, 1978, Father Barrera Motto was martyred; and on January 20, 1979, Octavio Ortiz died. This does not include the many lay people killed in the same incidents. Alongside Father Ortiz, for example, the following lay people were killed by the Army in the parish of San Antonio Abad: David Caballero, 14; Angel Morales, 22; Roberto Orellana, 15; and Jorge Gómez, 22.[21]

On February 22, 1977, Oscar Romero took charge of his archdiocese. He soon displayed a courage rarely seen in the church, as he undertook to defend his people from paramilitary groups and the government itself. On March 5, 1977, his bishops declared: "This situation has to be called one of collective injustice and institutionalized violence."[22] This does not mean that there are no disagreements or contradictions. Whereas Archbishop Romero celebrated a liturgy over the corpse of Rutilio Grande, Bishop Pedro Aparicio supported the government and criticized both lay people and priests at the 1977 Synod of Bishops in Rome.

Some still have the New Christendom model on their minds. Others are already implementing the model of a people's church. That is why, as Archbishop Romero put it: "The church of El Salvador is finding itself obliged to go back to the days of the catacombs." The early church could not use the state as a pastoral go-between; nor could it establish an alliance with the dominant classes. Such is the case with the church in El Salvador.

Archbishop Romero's death as a martyr may perhaps perdure as the symbol of the liberation struggle that Christians have undertaken in the second half of the twentieth century.

The Church in Socialist Societies (Cuba, Nicaragua)

The victory of the Sandinista Front for National Liberation in Nicaragua came on July 19, 1979. Thus began a new phase of church history in Latin America, and perhaps in the history of the universal church. For the first time in history a country moving slowly but surely toward a Latin American brand of socialism has succeeded in posing the question of religion in a positive, innovative, revolutionary manner. Quite obviously this is not just the result of pragmatic prudence on the part of the Front's leaders. It is also due to the revolutionary stance and active participation of thousands of Christians in the "war" against Somoza. Both before and after the revolution these Christians have taken an active part, many of them belonging to CCBs or other ecclesial or Christian institutions. Moreover, in contrast with Cuba in 1959, the Latin American church has progressed greatly in the past twenty years. The issue of religion has assumed strategic priority because of Christian grassroots praxis, the theology of liberation, and the committed involvement of many Christians in revolutionary movements. By virtue of its prophetic nature, Christianity will definitely not disappear in tomorrow's socialist society. It will probably bear fruit in new, revitalizing experiences.

The whole question is not only political but *theoretical.* Marxist thought must revise its theory of religion. Using its own categories and methodology, it will have to formulate a positive Marxist theory of religion. And obviously we Christians, like the Fathers of the Church when confronted with pagan Greek thought, will have to go to work on this major task. In Nicaragua some solution to this question must be worked out, or else decades will be wasted in trying to solve it.

But some Christians, including top-level hierarchical churchmen in Latin America, are trying to preach a conservative, reformist, anti-revolutionary brand of Christianity in Nicaragua. They are backed up by the hundreds of thousands of dollars supplied by certain American foundations, and by the efforts of priests and intellectuals who seek the triumph of a counter-revolution. The situation is serious, but Christianity will not lose this evangelizing battle. It will succeed in proclaiming the gospel message for a post-capitalist, Christian, Latin American society geared to the common people. Needless to say, this Christianity will no longer be identified with capitalism, private property, and the platform of Christian Democracy—all part of the system of capitalist dependence in Latin America.

The church in *Cuba* finds itself in a difficult situation. Under Batista the church cherished the idyllic dream of a New Christendom. It cost the church a great deal to abandon its class instincts and gradually get used to the irrevocable situation of living in a socialist country. The worst of the crisis had passed by 1973, insofar as accepting the real situation was concerned. But the church was still far from being able to accept the real situation in positive terms. For one thing, the Cuban church was isolated from the rest of Latin America, and that situation continues. Hence it is also isolated from such things as grassroots church movements and liberation theology. Its exclusivist connection with Rome also prevents it from having direct knowledge of other Latin American churches that are faced with similar situations. It is isolated and alone.

Direct contact between the Cuban bishops and the Holy See was established on March 27, 1974, when Agostino Casaroli visited Cuba. This contact enabled Cesare Zacchi to serve as papal nuncio until the end of 1974, when he was replaced by Mario Tagliaferri as pro-nuncio. However, this link is primarily diplomatic and political, not specifically pastoral and theological.

The church felt very uncertain about accepting socialism and weak in trying to criticize certain one-sided features of the religious issue as embodied in the new Constitution. It realizes that it should first make some contribution to the revolution so that it will have the right to demand corrections. In terms of humility the church has made positive statements. For example, "José Domínguez, bishop of Matanzas and president of the episcopal conference, expressed the view that justice would be done to Cuba by lifting economic and political sanctions."[23] The same can be said of the church's condemnation of an attack on a Cuban plane on November 9, 1976.[24]

Nevertheless the Cuban church has not yet discovered its strategic importance in the overall destiny of Latin America; nor has it made a firm decision to implement fully the people's church model, though it finds itself in an ideal situation to take the lead in doing so. More than any church in Latin America, it has autonomy vis-à-vis the state and can work in and with the people in civil society, allying itself with them in their revolutionary process.

It is a difficult task, calling for much moral strength, extreme poverty, and eyes fixed on the future. If the church turns to look back, it will turn into a "pillar of salt."

In *Nicaragua* the earthquake that destroyed Managua also shattered some of the support that Somoza had still been getting from some groups among the bourgeoisie. Somoza robbed the aid funds meant to rebuild the city, took over construction companies, and assumed a personal monopoly over various enterprises that he had once respected as belonging to other members of the national bourgeoisie. Thus his economic and political power reached its peak, but Somoza found himself completely alone and isolated. In February 1973, around the time of the earthquake, the episcopate pointed out that the needed material reconstruction symbolized the need "to construct a new society" that would be more just. On May 27, the episcopate again denounced the violent acts and abuses perpetrated by the authorities against human rights. Bishop Obando y Bravo accompanied the guerrilla group that left for Cuba with thirteen hostages. Gradually the church began to become a target for persecution.

On June 13, 1976, thirteen priests under the leadership of North American Capuchins on the Atlantic coast sent a letter to the Somoza government. In it they denounced acts of detention, torture, and kidnapping committed in Nueva Segovia, Matagalpa, Jinotega, Zelaya, and elsewhere. The only response was the expulsion of Father Avaristo Bertrand as a subversive.

Meanwhile Father Fernando Cardenal was bravely condemning the Somoza government before the United States Senate. Ernesto Cardenal had become plenipotentiary minister for the Front, travelling around the world to inform world opinion about what was happening in Nicaragua. In 1976 Father Miguel d'Escoto, one of "The Twelve," declared that a priest's work "on behalf of justice is a thoroughly Christian and priestly mission. Denunciation of injustice is an inherent part of the proclamation of the gospel message. It entails representing the weak and acting as the voice of those who have no voice, as the documents of the Medellín Conference asserted."

Sandino had fought against the North American invasion of Nicaragua at the end of the twenties. In 1934 he was treacherously assassinated by the recent Somoza's father. The Sandinista movement began anew in the mountains around 1956, and a growing number of students joined in from 1959 on. Carlos Fonseca Amador was one of the first. First it was called the National Liberation Front, then the Sandinista National Liberation Front (FSLN). In 1970 members of Catholic University Youth who were working in some of the poorest neighborhoods began to dialogue with the Front. In 1972 many of them joined the Front, including Luis Carrión and Monica Baltodano. Some of them formed the "proletarian" fraction of the Front in 1975. It concentrated on working with urban people and manual laborers. Another faction, the Ongoing People's War (GPP), one of whose members was Tomás Borge, remained amid the peasantry and in the hillsides.

In November 1977, the National Guard destroyed Ernesto Cardenal's community at Solentiname. Persecution, torture, and assassination increased. The first insurrection took place in 1978. In Estelí alone during that year there were some 2,400 wounded, 2,500 killed, 4,200 orphaned, and 12,000 abandoned. On Christmas 1977, Gaspar García Lavina, a Sacred Heart priest, joined the Sandinista Front. He would soon die a martyr's death and be especially commemorated as a hero of the Revolution.

On January 1, 1978, Bishop Obando y Bravo led a procession in which more than 2,000 people participated. The government responded by assassinating the leader of the bourgeois opposition, the journalist Pedro Joaquín Chamorro Cardenal. That moment marked the beginning of the countdown that arrived at zero on July 19, 1979. Somoza found himself alone and isolated in the face of the Sandinista Front, the spontaneous mobilization of the masses, an aroused church, the opposition bourgeoisie, and a United States advocating the Trilateral policy of human rights.

The prolonged strike began. On January 27, the cities stood empty. The whole population was opposed to the regime. Yet the papal nuncio, Gabriel Montalvo, of Colombian nationality, was drinking a toast with Somoza while León was being bombarded. One paper noted: "It is nationally known that the nuncio has publicly identified himself with the Somoza regime" (*Excelsior,* Mexico City, November 4, 1978).

The base-level ecclesial communities participated in the revolution, and the church committed itself to the anti-Somoza war. Victory was finally achieved, and the Sandinista Front entered Managua unconditionally on July 19. The work of national reconstruction and the organization of a new society began. It is over the latter issue, the organization of a postcapitalist society, that Christians of Nicaragua are now divided. The issue is of the greatest importance for the worldwide church. I shall come back to it after I discuss the Puebla Conference.

THE PUEBLA CONFERENCE (1979)

Ecclesial Context

It can be said that the whole Puebla process began in 1973. At the start of the year it was said that "for the moment there would be no third Conference. Observers got this meaning from some statements issued at the beginning of the year here in Rio de Janeiro by the new Secretary General of CELAM."[25] Some bishops were also suggesting that there were both false and true interpretations of the Medellín Conference. One Mexican bishop went so far as to say: "Medellín is more a matter of what people say about it than of what really happened there. Read carefully, the commitments of Medellín do not oblige the church to side with the poor."[26]

Thus a new ideological platform had to be erected so as to be able to sidestep Medellín. In any case CELAM was entrusted with the task of organizing a third conference. It was the start of a long process that would terminate on February 13, 1979. More than two years of preparation enabled people to take cognizance of the importance of Puebla—first, the Latin American church; then, the European church; and then the African and Asian churches.

The whole process can be divided into four stages: (1) from the announcement of the Puebla Conference to the publication of the preliminary consultative document (November 1976 to November 1977); (2) from the consultative document to the publication of the working-draft document in September 1978; (3) from there to the actual start of the Puebla Conference on January 27, 1979; and (4) the Puebla Conference itself from its start to its conclusion on February 13, 1979. The first stage lasted one year; the second, ten months; the third, four months—due to the unforeseen death of Pope Paul VI on August 6, 1978, the sudden death of Pope John Paul I a little more than a month later, and the election of Pope John Paul II. If the third stage had not been delayed and protracted by those unforeseen occurrences, it is quite possible that the Puebla Conference would have turned out differently. For the extended time-period enabled people to learn much more about the upcoming conference and study its details.

There is no doubt whatsoever that the Secretary General of CELAM had formed a plan, was counting on his own experts, and hoped to achieve his aims in satisfactory fashion at the Puebla Conference. In the first stage, however, nothing was clear as yet. There were indications: e.g., the document of the Colombian bishops on "Christian Identity" (November 1976) and the conclusions of a lay people's meeting in Buenos Aires that lasted from July 2 to July 8, 1977. One could see that the theoretical backdrop was the whole idea of the transition from a rural society to an urban, industrial society. Here was the start of Ariadne's thread. The grassroots began to organize and take cognizance, waiting for the preliminary consultative document.

The second stage began in December 1977, when the consultative document appeared with its 1,159 sections. Earlier suspicions were largely confirmed. It contained attacks on the Medellín Conference. Its theoretical framework was developmentalist and even close to that of the Trilateral Commission. It did not speak out clearly to condemn the violations of human rights, multinationals, and National Security regimes. Beginning in January 1978, the most important theological reaction ever to take place in the history of Latin American theology occurred. It was not only theologians who wrote, however. So did bishops, groups of prelates, priests, religious, base-level ecclesial communities, peasants, and natives. It was a spontaneous reaction of dissent. Two brief alternative documents gained recognition. One came from the bishops of Brazil's Northeast, from a team headed by Bishop Marcelo

Pinto Carvalheira; it was entitled: "Aids for Reflection." The other document, from a Venezuelan group, was entitled: "A Piece of Good News: The Church Is Born of the Latin American People."

But another event also took place for the first time in the history of theology. A sizeable group of theologians, pastors, and Christians in Europe, the United States, Africa, and Asia expressed support for the course opened up by the Medellín Conference. They condemned the effort to depart from that tradition. The ground was broken with the famous Memorandum from German theologians (November 1977). Other theologians followed: French, Spanish, Italian, North American (including Chicano bishops), Canadian and, finally, more than seventy theologians from Asia and Africa who met in Colombo, Sri Lanka, shortly before the Puebla Conference itself opened. Puebla took on universal significance because at stake were the interests of church members living on other continents. Puebla would undermine or reinforce positions directly or indirectly affecting Christians all over the world, because in a few short years 50 percent of the world's Catholics would be living in Latin America. In 1975 the number of Christians in America surpassed the number in Europe, and the weight of Catholicism shifted to this side of the Atlantic.

Here is not the place to detail all that took place.[27] The strong reactions against the preliminary consultative document bore fruit. Cardinal Aloisio Lorscheider assumed personal responsibility for drawing up the working draft for Puebla, which was the fruit of much consultation. But we must not forget that liberation theologians were excluded from the whole official consultation process and the work of drafting. It was the same as if Rahner, Congar, and all the major theologians of Europe had been excluded from Vatican II.

The death of two popes and the election of John Paul II, the first non-Italian pope in four centuries, delayed the convening of Puebla. People became better aware of the setup of the Puebla Conference, of who was included and who was not. All this enabled people to prepare better for the actual sessions.

Some sought the condemnation of liberation theology and of what they understood by "people's church," "parallel magisterium," "Marxist analysis," and so forth. Others wanted to defend the experiences of the church at the grassroots level and its work with the poor. They wanted to see condemned the violations of human rights, the existence of National Security regimes, the expansion of multinational corporations, etc. Confrontation was inevitable, for there were different options based on differing class interests and ideologies and even specifically national stances. The churches of Argentina, Colombia, Mexico, and Venezuela (a later addition) seemed to have one posture. The Brazilian church and groups of bishops and church members from Peru, Central America, the Caribbean, Ecuador, Chile, and elsewhere upheld the church's committed involvement with the sorely repressed people.

The Puebla Conference Itself [28]

Pope John Paul II's arrival in Santo Domingo on January 25, 1979, drew the attention of the world; so the Puebla Conference, which began two days later, could begin its work in an atmosphere of greater tranquillity. The pope's words, in more than forty speeches from the time he left Rome, sparked excited commentaries. The Puebla Conference had to ponder them calmly and take them up in mature fashion. Almost at once liberation theologians made their presence felt. They had not been invited as conference participants, but various bishops had invited them to come to the vicinity of Puebla as advisors. As early as the afternoon of January 28, these theologians responded to a request from the bishops by sending them a theological commentary on the pope's "Opening Address" to the Conference. The ten-page commentary was entitled: "Discurso de Juan Pablo II en la inauguración de la III Conferencia: Breve comentario de un grupo de teólogos."

No support for the New Christendom model was to be found in the essential structure of the pope's discourses. He was not suggesting that the church station itself in political society or make alliances with the dominant classes. Nor was he suggesting that it was to be the state that would help the church to carry out its pastoral function. On the contrary, the pope demanded religious liberty and noninvolvement on the level of political society. Of course the system would manage to find support for its own position in the pope's words. Banks and the Mexican bourgeoisie, among others, were struck and even taken aback by the pope's popular appeal; they quickly interpreted his words as support for the New Christendom model of the church. As the days passed, however, one could see that the pope was not supporting capitalism or condemning socialism. He was upholding the freedom of the church and the transcendence of its mission, whichever system might be in effect. His language and his way of developing a theme did not make for quick, easy comprehension. But if we look at the papal words that made their way into the Puebla Final Document, we can see that they were the ones that were most pastoral in nature, and that spoke most clearly on behalf of an option for the poor.

I am not going to give a day-to-day account of events. I am not going to talk about the makeup of committees, the various drafts of the final document, or the points of high tension. For example, I will not go into details about the letter of Archbishop López Trujillo to Bishop Luciano Duarte, which caused a great sensation because there was no doubt at all about its authenticity. I shall simply offer some reflections on the Puebla Final Document.

Viewing the Final Document, and indeed the whole course of the conference proceedings, we can draw certain conclusions. The various groups that hoped to condemn Christian movements of the common people, grassroots communities, the "people's church," liberation theology, and supporters of a "parallel magisterium" (who they were was never made clear) were unsuccessful. They were defeated, at least at the Puebla Conference itself. More successful, however, were those who sought to "choke off" the voice of the Latin American church, so that it would not embarrass them with its denunciations. The fact is that little was said at Puebla, and what was said was not very forceful. The Final Document was a "compromise" document, voicing minimal statements on which all could agree. This was very different from Medellín. Many of the documents of Medellín were not too clear, but none of them was weak, timid, inarticulate. Still, those who were expected to be the sure losers at Puebla came out stronger: people's groups, base-level communities, liberation theology, and prophetic bishops. They managed to take control of the adverse situation.

In the end Medellín was adopted as the starting point and inspiration. The Puebla Conference can be placed in the tradition of Medellín. It was not as original and creative as the Medellín Conference, but it was in the same tradition. That in itself is a great deal, and in many quarters it was not expected or hoped for. The door remains open for Christians to keep opting for the interests of the poor and oppressed.

STATUS OF THE "TEXT" AND THE "PUEBLA EVENT"

I should like to make a few observations on the difference between a mere "text" and an ecclesial "event." All too often we tend to equate an ecclesial "text" with the totality of an ecclesial "event" that encompasses many other aspects and moments. The Puebla "event" is much more than a Puebla "Final Document." If we fail to realize this, then we will be giving the Final Document a centrality that it does not possess; and we will be overlooking where the "event" itself really takes place.

It can be said, in fact, that the "Puebla event" has only begun to take place. Its earliest antecendents go back to early 1973, as I noted above. But its full realization will take place only in the decade of the eighties, and its impact will perdure after that.

The important thing to realize is that the Puebla Final Document is only *one* aspect, and not the chief one, of the whole Puebla "event." So analysis of the "text" of the Final Document can be done in two ways. It might be viewed as the Puebla "event" itself, in which case one would study the document thoroughly in order to implement it, apply it, and critique it. Or, on the other hand, one might view it as simply a part of the historical process involved, a process that has only begun. If we adopt the second alternative, then the contradictions in the Puebla text are not impossible obstacles but enriching incentives. In other words, the text becomes a *quarry* where we can find things we need to shed light on ecclesial praxis centered around the common people. The people's praxis will be the support system of "discernment" and its orthopraxis. It will not be a Machiavellian use of Puebla, or a misdirected interpretation. It will be the people of God's way of discerning and implementing Puebla.

In that case, Puebla will be what the people's church makes of it. When peasants are imprisoned, when they offer the defense that Puebla inspired their actions, then the oppressors involved will form the conclusion that the Puebla "event" is the root-cause of subversion and popular unrest. That, in fact, is how Medellín became a historic event—not in its seminary walls, but in thousands of grassroots ecclesial communities, in courts and torture chambers, and through its many martyrs. Medellín became real and historically meaningful *in the praxis of the people's church.*

Many factors intervened in the Puebla "text": e.g., consultations, a preliminary consultative document, a working draft, contributions from the Christian people, the words and "gestures" of the pope, and so forth. At the Puebla Conference itself, liberation theologians also played a role, speaking on behalf of the people. All the contradictions in various Latin American countries and among the different classes within the church were evident in the Final Document, where the tensions were not resolved. To some this is a scandal; to others it makes the document a rich quarry.

Since February 1979 the most pressing and immediate task has become one of "discernment." On the basis of the text we must formulate *a discourse that is valid and worthwhile for the praxis of the common people's church.* We must have anthologies of Puebla statements so that the common people can *take possession* of the Puebla "event," which is theirs by right even though Puebla may have originally been organized against them. The *appropriation of Puebla by the common people* is the most immediate task facing us.

The matter of the people's appropriation of the text makes clear the difference between Medellín and Puebla. When we consider the originators of Medellín (the CELAM of 1968), many of its texts, and its surrounding atmosphere, we realize that from the very start the conservative groups in the church had handed it over to the more prophetic groups in the church. There was hardly any need for the common people to work at taking possession of Medellín. It was born in the hands of the oppressed.

Puebla was not. It came from hands that had no desire to see Puebla become an event belonging to the Christian common people. Those hands wanted to bury Medellín and condemn many issues that entailed the church's commitment to the poor. But they failed in their attempt. As a quarry, the Puebla text contains precious stones and abundant marble. So we must not make the historical mistake of letting Puebla be taken over by the dominant classes, National Security regimes, or a church unwilling to opt for the poor. It would be a crime to hand over the text to them when the Christian people fought for it in hundreds of meetings, demonstrations, written pieces, and experiences of suffering. The text cannot simply be surrendered without a fight. The common people have a right to the Puebla text, and a duty to flesh it into a historical reality.

GENERAL CHALLENGES AFTER PUEBLA

History has continued its course since February 1979. The victory of the Nicaraguan people has opened a new phase in that history. Christian praxis, and hence theology, finds itself involved in a set of problems that follows the basic structure of the previous phase but that also underlines certain aspects that I would like to point up here.

The People's Church

Since Puebla the whole experience of a new model of the church being applied to political and civil society has continued and indeed been reinforced. It is becoming quite clear to people that it is a grassroots ecclesial task. In extremely repressive countries the church is the only place that provides "space" for dialogue, criticism, and political awareness. There the people's church is growing.

The same can be said of Brazil. Its church has grown in stature insofar as it gave a prophetic and people-oriented sense to the visit of Pope John Paul II in 1980, making it part of the fight for human rights against a repressive government. This is also true in Peru, and in Colombia in particular, where the national conference of base-level communities at the start of 1980 gave great impetus to the movement throughout the country. It is also true in Mexico and almost all the countries of Latin America. Certainly it is true in Nicaragua, where such base-level communities have begun to redefine their function within a socialist nation geared toward the common people.

Puebla lent support to this ecclesial experience. Now it is not just prophetic groups but the church as a whole that is supporting the grassroots movement. But clearly the confrontation between two different models of the church goes on, and it is quite possible that the tension will increase.

Confusion in the Face of the "Opening Up"

Some countries have seen a sudden degree of political "opening up" in their regimes of "controlled democracy." This is true in Brazil, where the control was complete; it is also true in such countries as Peru, where there was greater freedom to begin with.

Whatever the case may be, Christians face an ambiguous situation. It is not a black and white issue, as was the fight for human rights against a repressing state. Now we have a multiplicity of "democratic" possibilities. There is always the possibility that we will end up with populism, capitalist reforms, or various forms of government proposed by Social Democrats or Christian Democrats as the proper political approach for Christians. Populism or third-way alternatives seem to be the greatest temptations facing Christians. Lacking any clear-eyed strategy for implementing a new historical project, people may succumb to capitalist projects entailing greater or lesser dependence on multinational capital. We must keep a close eye on the policies of the Trilateral Commission and conservative progressivism. Although some of their means seem to be modernizing, they tend to install new levels of dependence and exploitation.

It is history that is the great teacher in life, however, and no warnings can substitute for personal experience. We must keep moving. Sooner or later we may realize more clearly that urgent changes are needed.

A New Theory and Praxis of Religion

I have already noted that a prototypical experience for Latin America is now under way in Nicaragua. In its pastoral letter of November 17, 1979, the episcopate had this to say:

> We want to start with a word about the achievements of the revolutionary process. They tell us that our people, through years of suffering and social marginalization, have been accumulating the needed experience to convert it all now into a broad-based and profoundly liberative action.

Further on the episcopate said:

> Sometimes we hear anxious and fearful talk that the present process in Nicaragua is heading toward socialism. . . . Now if socialism means power exercised from the standpoint of the vast majority and increasingly shared by the organized people, so that there will be a real transfer of power to the common classes of the people, then once again it can only find motivation and support in the faith.

This is the most important text coming from an episcopate in many years, perhaps in decades, perhaps in the whole twentieth century. It marks the *positive* entry of the church into the coming society of the future.

In this highly complicated and important situation Christians clearly have a responsibility to resolve the question of religion in an innovative way. We know that in dogmatic Marxism religion is alienation and will disappear with the coming of socialism. By the same token, we also know that conservative Christians are seeking to bring together the church and those groups or classes that oppose the socialist revolution in Nicaragua. All of a sudden, pragmatic factions of the Sandinista vanguard can appreciate the contribution and support of the prophetic and people-rooted Christianity that has been gestating in Latin America over the past twenty years. (Such Christians did not exist in Cuba in 1959, remember.) We are seeing pragmatic Sandinistas (i.e., socialist revolutionaries, which include people who were Christian leaders) join together with Christians who have made a clearcut commitment to the poor, the oppressed classes, and criticism of capitalist society. This union offers sound reasons to be hopeful about the Nicaraguan revolution and an innovative resolution of the religious question.

Going against the views of dogmatic Marxists, those involved must spell out a *theory of religion* advocating *liberation*. Such a theory would explain an existing and growing praxis, showing that this type of religion is a necessary support for every revolution, for the process of reconstruction, and for the future socialist society. In that future society democracy is an ideal to be achieved through criticism and self-criticism; and it is to be people's democracy rather than democratic centralism.

This would be a positive theory of religion based on a theology of work, where religion is situated on its essential level of cult. In the eucharistic cult we offer God a piece of bread, which is the fruit "of the earth and of work." The productive relationship between human beings and nature finds embodiment in the product whose real-life symbol is bread. If that bread has been snatched away from the poor, it cannot be offered as sacrifice. In other words, economic justice between human beings is required before one can offer a sacrifice to God. So we need a *theology of work* within which religion will find its place in the socialist society of the future.

This notion frightens Marxist dogmatists and Christian conservatives. But as far back as 1514, Bartolomé de Las Casas read the famous biblical passage that suggested the link between Eucharist and economics. That passage could well serve as the starting point for a new theory of religion in a dialectical, anti-fetishist vein:

> If one sacrifices from what has been wrongfully obtained, the offering is blemished; the gifts of the lawless are not acceptable. The Most High is not pleased with the offerings of the ungodly; and he is not propitiated for sins by a multitude of sacrifices. Like one who kills a son before his father's eyes is the man who offers a sacrifice from the property of the poor. The bread of the needy is the life of the poor; whoever deprives them of it is a man of blood. To take away a neighbor's living is to murder him; to deprive an employee of his wages is to shed blood [Sirach 34:18–22].

In his *History of the Indies* (Book III, Chap. 79), Bartolomé tells us the effect the passage had on him. Closing the text, he freed his Indians and began his fight in their defense. Today, too, the church is summoned to prophesy against the oppression of the poor and to opt for them, as both Medellín and Puebla stated clearly.

NOTES

1. See my book, *De Medellín a Puebla (1968–1979)* (Mexico City: Edicol, 1979), 620 pp.
2. This is the thesis I proposed in my book, *Hipótesis para una historia de la Iglesia en América Latina* (Barcelona: Estela, 1967). Pablo Richard has recently spelled it out clearly in his thesis, *Mort des Chrétientés et naissance de l'Eglise* (Paris: Centre Lebret, 1978).
3. *Excelsior,* October 7, 1977, p. 2.
4. Ibid.
5. Ibid., October 8, 1977, p. 3.
6. *ICI,* 388 (1971), p. 17.
7. Ibid., 428 (1973), p. 12.

8. *La Nación* (Buenos Aires), November 15, 1972, p. 9.

9. *Marcha,* 1620 (1972), p. 20.

10. Spanish text in *Uno más uno* (Mexico), December 26, 1977, p. 3.

11. Galet y Ordoñez, *Liberación de la liberación* (Bogotá: Paulinas, 1976), p. 38.

12. R. Roncagliolo and F. Reyes Matte, *Iglesia, prensa y militares* (Mexico City: ILET, 1978), p. 91.

13. See F. Hinkelammert, *Ideología del sometimiento* (San José, Costa Rica: EDUCA, 1977), p. 41f.

14. For the text of this document and background and documentation on the Christians for Socialism movement in Chile see John Eagleson, ed., *Christians and Socialism: The Christians for Socialism Movement in Latin America* (Maryknoll, N.Y.: Orbis Books, 1975).

15. *Signos de lucha y esperanza* (Lima: CEP, 1978), p. 278.

16. Jose Marins et al., eds., *Praxis de los Padres de América Latina* (Bogotá: Paulinas, 1978), p. 847.

17. *Brasil: ¿Milagro o Engaño?* (Lima: CEP, 1973), p. 110.

18. *Identidad cristiana en la acción por la justicia,* no. 17.

19. *Documentos colectivos del episcopado mexicano* (Mexico City: Paulinas, 1977), pp. 313–69.

20. *Praxis de los Padres,* p. 858.

21. *Excelsior,* March 20, 1979, p. 9.

22. *Praxis de los Padres,* p. 967.

23. *Noticias Aliadas,* November 20, 1975, N43, p. 9.

24. CELAM *Boletín,* 113 (1977), pp. 14–15.

25. *Noticias Aliadas,* 26 (1973), p. 2 and p. 9.

26. *Proceso,* Mexico City, 86, June 26, 1978, p. 13.

27. See my work cited in note 1.

28. See my article, "Crónica de Puebla," in *Christus,* March-April, 1979. For extensive coverage of the Puebla Conference in English, including the Puebla Final Document, papal talks, and commentaries, see John Eagleson and Philip Scharper, eds., *Puebla And Beyond* (Maryknoll, N.Y.: Orbis Books, 1979).

9

Latin American Protestantism (1969–1978)

Carmelo E. Alvarez (Costa Rica)

In treating Latin American Protestantism during the stated period, I would not be so rash as to claim that this is an adequate, much less complete, coverage of the subject. I shall simply attempt to offer a few indications of what is going on in several sectors of Latin American Protestantism. One is the sector that has organized itself into a Protestant ecumenical movement; the other is the "evangelical" sector. The distinction is more formal than real, but at least it does enable me to make a few distinctions and to detail a few important historical developments. However, it has also caused some confusion, one being the famous distinction between "civil-oriented" missionaries and "evangelizing" missionaries. My aim here is pedagogical rather than polemical. I would like to offer a somewhat clearer profile of Latin American Protestantism, with its contradictions, divisions, and positive aspects.

For the purposes of this brief paper I can describe what has been going on in Latin American Protestantism in terms of two key events that took place in 1969. One was the first Latin American Congress on Evangelization (CLADE), held in Bogotá, Colombia; the other was the third Latin American Evangelical Conference (CELA), held in Buenos Aires, Argentina. Both were important landmarks in the life of the Protestant churches on the continent. Then I will comment on the impact of various ecumenical movements of Protestant origin during this period: i.e., ISAL, ULAJE, CELADEC, and FUMEC—A.L. Finally, I will mention the Assembly of Evangelical Churches held in Oaxtepec, Mexico, in 1978. That gathering was the moment when the churches finally came out in favor of a *process* aimed at forming a Latin American Council of Churches. I will briefly *describe* what happened at the gathering in Oaxtepec, and I will suggest where Latin American Protestantism may be heading in the future.

The Latin American Congress of Evangelization (CLADE), which was

103

held in Bogotá in 1969, marked the end of a stage in Latin American Protestantism. It was a very heterogeneous meeting, but it was marked by a search for a pertinent type of evangelization. Criticisms and challenges were voiced in favor of real commitment to Latin America. There were repeated appeals to the social responsibility of the Christian on a continent facing crisis. The basic idea was the renewal of the church for the sake of the task of evangelization.

It has been said that this Congress was more an encounter than a convention. There were encounters and confrontations between Christians who were all deeply concerned about the task of evangelization, but who had different views of this task and different strategies for carrying it out. Although a theological consensus was evident, this could not hide the fact that people disagreed as to how to formulate and implement the task of evangelization. Thus a wide diversity of options was evident at the CLADE conference. But so was the undeniable fact that the participants wanted to heed the outcry caused by the reality of oppression on our continent. The task of evangelization is framed in this basic context of turmoil and yearnings for liberation.

The third Latin American Evangelical Conference (CELA III) in Buenos Aires was the last in a series of conferences. Their common aim had been to try to overcome the identity-crisis of Protestantism and to work toward a continent-wide organism that would give cohesion and representation to the Protestant churches of Latin America. Recognition of this twofold crisis— crisis of identity and crisis of unity—was the basic focus of the CELA III meeting. It entailed an agenda based on the political, economic, and social realities of Latin America.

This raised a whole new issue. The lack of committed involvement to Latin America was criticized. The churches had not been truly effective and operative in this respect in their dealings with the world. Thus they had a debt to pay, a debt imposed by the gospel message and claimed by the people. The theme of the Conference was: "Debtors to the World."

CELA III stressed the reality of injustice in Latin America and the urgent need for structural changes. The need for a transformation in Latin America was clearly perceived. Participants shared a vision that is expressed, in theological terms, by a necessary fleshing out with a Christian presence. Though this conception of Christian presence does break with the old non-involvement, it emphasizes the committed involvement of the individual rather than that of the church as such. The thinking is that the liberal, democratic ideal is the best one for Latin America.

What balance-sheet can we draw up with regard to these two meetings? Both CLADE and CELA III took place at a time when Protestantism was going through a crisis. Underlying the two meetings was the yearning to fashion an authentic Protestantism that possessed both unity and strength. What was not foreseen was that it takes more than a congress or a conference to dispel historical divisions, failed initiatives, and aborted aspirations. The division within Latin American Protestantism goes much deeper. However, these efforts do fan the existing yearning for unity, which must entail real, authentic involvement in the situation through which our nations are living. We must take seriously the yearnings for unity evident among the people of Latin America, as well as their struggles and their defeats.

Protestant ecumenical movements—in their origins at least—have played an important pioneering role in the efforts of Latin American Protestantism to be historically relevant and effective. Within the broad context of social concern and political involvement, these movements have been a force working to shake the churches out of their lethargy and comfortable position.

There is a tension between the church as institution and the church as a movement. This has led to estrangement, breaks, and mutual expulsions between movements and the churches as such. The churches were not able to discern the prophetic element being posed in the outlined programs and strategies of these movements, much less to identify themselves with the movements' lines of action. Even ecumenical movements themselves would admit that there have been tactical errors, verbal scare tactics on both the theological and political level, and a tendency toward divisiveness that was hardly conducive to overcoming the divisions existing between the churches. But even though the churches may not admit it, these movements have made important contributions to the churches with their theological work, their educational programs, and their analyses of Latin America in sociological, theological, and historical terms. If the churches could bring themselves to acknowledge the worthwhile contributions of the various ecumenical movements, then they would have a rich store of lessons and experiences to utilize at this critical juncture in Latin American life.

By the same token, ecumenical groups must recognize that the ecumenical movement is truly worthwhile and effective where it is giving shape to the struggle of the people, to their yearnings rooted in the life of faith, and to their hope in a new dawn. Ecumenical groups must formulate their strategy to serve that process and that way of life. Only then do we get convergence and true ecumenism.

As the decade of the seventies drew to a close, Latin American Protestantism accepted a challenge which has unleashed a process that cannot yet be evaluated satisfactorily. By the time the Assembly of Churches met in Oaxtepec, Mexico, in 1978, there were more questions than answers. It was obvious that earlier efforts at unity had failed, including UNELAM (Latin American Evangelical Unity). UNELAM had been organized as a provisional committee aimed at working toward a permanent council of churches. Certain intraecclesiastical conditions prevented agreement regarding the proposed council. Even efforts to "copy" the model of the World Council of Churches encountered various kinds of resistance and suspicion. What is obvious is that the Protestant churches felt themselves to be without a leader.

In such a brief space I cannot say much about the Oaxtepec documents. A distinction must be made between the positions presented at the conference and the documents that were officially approved. Nevertheless I think we can point up four worthwhile things in what was affirmed and approved by the Assembly of Latin American Churches at Oaxtepec.

First of all, the Assembly felt obliged to give concreteness and specificity to its documents. When it came to the question of human rights, the concrete case of Nicaragua surfaced immediately. During that very week Nicaragua was suffering through one of the worst moments in its history. The Assembly took the situation of Nicaragua seriously, sending telegrams to different levels of government and calling attention to particular matters. One of the telegrams was sent to Somoza himself.

Second, the presence of native Indian representatives as duly authorized delegates meant that the Assembly could not bypass the whole issue of the *forgotten sectors*. The presence of women made clear once again that there was an urgent need to give serious consideration to problems that afflicted Latin American society and hence the church of Jesus Christ. Many young people participated actively at the meetings, thus reminding the churches of the decisive role young people can and should play in the task of building the kingdom.

Third, the whole issue of *power structures* had to be broached, recognized, and treated as one that was clearly relevant to the Latin American situation. The document in question suffered from certain imprecisions and over-generalizations. But in my opinion it also examined, from a biblical-theological perspective, what exactly the mission of the church is to be right now vis-à-vis power structures, and what its proper role is as a prophetic agent on the Latin American continent.

Fourth and finally, the open letter to the churches of Latin America was a challenge and a statement of commitment laid down by the Assembly. It was a challenge because the churches will have to spell out clearly where they want to go, whether they really want unity, and whether it is their conviction to participate actively in the liberation processes that should arise among our people on the basis of the gospel message. It was a statement of commitment because if Oaxtepec does not succeed in creating organisms to channel these concerns effectively, then it will prove to have been just another ecumenical meeting on the continental level.

Oaxtepec produced many formulations and made various plans. I don't think it has changed anything up to now. We will have to wait and see. Our hope is that CLAI, which is now being formed, will assume responsibility for the commitments that Oaxtepec made. We hope that it will foster *authentic ecumenism* and responsible action among Latin American Protestants.

What was said is one thing. What has been done, and what remains to be done, is something else again. Let us trust that the churches will take up this challenge.

10

The Irruption of the Poor in Latin America and the Christian Communities of the Common People

Gustavo Gutiérrez (Peru)

I would like to indicate the context and thrust of my presentation. The points I want to offer for your consideration will be framed in the perspective of *Latin America*. The aim is to pool our problems so that we can better compare them with the experiences of companions from other countries and continents. I beg your pardon for restricting my references exclusively to our realities, but I want you to know that we wish to engage in comparison and dialogue with other people's experiences.

I shall present my considerations under three main headings: (I) the irruption, or breaking-in, of the poor; (II) an oppressed and believing people and Christian communities of the common people; (III) some ecclesiological indicators.

I. THE IRRUPTION OF THE POOR

One of our colleagues, after hearing the committee reports, drew the following conclusion: we are experiencing enormous vitality in the sectors composed of the common people of Latin America; we are also seeing great vitality in the church that is taking root in those sectors. He also saw, and with good reason, progress in the practice of the common people with respect to theological formulations. In the circular relationship between commitment and theological reflection, this progress is an ongoing stimulus and summons to creativity.

I think that this vitality comes from what could be called the irruption, or breaking-in, of the poor within the historical process of Latin America and within the life of the Christian community that constantly wells up from it. It is a tough entry that asks permission of no one, and it is sometimes violent. The poor come with "their poverty on their back," as Bartolomé de las Casas put it, with their suffering, their culture, their odor, their race, their language, and the exploitation they are experiencing. When the poor break in, they do so with everything they are.

The "Absent Ones" Make Their Presence Felt

This is the most important event in the recent history of Latin America. I put the term "absent ones" in quote marks because obviously the poor have never been outside the concrete history of our peoples; their lives, their blood and sweat, are part of that history. My point is that history has not been fashioned and interpreted in terms of the poor but in terms of the privileged people who have humiliated and exploited the poor. So we talk about a presence in the strong sense when the poor move to center stage in society and the church, claiming their rights, calling attention to their interests, and launching a challenge through their struggles and their hopes.

It is only from them, from the common people at the bottom who are often anonymous, that we can read the pulse of our continent's history. Analyses which take off from, and often go no further than, the top levels of politics and the church miss the mark. So let me say something about the historical process and then about the life of the church. Distinguishing the two helps us to organize our thoughts, but we know that they are deeply interconnected.

a. Their presence in the historical process of Latin America. The presence of the poor is making itself felt first of all in the struggles of the common people and the new historical awareness associated with those struggles.

First of all, then, we have *the struggles of the common people for liberation.* Such struggles have always been a part of the history of our continent. There are notable examples in different countries. Today people are trying specifically to recover the memory of those efforts. Those exercising domination seek to erase that memory because they know it is a historical force that can subvert the existing social order.

Today we confront new facts that have been gestating for some time but that have surfaced in Latin American history only in the last twenty or thirty years. It is very difficult to establish exact dates in these matters. The struggles for the liberation of the people, arising on different sides of the continent, have created a new situation that varies from country to country. It is a difficult situation, to be sure, marked by the efforts of poor people to free themselves from new forms of despoilment that would rob them of the fruits of their toil, their identity as a people, their land, their country, and even their very lives. This despoilment is an old story in Latin America. But today we see new and more refined ways of despoiling the poor being practiced by imperialism and its allies within our own countries. I simply want to point out that these new forms of exploitation have led to the struggles of the common people. The latter, in turn, have provoked a response from the oppressor, whose aim is:

—to hide the historical import of these struggles by blaming them on small groups that are dissociated from the masses and that are motivated by ideological considerations;

—or to make people believe (and perhaps convince themselves) that it is just a bad moment, a nightmare, that will soon pass and give way to "the normal situation";

—or to repress them brutally by instilling fear and sowing death.

Many of our brothers and sisters have endured prison, torture, and death; and they still are. The price being paid for these liberation struggles is very high. I hope we will never accept it as a matter of course, even though it is an everyday occurrence. But it is also true that this brutal repression would not be taking place if the dominating party did not realize what the awareness and struggles of the people meant in terms of its privileges. We all know the oft quoted remark of Don Quixote: "They inflict wounds, Sancho, a sign that we are advancing." We can say, with realism if not without regret: "They repress—a sign that we are winning our freedom."

The fact is that the oppressors, perhaps for the first time in the history of Latin America, have begun to think that they could lose their age-old privileges on this continent. That is why the repression is so severe. And there is good reason for thinking thus. Cuba, Nicaragua, and other processes under way are there to prove that things are changing, that the moment has come, that a fresh burst of generosity and solidarity is out to eliminate old injustices and begin, however imperfectly, the construction of a different sort of society.

Secondly, we have before us *a new historical awareness*. These liberation efforts are accompanied by a greater awareness of our reality, of the real life of the poor people in particular. Analysis of reality is a precondition if we are to be able to change it. We are getting increasingly precise and detailed analyses of many things: e.g., the underlying causes and forms of the exploitation of the common classes; the scorn heaped on various races present on our continent (to say that there is no racial problem in Latin America is to lie); the marginalization of the ancient cultures surviving on our continent; the discrimination and undervaluation directed against women, particularly women of the common classes who are doubly oppressed as Puebla affirmed.

This new awareness accompanies and nourishes the liberation efforts in which the people express their strength and an awareness of their identity.

b. Their presence in the churches. This shift from absence to presence is also taking place in the churches. There, too, the poor people are increasingly getting across their right to live their faith and to think about it in their own terms. The outlines of a theology of liberation that we possess today are simply an expression of the poor and oppressed people's right to think. And that right to think is merely a manifestation of their very right to exist.

We are really seeing changes in the churches. The CCBs (*comunidades cristianas de base*—Christian communities of the common people), one of the richest experiments in the Latin American church, point up the irruption of the poor. But it is worth pointing out that those communities themselves, in the course of their development over the past twenty years, have been marked by the presence of the poor. Indeed they have been radically transformed by it, so that they have been opened to new possibilities.

There are many, many shortcomings insofar as the presence of the poor in the church is concerned. Moreover, the process is also provoking suspicion, distrust, and hostility, as we all know. Some ask whether a church born from below, from the faith response of the poor, will always be the church of Christ. When all is said and done, that is an odd question because the Scriptures tell us that Christ became a servant to announce the Father's love (Phil. 2:7). Here we clearly have a question of Christology that is important for any ecclesiological reflection.

Perhaps such reactions are due to something deeper, to something that cannot be readily detected at first glance. I have the impression—perhaps you do too—that in the church we have what might be called our house, our home, the place where we feel secure and comfortable in a world that is not the world of the poor. I am talking about mental categories, and also about affective and emotional activities. I am talking about a deep, subtle complicity with a milieu that is distinct from, and even opposed to, that of the poor. That is why the world of oppressed people who are conscious of their situation and fighting for their rights is alien and sometimes hostile to the church. One finds it difficult to relax there, to feel at home in it. The world of the poor is a place where we go to work rather than a place in which we live mentally, emotionally, affectively, and recreationally. Please excuse these images, but I hope they help to get across a hint of the saddening and exacting sense we all have.

What is demanded or exacted is this case in conversion. Taking cognizance of oneself means going through the mediation of another. Without that we do not see ourselves for what we are: persons in relationship with other persons. Around the time of Vatican II there was much talk about the church having to develop self-awareness. But clearly the church could not do that without subjecting itself to the mediation of the other and the world; otherwise it would fall into the very ecclesiocentrism from which Vatican II wished to detach it. But how can we develop ecclesial awareness in Latin America today, through the mediation of the world of the poor and the oppressed, without in some sense experiencing a "bad conscience," without feeling and knowing that today we are still strangers to the universe of the poor?

Who or What Are "the Poor"?

This is not the moment to go into a detailed discussion of this subject. It is a familiar one, and it was much debated in connection with the Puebla Conference. But there is one curious fact. If you get thirty people who are not poor together, they will debate interminably and never agree on the notion of "poor." Each has his or her own idea, the qualifications are endless, and the result is confusion. But if you bring together thirty poor people, it will only take them a minute or so to agree on who or what a rich person is. Here I simply want to make two basic points.

First, when we talk about the poor, we are talking about something *collective*. The isolated poor person does not exist. The poor belong to social groups, races, classes, cultures, sexes. That is precisely why the irruption of the poor is so tough and aggressive. If it were simply a matter of individual poor people, there would be no problem. But since it has to do with classes, races, cultures, and the condition of women, tension and conflict are entailed. Something very important is at stake in all this: the identity of the poor people. Awareness of the injustice amid which they live and efforts to free themselves from it are part of the very identity of the poor and oppressed. It is a necessary identity, one opposed to the alienation suffered by the despoiled and exploited. (Indeed alienation refers to the fact that they are not their own masters.) Individual, personal awareness of one's situation of poverty and oppression is not enough. One must perceive the solidarity of race, class, sex, and culture.

Second, to talk about the poor is also to point up the element of social *conflict*. The word "poor" is not a tranquillizing one. It reminds us, as the Puebla Conference did, that poverty, "inhuman poverty," as it is experienced in Latin America, has structural causes. The poor person is the product, or byproduct, of an economic and social system fashioned by a few for their own benefit. So a structural conflict is imbedded in the reality of the poor. What is more, perception of those causes leads to a fight against them. That is why talk about the poor means talk about poor people who are fighting for their liberation, radically calling society into question, and presenting a challenge to the meaning attached to the word "church."

Because the term "poor" signifies all this, the oppressor is crushing every witness to the fact that there is poverty in Latin America. That is why so many of our companions are being subjected to prison, exile, torture, and death. In meetings such as this one, we have shared experiences and reflections with many of them. These brothers and sisters, these martyrs, bear witness to the fact that the poor die before their time, victims of hunger and of bullets. That is why their very corpses are subversive, why so often on this continent the repressive authorities do not hand them over and lie about the exact circumstances of their death. Those exercising domination fail to realize that it was the experience and crisis of the "empty tomb" that enabled the friends of Jesus long ago, as it does his followers today, to comprehend the fullness of life of the risen one that conquers death completely.

I should like to conclude this first section with a few brief observations.

It seems to me that the important and irreversible happening of these recent years in Latin America is this irruption, or breaking-in, of the poor. Around this happening turns the sociopolitical life of our countries and also the life of the church and theological reflection. It should also leave its impress on our work at this Convention. It is at bottom an irreversible process, but that does not mean it will not experience the impasses, failures, and stagnation that are part of every historical process.

The Quechua people of my country considered the arrival of the Europeans in the sixteenth century to be a cataclysm. It broke the existing order and turned the world upside down. The Quechua Indians began to live as downtrodden, enslaved, oppressed people. They had a Quechua word for this great reversal. It was a *pachacuti*. They also felt that a new *pachacuti* would be needed to turn things right-side-up again. Well, we are beginning this new *pachacuti* in the efforts to fashion a society from below: from the exploited classes, the women suffering discrimination, the despised races, and the downtrodden cultures.

All this poses serious and challenging problems for the proclamation of the gospel message, of the Father's love for every human being and for the Church's essence and activity.

II. AN OPPRESSED AND BELIEVING PEOPLE AND CHRISTIAN COMMUNITIES OF THE COMMON PEOPLE

The poor and oppressed who are breaking into the history of Latin America and its church constitute a people who are simultaneously oppressed and believing. This twofold character of one and the same people is of major importance in trying to understand the import and function of the basic ecclesial communities. In this section I should like to deal with both matters.

An Oppressed and Believing People

As I indicated earlier, the word "poor" has a collective connotation and entails an element of social conflict. In the Bible the poor are part of a social group; they are the poor or lowly of the land. They are a people: poor, harassed, robbed of the fruit of their labor, and oppressed by injustice. It is to this complex and fecund notion of the poor that we are referring when we say that in Latin America ecclesial life and theological reflection find a concrete and richly consequential point of departure in the people who are simultaneously poor and Christian. That is the precise condition of the poor on our continent. Here we have two dimensions, but also two possibilities, of one and the same people.

a. A situation of exploitation. We know the situation well enough, but we must examine its present forms. It is a concrete situation that requires concrete analyses. Nothing excuses us from seeking serious, scientific knowledge of the character of the exploitation to which the common classes are being subjected. It is just as urgent for us to know how to differentiate sectors and levels among them, to know which are ahead and which are behind. Basically this has to do with their relationship to the production process; but their possibilities for mobilization and experiences in that area under certain circumstances are also relevant.

The exploitation suffered by the poor people and the presence of the prevailing ideology in their midst undoubtedly foster social climbing and a search for individual, egotistical solutions to their problems. This is the way out which the capitalist ideology seeks to inculcate. Capitalism takes delight in the stories of poor individuals who become millionaires through their own efforts. It happens. But such happenings are only obstacles on the path of a more important and decisive thrust that arises out of the same situation of exploitation: the quest for radical change, the potential for revolution. It is not enough, you see, to point out and denounce the despoilment and oppression of the lower classes. One must also realize that this situation is creating the objective conditions that will allow the people to initiate the fight for their rights and ultimately aim for the takeover of power by the common people— in a society that refuses to recognize them as human beings. In this struggle the people are gradually going to take cognizance of the fact that they are a social class, a race, a culture, an active subject of revolution and the construction of a different society.

The individualistic way out must be combatted, just as the capacity to make revolution must be developed and organized with a view to historical effectiveness. Hence organizations of the common people must set the task of developing their identity and revolutionary capability, and they must help the common people to achieve this.

b. The people as believers. The second dimension, intimately linked with the first, is the character of the people as believing Christians. I am speaking here in general, overall terms, without going into details. This trait is evident not only in their specifically religious forms of expression but also in their lives as a whole. It is what José Carlos Mariátegui, the student of Peruvian reality, called "the religious factor" in the life and history of the Peruvian people. What we know as popular religiosity is one expression of it, but not the only one. Often the religious factor has been, and still is unfortunately, an obstacle preventing the people from getting a clearer view of their oppressive situation. Much in it still mirrors the prevailing ideology. Often the religious element is used by the oppressor to justify the existing social order—for example, by encouraging resignation or the individualistic solution mentioned above. Hence we must avoid all forms of "religious populism," of romanticism, that do not take into account the aspect we have just brought up. But we are facing a complex fact, so our approach to it must be conscious of that complexity.

The dimension of religious belief in the people also implies, as their practice displays, the presence of an immense possibility for liberative faith. It has found different forms of expression in the course of history, accompanying and inspiring both firm resistance to oppression and open action against it. The oppression has been inflicted on our people, who have faith in the God of the Bible, and in a certain sense on that faith itself, which is oppressed and held captive in a dehumanizing, capitalist society. The liberative potential of the faith must also be developed. Otherwise the richly complex life of the Latin American people will be mutilated, and we will be depriving ourselves of the message that God is revealing to us through the understanding of God that poor and simple people possess. It is in the service of such development, and by the intrinsic dynamism of that faith itself, that we are seeing the rise of Christian communities of the people and a people's church, rooted in the poor sectors, under the impulse of the Spirit of truth and liberty.

This liberative faith disconcerts those exercising domination. They prefer not to believe in its existence or its ability to reveal God in our concrete history. Denying it, they reveal who they truly are: the fools of whom the Bible speaks, the atheists who reject the God of liberation.

c. One and the same people. It must be stressed that the above two dimensions and possibilities cannot be separated. The situation of oppression does not eliminate the people's character as believers. The possibilities of a liberative faith are bound up with their revolutionary capacity, and vice-versa. This is the reality in the concrete life of the poor, oppressed people. Hence one cannot try to develop one of these capabilities without taking the other into account. Herein lies the real meeting ground between organizations of the common people and Christian communities of the common people. This is what is disturbing about the growth of political awareness and Christian awareness in the people's movement of Latin America. The exploited, Christian people as the starting point: this is the unifying perspective that has marked the growth and work of many CCBs in Latin America. From this real ground it is possible to move beyond the dichotomy imposed by certain theologies, without succumbing to oversimplification. For some time that sort of dichotomy has been ignored by the people's practice and criticized by their reflection. But the oneness or unity of these dimensions in the selfsame people is a process. It is inevitable that the dimension of politics and the dimension of faith will be out of phase with each other at times. Sometimes one aspect will enjoy more growth than the other. The requirement of unity is a basic one, rooted in the biblical message and the people's situation; but it must be pondered, worked out, and systematized. This complex reality conditions our work, but it also points up a task.

To adopt this point of departure and its consequences means to forth-rightly reject any attempt to subject the task of evangelization to "reduc-tionism." Let us be very clear about that. It means rejecting a disembodied spiritualism posing as the religious sense, and it means rejecting a political-action approach that idealistically ignores the reality of our people's faith. Both types of reductionism, being one-sided and unreal, betray an ignorance of the situation and the capabilities of the common classes; we know what dangers they entail. We remain convinced—and the practice of the poor con-firms this—that the truly fruitful and imaginative challenge lies in a "con-templation in action," in action that will transform history. It has to do with encountering God in the poor, in solidarity with the struggle of the oppressed, in a faith filled with hope and joy that is lived within a liberation process whose agent is the poor people. Proclamation of the Father's love is some-thing to be done at every moment, "in season and out of season," as St. Paul put it (although, as we know, there are some who follow half of this counsel). And evangelizing means proclaiming the Lord with words of life and acts of solidarity from the world of the poor and their struggles.

So rejecting political "reductionism" does not at all mean disregarding the role of revolutionary political activity. Still less does it mean overlooking its character as gesture or action, within the framework of a unitary perspective, in the task of evangelization. The unity of the latter, indeed, is one which stresses the dialectical character of the word-action interrelationship, proper to any proclamation of the Word made flesh. The various forms of reduc-tionism ignore this dialectic; they also fail to perceive the relationship be-tween the will to achieve social transformation and a faith that liberates the concrete life of the people. Thus they mutilate a rich historical reality, mis-construing it idealistically and going against the current of a growing prac-tice. They fail to go to the root of the matter, where political and evangelical radicalism meet and reinforce each other.

Basic Christian Communities (Comunidades Cristianas de Base—CCBs)

The CCBs are one of the most fruitful and significant events in the present-day life of the Latin American church. Their growth throughout our conti-nent has helped to raise the hopes of the poor and oppressed. They are a privileged meeting place for a people trying to familiarize itself with its situa-tion of misery and exploitation, to fight against that situation, and to give an account of its faith in a liberating God. We also know that they were an issue debated at the Puebla Conference. After some misunderstandings had been cleared up, Puebla accepted and hailed base-level ecclesial communities as an event of primary importance in the life of the church.

I want to make clear at the very start that my observations derive from personal experience within the CCBs. I work with them in my country and I personally owe them a great deal.

a. From within a poor people. Here I would like to offer a few questions, open questions, which may contribute to the discussion.

First of all, what do we mean by "base" or "base-level" when we talk about base-level Christian ecclesial communities? It seems to me that we are referring to the oppressed and believing people of whom I was just speaking. The "base" of such communities is made up of those people and their ties of class, race, and culture. In other words, here the word "base" does not primarily refer to persons without authoritative functions in the church who come together, perhaps even in opposition to church authority. To view it thus would be to remain confined within a mistaken intraecclesiastical formulation of the issue: i.e., base and apex of the church pyramid. That does not accord with the experience of such Christian communities. To understand the word "base," we must realize that the first point of reference, strictly speaking, lies outside such intraecclesiastical boundaries. It is to be found in the world, where the church is present and where it must witness to the love of the Father.

"Base" means the poor, oppressed, believing people: marginalized races, exploited classes, despised cultures, and so forth. It is from them that these Christian communities are arising. From these poor, oppressed sectors the Spirit is bringing to birth a church rooted in the milieu of exploitation and the struggle for liberation. These Christian communities are not parallel organizations operating alongside those of the people's movement. Rather, they are communities and a church made up of persons involved in that movement who seek to live their faith and break bread together in such communities.

The "base," then, refers to persons from the common classes who have made, and are making, an option to join in solidarity with their brothers and sisters of the same class, culture, and race, and who proclaim their faith in the Lord. It also refers to all those, whatever their ecclesial responsibility might be, who make their own the life, the interests, and the aspirations of the poor and oppressed. They thereby answer the demands of the gospel message, which proclaims a God whose love goes out to the poor by way of preference. These points need to be further explored. Here I simply want to broach them without going into details.

There is a second matter. Sometimes when we talk about base-level Christian communities we say that they are a response to the massification that is taking place in our big cities. These communities are cut down to human size, we say, and in them people can meet and find identity as persons. Thus they favor personalization.

The first point above, dealing with the meaning of the "base," of the believing common peoples touched upon the scope of this function for such communities within the context of the lower classes, their lives and aspirations. There can be no doubt that the aspect of community and encounter to be found in such communities is of great richness and significance for a poor people whose identity aims at destroying the system that exploits it. Anyone who knows these communities from experience realizes and appreciates the importance for the poor of their encountering themselves on the basis of their human and Christian values.

But this issue must be explored more deeply, and so I think we must consider what we mean exactly by evangelization.

b. *Making disciples of all nations.* The proclamation of the gospel is intrinsic to the Christian faith. It is not optional; it defines us as followers of Jesus Christ.

Let us recall the formula of Matthew's Gospel (Chapter 28). Where today we would use the term "evangelize," it talks about "making disciples." People are to be disciples, followers of Jesus. Discipleship is a key category in Matthew's Gospel. It clearly corresponds to an ecclesial experience, the experience of a community of disciples.

Matthew's Gospel adds that it is necessary to make disciples of "all nations." The universality of Jesus' message is affirmed. This universality, this addressing oneself to all peoples, is another feature characteristic of Matthew's Gospel (see Chapter 25). However, this universality does not suppress the particularities of those various peoples—it is a question of nations, not just individuals. This last point need not be examined in detail here. My concern is rather to underline the fact that the gospel message is addressed to all peoples. Its proclamation is always *mass-directed;* it is a summons to all to be disciples.

It is not enough, however, to point up the public, universal, mass-directed character of evangelization. We must also keep in mind the fact that this proclamation has a thrust, a perspective, rooted in a specific historical locale. Matthew's Gospel also brings this out. Christians are to make disciples of all nations by teaching "all that I have commanded you." The "I" establishes the identification of the risen Christ who is now speaking to his disciples with the historical Jesus who proclaimed and lived out his message in the company of his disciples. Now then, we know that his message entailed an inescapable preference for the poor. The God revealed by Jesus is One who expresses preferential love for the humiliated, oppressed, and marginalized people of history. This God is revealed, therefore, to the simple people, and this manifestation leads Jesus to give thanks (Luke 10:21). Without that option one cannot clearly see the import of the universality attached to evangelization. It is not some facile, conciliatory universality. It is a summons to all that they evangelize in terms of God's proclaimed preference for the poor and the oppressed. This is the perspective, the thrust, embodied in Jesus' command to his disciples. His own messianic practice clearly witnessed to it and lead him to his death at the hands of the powerful. But by the same token these powerful ones will leave life and history empty-handed, as the Magnificat prophesied.

Making disciples of all nations is a task marked by this option for the poor, the downtrodden, and the oppressed. This is what has prompted people in some quarters to talk about a *mass-directed evangelization,* an evangelization aimed at all peoples *in terms of this perspective.* It entails the free and gratuitous love of God that is revealed in an option for the poor and a life of concrete, day-to-day commitment to their interests and struggles. Here I need not detail all that implies in historical, social, and political terms.

c. *A question for further discussion.* Let me go back briefly to the matter of the Basic Ecclesial Communities. Their relationship to evangelization, in terms of the perspective just described, is central for any understanding of what they mean. Are we moving toward a model that envisions something like a church that is totally and completely made up of small communities? Perhaps I might call it a chess board, if you will pardon the extreme comparison. The point I want to make here is that the experience of many base-level Christian communities in Latin America is making us realize that they are the active agents of the evangelization of a whole people in the very midst of their struggles for liberation. These Christian communities, which represent an enormous contribution to the identity and organization of the poor people, would thus be *evangelizing cadres.* They would be made up of persons who assume a function within the evangelization process. By evangelization we certainly mean the proclamation of the word. But we also mean the gesture of solidarity that gives authenticity to that proclamation, the commitment to the poor and oppressed of this world in their lives and their struggles.

Only these base-level Christian communities, rising up out of the oppressed but believing people, will be in a position to proclaim and live the values of the Kingdom in the very midst of the common masses who are fighting for their liberation. The practice of these communities continually leads them beyond themselves. The CCBs are a means, a tool if you will, for the evangelization of all nations from the standpoint of the poor and exploited. That is why they are transforming our way of understanding Christian discipleship. These communities do not tend to take shape as extensions of the church's pastoral agents, assuming tasks that the latter cannot or should not carry out. Nor are they merely the first stage in a process. The matter goes much deeper; it is more complex and novel. They arise in the very process of living out what Christ means for the common masses, of showing how the gratuitous gift of the Kingdom is accepted in their efforts to free themselves from exploitation, defend their rights as poor people, and fashion a human society that is free and just.

The necessary consequence of all this is that the CCBs are places for reflection within a church born of the faith of the people; where we assume the task of reviewing and revising our life of faith in commitment; where we celebrate our hope and share our bread, the bread which so many of our fellow human beings lack and in which the life of the risen Jesus is made present and acknowledged. The CCBs are privileged places where the poor people read the Bible and make its message their own in their own terms. They are moments of fraternal encounter when we recognize God as our Father. Thus the community aspect is linked up with the task of evangelization, with Jesus' summons to his disciples to form a gathering of disciples, an *ecclesia,* grounded the poor, on those whom James Cone called the "victims of history." The CCBs are evangelizing cadres that necessarily come together as communities for a task that continually thrusts them beyond themselves, placing them there where we meet Christ in our needy fellow humans, the poor. It is there that eschatology is applied to human history (cf. John Paul II, *Redemptor Hominis,* no. 16).

Here again we come to a point which we must discuss further: the rich experience of the Christian communities of the common people. The maturity already achieved by them poses serious challenges, but there is still a long way for them to go.

III. SOME ECCLESIOLOGICAL INDICATORS

All I shall offer are a few indicators based on the points already presented. Our preoccupation with some sort of theological reflection on the church grows out of the very dynamics of our social and ecclesial practice. It is something demanded by the growth of this perspective in Latin America and in the church. A debate on ecclesiology has even been opened up by efforts to show that to be born of the people is the vocation of the *whole* church, not some parasitic or fruitless alternative to it. Such efforts could not help but provoke questions, fears, false interpretations and even hostility. Many things are at stake. But let us not forget that reflection on the church, ecclesiology, always arose amid situations of questioning and crisis (in the sixteenth and nineteenth centuries, for example). This should stimulate our reflection, prompting us to formulate a theology, not of what the church ought to be but of what the church is in the concrete.

Right now I simply want to deal with several points that are brought up in discussions arising out of commitment to the common people. They derive from the irruption of the poor and oppressed which I mentioned earlier.

A Church Springing from the Uninvited

The church, the community of disciples who adopt the messianic practice of Jesus, should constantly arise from those that one gospel parable describes as the "uninvited." Remember the gospel text. Those invited to the banquet refuse to attend. The master then orders his servants to go out into the streets and the byways to invite the lame and the blind, "both bad and good" (Matt. 22:10). (Note: not just the good, or good and bad, as we might tend to put it.) These downtrodden, marginalized people are the *uninvited,* who are called to the Kingdom. They are called because they are poor, not necessarily because they are good. In that summons is revealed the God of the Bible, the King in all the parables about the Kingdom. He takes the initiative on the basis of his gratuitous love, which is not conditioned by prior merits.

The church directed toward that Kingdom should always arise out of the uninvited: the sectors of the common people, the oppressed and believing people. As our practice now enables us to see more clearly, being born out of the faith of the poor and oppressed is a profound, decisive evangelical demand from the standpoint of the Kingdom of God.

The Poor as Evangelizers

After Vatican II and the stimulus of the Medellín Conference, we creatively reappropriated the gospel expression about evangelizing or "preaching the good news to the poor." Reinforced by an option for the oppressed and a commitment of solidarity with them, a series of rich and promising initiatives took place all over Latin America.

Then came the irruption of the poor. At a terrible price the common people began to become the active protagonists of history. This fact gave us deeper insight into the whole matter of evangelization. Working in the midst of the poor, exploited people, whom we were supposedly going to evangelize, we came to realize that we were being evangelized by them. Here the CCBs played a major role. The Puebla Conference commented on this when it noted that the church discovered the "evangelizing potential of the poor" through its involvement with the poor and such communities.

This fact is coming to dominate our work and our view of the church more and more. Experience has shown us that it is the poor who are doing the work of evangelization. We are coming to realize in a new way that God is revealed in history and that God is revealed through the poor. It is to them that God's love is revealed. It is they who accept, understand, and proclaim God's message. Remember the text cited by Sergio Torres about the revelation that is hidden to the wise and prudent but open to the simple. Viewed in this light, the task of evangelization consists in involving oneself in the process of proclamation carried out by the poor. The latter are not just the privileged addressees of the gospel message. They are also its bearers by the very fact of who they are.

By the same token we know that the poor, the classes of the common people, are the force that transforms history, the active subject of liberation praxis. This statement does not stand in mere juxtaposition to the previous one. The relationship between the two is profound, imbedded in a history which the poor simultaneously subvert and evangelize. To say this is not to succumb to illusory triumphalism or false reliance on some automatic historical mechanicism; it is to call attention to demands and tasks that await us.

Evangelization, the proclamation of the good news of the Father's love, takes place in the very process of liberation where brotherly love finds expression. Practice has led us one step further, so that we now say that the poor evangelize by liberating themselves. This deep, reciprocal relationship between evangelization and liberation occurs first and foremost on the concrete level, in the real lives of the poor, exploited, Christian people.

Kingdom and Church

The question is a traditional one. Our current practice has led us to re-examine the matter in biblical perspective. Here I want to stress only one point.

Let us consider Matthew's Gospel. Its first four chapters deal with the birth of Jesus and the preparation for his mission. Its last three chapters deal with his death resulting from that mission and with the resurrection; through the resurrection the Father confirms the meaning of Jesus' task. The twenty-one chapters between these two sections give us the preaching of Jesus. They begin with the blessing of the poor (Matt. 5); they end with the assertion that we meet Christ himself when we go out to the poor with concrete acts (Matt.25). So the teaching of Jesus is framed in a context that moves *from the poor to the poor*. This shows us that only in such a perspective can we compre-hend the meaning of the Kingdom promised to the poor. The poor and the Kingdom are linked realities. It is in their relationship that the Father's gratui-tous love is revealed.

The life of a disciple is worked out in the dialectics of *grace* and *demand*. The latter presents itself in time, in history, to the disciple—which is to say, to the community of Jesus' followers, the church. His disciples are required to be loyal to his own practice. All this is bound up with, and is a consequence of, grace: the gift of the Kingdom. This basic gratuitousness is the start of everything. It is within this dialectics of grace and demand, which constitutes the life of a disciple, that the relationship between church and Kingdom finds a place.

The issue is broad. I shall restrict myself to a point that is traditional in the best sense and that we find throughout the Gospels: the Kingdom *judges* the church, the community of disciples who announce the Kingdom in history. This point is stressed by Matthew in various passages. The criterion of judg-ment is also indicated: "You will know them by their fruits" (Matt. 7:20). The absence of these fruits invalidates the exercise of any and every charism (see 1 Cor. 13). And these fruits are technically described in the Bible as "works of mercy" or "good works." They are concrete acts on behalf of the poor: e.g., offering food and drink. The characteristic thing about Matthew's Gospel, which gives definitive force to this criterion, is the assertion that in these works on behalf of the poor we encounter Christ. That ultimately is what grace is.

It is important for us to recapture this idea in the present-day life of the Latin American church. We must deepen our way of living out the dialectics of grace and demand. In the Christian communities of the common people we find a fruitful living out of the values of the Kingdom. It entails the mass-directed task of evangelization and the gathering together of people as "church." To be sure, we find a wide variety of situations in Latin America. We also find novel situations, such as those of Nicaragua and Cuba. Granting that, we might ask ourselves what fruits should be displayed by the church of Christ.

In any case I would sum up what I have been saying in this brief diagram:

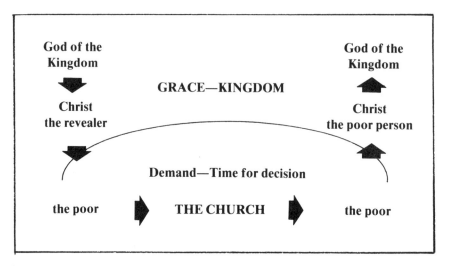

The God of the Kingdom

The fourth and last ecclesiological point is perhaps the most important one. It has to do with our way of understanding God.

In recent times some have reminded us that the God proclaimed by Jesus Christ is the God of the Kingdom, not a God dissociated from the Kingdom. The Kingdom itself is understood as the global sense and meaning of history, both in the present and at its ultimate end. It is a Kingdom of justice and life. It reveals God to us as the *Go'el*, to use the biblical term: i.e., the defender and vindicator of the poor and oppressed. To dissociate God from the Kingdom is to turn God into an idol, to fall into idolatry. And, let's face it, such idolatry is a reality in many sectors of Latin America that consider themselves to be Christian.

Our way of understanding God is related to our way of understanding ourselves. To put it in somewhat oversimplified terms, we might say that classical theology long stressed an omnipotent and omniscient God standing over against a finite, limited human being. I need not stress the point since it is familiar to us all. More recently, and particularly in North Atlantic countries, people have taken cognizance of what is called the adulthood or maturity of the human being. This led them to the theme of the weakness and suffering of God (Bonhoeffer, Moltmann). It has enabled us to recapture important points from a christological perspective.

The perspective of the poor and oppressed struggling for their liberation is different. Living out one's faith amid those struggles enables one to see things from a different perspective. It is evident in such expressions as the "black God," used forcefully by black liberation theology, or the "God of the poor and oppressed," or "God the liberator, or "the God of life."

They are not mere expressions, however. These are deeply lived experiences, which are celebrated with paschal joy. They pass through death to rise and affirm life. In Nicaragua, for example, one of the most impressive things is the joy of a people who are fighting unto death to be masters of their country and to construct a just society. This joy is also evident in their celebration of the faith. It is the subversive joy of the poor, who know that they will rejoice tomorrow even though they may be weeping today (see Luke's Gospel). Their joy subverts a world of oppression. It upsets those exercising domination, denounces the fear of the hesitant, and reveals the love of the God of hope.

Here we confront something decisive. For when we talk about God, we are touching the basis of our faith and our theology. In the last analysis all theology is reflection about God. I simply want to make the point that this issue, brought back so forcefully today in and through the process of liberation, has enormous consequences for ecclesiology (see, for example, *La lucha de los dioses,* published by DEI in San José, Costa Rica, and the Centro Valdivieso in Managua; to be published by Orbis Books in English translations as *The Battle of the Gods*). The very notion of the people of God must be considered in terms of the God of the oppressed, believing people. José María Arguedas was right when he said that "the God of the masters is not the same God." He is not the God of the poor.

I would like to conclude by noting that many people now feel they are facing an either/or situation. Either the church will sink its roots into the poor people, into their faith and their hope, or else it will cease to bear witness to the death and resurrection of Christ in history. Today history is structured in a way that assassinates the poor on the one hand. But it is also the locale where the poor are carrying out their liberation practice, expressing their historical force, and taking hope in the God who liberates and gives life.

11

Theological Characteristics
of a Grassroots Church

Leonardo Boff, O.F.M. (Brazil)

In this effort at reinterpretation I am going to try to identify the main characteristics of a church that fleshes itself out at the basic, or grassroots, level. My aim is to show the new face of the church, which in turn points up the new features of Christ's own face insofar as the church seeks to be the sacrament of Christ.

Concern about the characteristics of the church goes way back. In ecclesiology those characteristics are referred to as "notes" or "marks" or "properties." We find such concern as far back as St. Epiphanius (315–403) and St. Cyril of Jerusalem (313–86). They had an impact on the elaboration of the Creed that was promulgated by the First Council of Constantinople (381),[1] and which is still recited today by the church. That Creed enumerated four basic notes (or characteristics) of the church: "I believe in one, holy, catholic, and apostolic church." Using these characteristics, the council fathers sought to offer criteria for discerning the true church of Christ.

WHAT "CHARACTERISTICS OF THE CHURCH" MEANS

The desire to set up criteria for the true church arose within a context of polemics and real confessional competition. In which group was the true church of Christ to be found? How were people to distinguish the true church from a false church? The question became critical from the fifteenth century on, when people had to debate the ecclesiology of such figures as Jan Hus and Martin Luther.

Operating in academic terms, theologians usually made a distinction between notes and properties of the church.[2] "Notes," as the word itself suggests, made something noticeable or perceptible. Thus the notes of the church

This article first appeared in SEDOC, January–February 1979, vol. 11, no. 118, pp. 824–42 were those qualities that *(a)* were accessible to all minds and spirits, including the most uneducated; *(b)* should therefore be more familiar than the church itself and help to make known the true church; and *(c)* should be inseparable from the true church so that they, taken all together, could not be found outside the true church.

The "properties" would be those qualities that indubitably belonged to the church, but that did not enable people to know the true church at first glance. Neither did they reveal the true church to people outside that church. Such would be the qualities of indefectibility, of the necessity of the church for salvation, and so forth.

The "notes" of the church were the four features mentioned above: oneness, holiness, catholicity, and apostolicity. Later, especially after the disputes with the heretical Waldensians in the thirteenth century (under Pope Innocent III: DS, 792), and most forcefully among the ecclesiologists of the late nineteenth century (Pasaglia, Mazzela, Perrone), a fifth note surfaced to prominence: Romanness. The church is one, holy, catholic, apostolic, and Roman.

The demonstrative force and result of this approach by way of "notes" *(per viam notarum)* was almost nil, since it was difficult to prove that they were to be found exclusively in the Roman Catholic church.[3] In the end the whole argument concentrated around the most obvious note: Romanness. But neither did this note, by itself, manage to guarantee the true church, since one got the impression that one was dealing with another church.

In taking up this matter of the characteristics of the church, I am not seeking to engage in any polemics. I am not proposing to prove that the base-level communities make up the true church of Christ because I start from the assumption that they are truly the church of Christ and his apostles fleshed out at the grassroots level. I do not propose to make a distinction between "notes" and "properties," such a distinction being merely academic and unfruitful in any case.

Here I shall simply write about characteristics of the church. By that term I mean certain qualities that reveal the features of the church as it arises from the people, through the work of God's Spirit, and that also give it concrete historical embodiment in the midst of social reality. Thus I am following in the tradition of the early medieval people who attempted to elaborate the treatise on the church, who wrote about the *conditiones ecclesiae* (i.e., the concrete conditions of the church). What relevant traits are to be perceived by those who look with sympathy and the eyes of faith at this ecclesial happening (ecclesiogenesis)? How do the characteristics of grassroots ecclesial communities convey to us the characteristics of Jesus Christ and his message? In the last analysis, that is the function of the church. It is meant to make visible and historical the salvific import of Jesus Christ and his mission. And in so doing, the church is to serve as a sacrament-sign and sacrament-instrument of liberation.

Before we get to that question, we must position the church within the world as the world happens to be organized socially. This matter has become basic since *Gaudium et spes* stressed a fact that we must take cognizance of: namely, that the church is in the world, not the world in the church. This fact is overlooked in almost all books on ecclesiology, even such recent ones as those of Hans Küng on the church.⁴ This omission prevents us from understanding the church in concrete terms. It opens the door to a brand of idealism that obscures the complex reality of the church. The problem we must broach, however briefly, is this: How are we to comprehend the church within a society based on classes? The characteristics of the church will depend on the way we pose this problem. In the case of a church born from the common people, the question is inescapable. To fail to ask it is to make it impossible to understand what base-level, or grassroots, ecclesial communities are all about.

THE CHARACTERISTICS OF A CHURCH
LINKED TO THE DOMINANT CLASS

We must broach the whole issue correctly.⁵ In the church we detect two dimensions. Each dimension has its own specific nature, but the two are mutually related. First, there is the church as an ecclesiastical-religious area: i.e., the church as an institution. Second, we have the church as an ecclesial-sacramental area: i.e., the church as a sacrament, sign, and instrument of salvation. When I talk about the church as an ecclesiastical-religious area, I am referring to the whole complex of ecclesiastical institutions, and also to the sum total of religious actors who interact with each other and with the various institutions.⁶ Since these are dimensions of one and the same church, they must be articulated properly to avoid any and all parallelism in either real life or linguistic usage.

Our basic affirmation, then, is that the ecclesiastical area or dimension is the support of the ecclesial-sacramental area. The institution is the vehicle for the sacrament. The social visibility of the church makes palpable the grace and kingdom of God.

Since our concern here is to identify the characteristics of the church, the ecclesiastical-religious dimension comes in for consideration. To what extent do the visible characteristics of the church reveal the invisible characteristics of evangelical salvation and the person of Jesus Christ? We see already that the two dimensions are linked. Now let us consider a brief analysis of the ecclesiastical-religious dimension.

The ecclesiastical-religious dimension is not a given, readymade structure of practices, actors, institutions, and discourses having to do with God, Christ, and the church as sacrament. It is the result of a production process, the product of a structuring effort in which two productive forces are at work. One productive force is society with its specific mode of production. The second productive force is the Christian experience with its content of divine revelation. In other words, the church is not born readymade in heaven. It, too, is the fruit of a specific history. At the same time it is the product of faith, a faith that in its own way assimilates the events of history. Let us, then, take a quick look at these two productive forces.

The Ecclesiastical-Religious Dimension and Society's Mode of Production

The church does not operate in some empty space. It operates in a society that is historically situated. This means that the church, willy-nilly, finds itself limited and oriented by the social context. That context contains a certain population and certain limited resources that are structured in a certain way. The ecclesiastical-religious dimension is a portion of the social sphere. The latter sphere exerts an influence on the former, but in a dialectical rather than a mechanical way.

Let us start off with an assumption that we will take for granted, without being able to justify it here because it would require a separate treatment of its own. The assumption is that the organizing axis of a society is its specific mode of production. By the latter term I mean the way in which a certain population is organized vis-à-vis available material resources in order to work up the goods needed for its subsistence and reproduction on both the biological and cultural levels. This activity is infrastructural; all the rest of the society is built on it. It is *constant* because it has to do with ever-present needs. It is *universal* because it is common to all societies and all ages. It is *fundamental* because it is the precondition that, in the last instance, makes possible every other initiative.

The church, too, is conditioned, limited, and oriented by the specific mode of production. In other words, the mode of production conditions which ecclesiastical-religious actions are impossible, undesirable, tolerable, acceptable, suitable, primordial, and so forth. Thus the mode of production confers specific characteristics on the church.[7] This is not to say that ecclesiastical-religious activities are merely social products under the religious rubric. Those activities possess their own specific nature. But insofar as they are expressed socially, they are suffused, limited, and oriented by the specific mode of production to be found in a given kind of society.

There are various modes of production. Some are more symmetrical, others are more asymmetrical. In the West and in Latin America we have a society organized by a *dissymmetrical mode of production*. It is the capitalist mode of production, and it has the following characteristics: private appropriation of the means of production by a permanent minority; unequal distribution of labor capacity (some people exercise no productive function); and unequal distribution of the finished products of labor. This dissymmetrical mode of production gives rise to a society of classes. Power is dissymmetrically distributed, relations of domination exist between the classes, and the classes have differing interests. There is a noticeable inequality in food, clothing, housing, sanitary conditions, employment, leisure, and so forth.

Obviously this class-based structure limits and orients any and all activities, quite apart from the wishes of the persons involved. That applies to ecclesiastical-religious activity as well.

Objectively speaking, the faithful occupy different social positions in accordance with their class situation, and they perceive reality in a way that corresponds with their class situation. They are led to interpret and live the gospel message in accordance with their class function because every class has its own needs, interests, habits, behavior patterns, and so forth. The activities that are possible or impossible, tolerable or commendable, necessary or urgent, vary from one class to the next.

But we should not imagine that class actions are mechanical or static. A given class finds itself continually in a process of construction or deconstruction, in accordance with its position in the social division of labor, the concrete set of circumstances, and the specific strategy required. Class dynamics is asymmetrical, just as the mode of production is. In other words, class dynamics is conflict-ridden and unequal. Unequal forces are involved in conflict and struggle. The dynamics is independent of the will of the participants; it is intrinsic to the objective position that each actor occupies in the whole class structure.

In a society composed of classes, there is always a ruling class, or a ruling bloc of classes, which is responsible for the running of the whole society. It is constantly at work to consolidate, deepen, and amplify its power. It seeks to persuade the ruled classes to accept its domination and to win an ideological consensus from them.[8] In this way the ruling class achieves hegemony: i.e., general assent to its hegemony. Thus is created what A. Gramsci called a historical bloc.[9] But such domination is never complete. Since it is fashioned in the course of a more or less lengthy process, the dominated classes continue to put up resistance, to work out a strategy of survival, and to make efforts to regain the power that has been stolen from them. There is a permanent, ongoing conflict, which is open or latent depending on historical circumstances, between the rulers and the ruled. This resistance imposes specific limitations and orientations on the classes exercising hegemony, because the subordinate classes can turn into revolutionary classes.

In their hegemonic strategy the ruling classes will try to enlist the church in the service of amplifying, consolidating, and legitimating their rule. In particular, they will try to use the church to win acceptance of their hegemony from all individuals and social groups. The ecclesiastical-religious realm is strongly pressured to organize itself in such a way that it will conform to the interests of the hegemonic classes. The strategy entails various types of measures: economic, juridical, political, cultural, and even repressive. In such a case the church serves the function of preserving and legitimating the ruling historical bloc.

But the church is not fatally doomed to conform to the hegemonic historical bloc. The subordinated classes, in turn, appeal to the church in their strategy to win more power and autonomy in the face of the domination from which they are suffering. The church can support and justify the breakup of the historical bloc, lending itself to a revolutionary service. The faithful are present in both camps. The church is inevitably riddled with class conflicts. It can assume a revolutionary function or the function of reinforcing the hegemonic bloc.

These two possibilities are not the object of sudden acts of will, nor are they options that can be taken *ad libitum*. It all depends on the kind of linkage that the ecclesiastical-religious realm has established with the various classes in the ongoing sociohistorical process. In that process the church may have slowly reproduced the structure of the hegemonic bloc in its own body. Thus the ecclesiastical-religious dimension, too, has been structured dissymmetrically; it is a reflection of the hegemonic social sphere. Obviously I am not talking about a mechanical reproduction here. There always remains the *relative autonomy* of the ecclesiastical-religious dimension. By that I mean that the latter dimension is neither totally determined by the social sphere nor totally independent. It has its own irreducible specificity: the Christian experience; its objective expression in discourses and practices; its institutional character through which it is reproduced, preserved, and spread—particularly through a corps of experts and hierarchical officials. On the basis of this irreducible specificity, the ecclesiastical-religious dimension *immediately* assimilates and works over various social influences.

Now let us briefly consider how the church linked up with the hegemonic bloc at one point and with the subordinate classes at another point. A dissymmetrical mode of production gradually took charge of the social setup, imposing a process entailing the expropriation of the means of material and symbolic production. This same mode of production ended up being predominant in the church as well. In a long historical process, which can be described in detail,[10] a dissymmetrical mode of religious production was created. This also involved—and here I am speaking in analytic terms rather than in moral terms—a process whereby the means of religious production were expropriated by the clergy over against the Christian people. In the beginnings of the church, the Christian people participated in the power of the church, in decision-making, and in the election of its ministers. Then they were consulted less and less. Finally, insofar as power and authority were concerned, the Christian people were totally marginalized and a capacity that had been theirs was expropriated. Just as there was a social division of labor, so an ecclesiastical division of religious labor was introduced. A corps of functionaries and experts was created. They were to take care of the religious interest of all through their exclusive production of the symbolic goods that were to be consumed by the now expropriated people.

Here I do not wish to discuss internal conflicts having to do with religious authority and power: hierarchy versus laity, higher clergy versus lower clergy, and so forth. Nor do I wish to discuss the various forms of ideological consensus created over the centuries, to the point where today—again I am speaking in analytical rather than theological terms—the corps of ecclesiastical officials holds a monopoly on the legitimate exercise of religious power.[11] But it is obvious that a church so dissymmetrically structured dovetails nicely with a social sphere that has the same dissymmetrical mode of production. The church readily tended to look like the legitimating religious ideology of the existing order. This was the type of link that existed between the church, civil society, and the state in Latin America until the time of the Medellín Conference (1968), giving rise to the system known as Christendom.[12]

I shall leave for later my description as to how the church linked up with the subordinate classes. For in talking about that subject, I will already be talking about grassroots ecclesial communities.

The Christian Experience with its Content of Revelation

The other productive force in the ecclesiastical-religious sphere is the Christian experience and its content of revelation. I am not going to go into this matter because it is amply familiar. But I do want to stress the irreducibility of the experience of Christian faith, which is attested and preserved in its foundational texts—i.e., the Christian Scriptures read and reread throughout the course of history (Tradition). There we find the history of a living person in whom the apostles detected the ultimate meaning of humanity and the world (salvation). The sustaining pillars of the Christian faith and the source and inspiration of the church are the deeds of the crucified and risen Jesus and his message. That message is one of love, hope, fraternity, service to human beings, and confident surrender to the Father. These content-materials form the positive core of the faith. They are not an *interpretandum* (i.e., something merely to be interpreted). Rather they remain the perduring criteria by which we are to pass judgment on the church, its practices, its discourses, and its mode of religious production.

Evidently, then, the ecclesiastical-religious sphere contains an undeniable contradiction within it. On the one hand it is fleshed out historically within the framework of a dissymmetrical mode of symbolic production, lending its support to capitalist society. On the other hand its basic complex of ideas summons us to a mode of production that would be symmetrical, participatory, and communal. Since the church lives this contradiction, it is always possible that the prophet and the spirit of liberty will break through within the church. Then the church will be led toward those groups that are seeking more just relationships in history and that are organizing in terms of revolutionary practice. That is what is happening right now with the church at the grassroots level of the common people.

Characteristics of the Church under the
Dissymmetrical Mode of Religious Production

In Latin America the church was present in the process whereby the hegemonic bloc sought to consolidate itself. The church tended to act as the agent of this bloc, insofar as it helped to preserve and legitimate it. In this arrangement the church forms a multiclass group in the ecclesiastical-religious sphere. Within it are reflected the conflicts that pervade the texture of society, but the church has its own ecclesiastical block exercising hegemony, with all power resting in the interrelationships between pope, bishops, and priests. This mode of ecclesiastical production is sharply dissymmetrical, and certain corresponding characteristics show up clearly. Let us take a look at the four basic (heuristic) notes of the church and see how they appear concretely under this system. I am referring to the notes of oneness (or unity), holiness, catholicity, and apostolicity.

Oneness appears as monolithic uniformity: one and the same doctrine; one and the same discourse; one and the same liturgy; one and the same ecclesiastical set of regulations (Canon Law); one and the same moral theology; and, if possible, one and the same language (Latin). This unification of the symbolic order reproduces the cohesion of the sociohistorical bloc, concealing and transfiguring social and intraecclesiastical conflicts. The oneness or unity of the church is defined as the communion of the people with the hierarchy. But the opposite is almost never stated: i.e., the communion of the hierarchy with the people. Church discourse is *unitary* and *ambiguous*. It is unitary, concealing the conflicts that of themselves would generate diversity of discourse. It is ambiguous, lending an ear to differing demands and thereby preserving the cohesive bloc. Partisan discourse would make possible the manifestation of conflict. This unitary, ambiguous discourse generally concentrates on nonconflictual topics; stresses harmony; explicitly denies the existence or importance of class divisions, or denies the legitimacy of the struggles of the dominated to see their expropriated liberty; and makes inflated appeals to the supernatural and moral observances. The unification of classes within one and the same church is merely symbolic; it functions sociopolitically in favor of the ruling classes.

In the dissymmetrical mode of religious production *holiness* is a characteristic of the church insofar as the faithful take part in, and faithfully carry out, the *ethos* of the historico-religious bloc under the hegemony of the hierarchy. The great virtues of the Catholic saint are obedience, ecclesiastical submissiveness, humility, and total reference to the church. That is to say, one is baptized or becomes a religious in order to serve the church. Hence almost all modern saints (in whom the hierarchical monopoly was fully embodied) are saints of the system: priests, bishops, and religious. Few of them are lay people, and those that are lay people were fully captured by the central hegemonic power (analytically speaking). The prophets and reformers, the people who criticize the existing power-relations in the church and call for mobilization, are subjected to all sorts of symbolic violence: e.g., canonical processes and excommunication. They never are seen as people typifying or *characterizing* church holiness.

In a dissymmetrically structured church, *apostolicity* is the property of only one class: i.e., the bishops, the successors of the apostles. It is not viewed as a characteristic of the whole church. Apostolic succession is more and more reduced to succession to apostolic authority and power. It is less and less associated with apostolic doctrine or teaching, as it had been in its original sense. One glosses over and obscures the fact that "the lay person, like the bishop, is a successor of the apostles" (Paul VI).[13]

Catholicity is strictly tied to unity (uniformity), and the quantitative aspect is stressed. The emphasis is on one and the same church present all over the world: *per totum orbem terrarum diffusa.* Catholicity is not to be defined in terms of its concrete elements: i.e., its incarnation in differing cultures and local churches. Instead it is to be defined in terms of its abstract elements: the same hierarchy, the same sacraments, and the same theology.

At this point one would be quite justified in offering a theological evaluation of this dissymmetrical structuring of the church. To what extent does it make visible and transmit the relevant experience of Jesus Christ and the apostles? To what extent does it serve as a vehicle for the ideals of love, participation, and communion that are evident in Jesus' own message and practice? For the sake of brevity I cannot go into that matter here. I simply want to stress its importance. I would also point out, however, that there is a widespread feeling and awareness throughout the ecclesial body that there is a contradiction between a dissymmetrically structured ecclesiastical-religious sphere on the one hand and the figure and message of Christ and the apostles on the other. Indeed to some the contradiction seems intolerable. Everything cries out for an internal restructuring of the church so that it may be more faithful to its origins and do a better job of carrying out its specific mission, which is theological in nature. And this would be achieved through the creation of mediations of power and authority that are more participatory, more symmetrical, and hence more just.

CHARACTERISTICS OF A CHURCH
LINKED TO THE SUBORDINATED CLASSES

The church is not condemned to perform a conservative function, as orthodox Marxism claims. By virtue of its central ideas and origins—the dangerous and subversive memory of Jesus of Nazareth, who was crucified under Pontius Pilate—it is revolutionary from the start. But that depends on certain social conditions and on its own internal situation. Given a certain degree of rupture in the historical bloc, the church can serve some function on the side of the subordinate classes, joining them in their struggles against domination. In particular, it can do this in conjunction with social groups that are guided by a religious vision of the world, as is the case with our Latin American people. These groups are seeking to create a *strategy of liberation*, starting off by elaborating an independent vision of the world—one that is an alternative to that of the classes exercising hegemony. This is an indispensable precondition if they are to create the objective conditions that will transform their downtrodden existence.

It is here that the ecclesiastical-religious sphere becomes relevant. If it helps to elaborate a religious vision of the world that conforms to the interests of the classes seeking liberty, that is opposed to the interests of the ruling classes, then it will be on the way toward performing a revolutionary function. The religious interest of the grassroots level is to make its own quest for liberation self-legitimating. It seeks to de-legitimate and de-naturalize the domination under which it is suffering. The ecclesiastical sphere can offer this legitimation, given certain concrete conditions both internally and externally. It may do so because it understands the righteousness of their struggle, or because it sees their struggle to be in conformity with the ideas and ideals of the gospel message.

Under the capitalist mode of production, religion is generally not the main reproductive instance of social relations. But due to the predominantly religious worldview of the common people in Latin America, the church there does perform a relevant function of either reproducing the existing order or protesting against it. Among predominantly religious groups of the oppressed classes, the elaboration of an independent Christian vision opposed to that of the hegemonic class signifies the start of their liberative process. That process will be historically successful, provided that it achieves a certain level of class awareness, organization, and mobilization. In theological terms, it recaptures the historical figure of Jesus of Nazareth, who gave priority to the poor and saw them as the primary addressees and beneficiaries of God's kingdom. It recaptures the original import of his life and death. His life is seen as a life committed to the cause of the downtrodden, in whom the cause of God met with frustration. His death is seen as something caused by a conflict that the ruling classes of the day were behind. The chief symbols of the faith are reinterpreted along these lines. This reveals the liberative dimensions that are objectively present in them, but that have been suppressed by religious structures based on domination and ties with the ruling social class.

Obviously this recapturing of the original import of Christianity entails a break with hegemonic religious traditions. Normally it is up to the *intellectual of the religious organism* to sew a new seam when the rupture takes place. On the one side, through their links with the oppressed classes these intellectuals help them to perceive, systematize, and express their great yearnings for liberation. On the other side, they take up these aspirations within a religious (theological) project, pointing up their coherence with the fundamental ideas of Jesus and the apostles. Thanks to this breaking of the ice, important segments of the ecclesiastical institution can ally themselves with the oppressed classes and make possible the emergence of a people's church with characteristics of the common people.

That is precisely what is happening, I feel, with the grassroots ecclesial communities. It is a real ecclesiogenesis that is taking place at the grassroots level of the church and of society. It is the genesis of a new church, but not one that is different from the church of the apostles and tradition. And it is taking place among the dominated classes, who had been stripped of both their religious power and their social power. In analytical terms, it is important to get a clear grasp of the novelty involved. These grassroots communities signify a break with the old monopoly of social and religious power, and the inauguration of a new social and religious process involving the restructuring of the church and society.[14] It entails a different social division of labor and a different religious division of ecclesiastical labor.

Let us consider some of the characteristics of a church rooted in this way in the oppressed classes at the grassroots level. As I see it, a church incarnate in the oppressed classes displays fifteen features. Robert Bellarmine, a famous ecclesiologist who dealt with the church incarnate in the hegemonic class, also presented fifteen notes of the church (in 1591). The coincidence may indeed by significant.

1. A Church as the People of God

By "people" here, I am not referring to a nation that takes in everyone indiscriminately and conceals the internal dissymmetries. By people I mean the oppressed class, the class that is defined by its exclusion from participation and its subjection to a process of massification (reification). "People" here constitutes both an analytical and an axiological category. Analytically, it describes one group over against another group. Axiologically, it proposes a value that is to be lived by all. In other words, everyone, not just the dominated class, is called upon to be the people. The dominated class turns the people into a reality insofar as it, through the mediation of communities,[15] ceases to be a mere mass, develops self-awareness, draws up a historical project of justice and participation for all (not just for itself), and undertakes practices that point toward the approximate realization of this utopia. The liberation strategy of the people seeks to get beyond the existing monopolistic structure of civil and sacred power; it aims toward a society with as much participation as possible.

Now this people becomes the people of God insofar as it forms communities of baptized people, communities of faith, hope, and love that are animated by Jesus Christ's message of absolute fraternity, and proposes historically to flesh out in the concrete a people made up of free, communal, participant human beings. This historical reality is not just the result of a symmetrical social process. Theologically speaking, it signifies an anticipation of, and a preparation for, the kingdom of God and God's eschatological people.

The grassroots ecclesial communities are this people on route. Their existence is a challenge posed to the hierarchy, which has monopolized sacred power and kept it all in its own hands. The hierarchy is called upon to see itself as a service rather than as an authority exercising power wholly on its own recognizance.[16] It is called upon to serve as a mediation for justice, community, and coordination among the people, to make sure that monopolistic and marginalizing structures are not created in their midst. It is clear that tension exists and persists in the church. We see a vast network of grassroots ecclesial communities on the one hand, a structure of parishes and dioceses on the other. We see a church of lay people on the one hand, and church managed and led exclusively by clerics on the other. We could have more balanced relationships, which would allow for greater participation by all in producing and enjoying religious goods.

2. A Church of the Poor and the Weak Reduced to the Subhuman Level

Most if not all of the members of grassroots ecclesial communities are poor and physically weak people because their labor is harshly expropriated. The communities have meager means, so they are inclined to combine their labor-power in various sorts of joint effort and mutual aid.

The fact of being poor and weak is not just a sociological datum. To the eye of faith it constitutes a theological happening. In terms of the gospel message, the poor person is an epiphany of the Lord. The existence of the poor person is a challenge posed to God, who has resolved to intervene to re-establish justice. Why? Because poverty expresses a breakdown of justice; because it does not just happen all by itself but rather is the product of an expropriative mode of production. It is the poor who are the natural bearers of the utopia of God's kingdom. It is they who bear the torch of hope, and the future belongs to them.

3. A Church of the Despoiled

By far most of the grassroots ecclesial communities are faced with various problems of despoilment. One need only read their reports to see that. They face the threat or the reality of their lands being taken away from them. They face problems with jobs, wages, housing, health, schooling, and labor unions. It is quite evident that our type of society was not made for them. It is a dependent, capitalist society of an elitist cast. Nothing in it functions to serve them: neither the laws, the courts, the police apparatus, nor the media of communication. They are really robbed and despoiled. Up to a short time ago they were the object of works of mercy by the church and society. They did not count in positive terms. They were simply raw material for political manipulation, numbers to swell the attendance at religious festivals.

Now they are getting together and forming communities. They are developing a critical-minded and transformation-oriented awareness with regard to both church and society. They are becoming active subjects of history. The ecclesial community is a point of departure for discovering the intrinsic dignity of the human person, whose rights are crushed by the ruling class when he or she is a poor person. These poor people are now discovering that they are subjects of rights and duties (citizens), images and likenesses of God, children of the Father, and temples of the Spirit. They are realizing that they are destined for full and complete personalization at the culmination of history, but that this culmination is to be anticipated right now by liberation practices.

As I see it, the grassroots ecclesial communities constitute the right form of the church for the victims of capitalist accumulation, as opposed to the traditional hierarchized church with its classic or more modernized associations. The lay apostolate would be an example of the classic mold; examples of the more modernized associations would be the Cursillo Movement, and the Charismatic Renewal Movement. Those older forms of ecclesial association fitted in better with a class society and the aims of the ruling classes.

4. A Church of Lay People

In its original Greek sense, the biblical term *laos* meant a member of the people of God. In that sense priests, bishops, and the pope are lay people too. But now, with the existing ecclesiastical division of labor, a lay person is anyone who does not have a share in sacred authority and power.

For some time lay persons have not been viewed as bearers or holders of ecclesiality, in the sense that they too could produce symbolic goods and be creators of ecclesial community. The lay person was one who benefited from that which the corps of sacred functionaries produced, and one who carried out their decisions. But in the base-level ecclesial communities, made up almost exclusively of lay people, it is obvious that they are real creators of ecclesial reality, communitarian witness, organization, and missionary responsibility. They are in possession of the word, they are creating symbols and rites, and they are re-inventing the church with grassroots materials.

5. A Church as a "Koinonia" of Power

The community itself, not just a few people in it, is viewed as the depository of sacred power. It is not anarchical, in the sense that it is trying to prescind from power, authority, and organization completely. But it is opposed to the monopolization of power by a corps of specialists who stand outside and above the community.

In the grassroots ecclesial community we see widespread diffusion of the roles of coordination, organization, and leadership. Power and authority is a function of the community, not of one person. Power in itself is not rejected. What is rejected is the monopolistic expropriation of power and authority for the benefit of an elite. Due to this basic stance, quite a few communities remain very suspicious of any terms that hint at authoritarianism or a concentration of power: e.g., leader, coordinator, guiding spirit, and director.

6. A Church Wholly Ministerial

Because the CEBs are more like communities than societies, they facilitate the circulation and distribution of power. The various services are not *a priori* givens, perpetuating a pre-existing structure. They are responses to needs that crop up. The whole community is ministerial, not just a few members in it. It has gone beyond the old hardening of lines that took place in the church's division of religious labor, where the hierarchy exercised management and gave orders whereas the laity simply obeyed and carried out orders.

Theologically speaking, we could say that in the first place the church is the representative of Christ, and that the ministers are representatives of the church. They are also representatives of Christ insofar as they are churches. So we should view power as something entrusted to the entire community. On that basis it is specified in different forms, as needs demand, right up to the supreme pontiff. So the various services are never outside and above the church. They are in the church to express the sacramental nature of the church and to serve the whole ecclesial community.

7. A Diaspora Church

In sociohistorical terms, the base-level ecclesial communities are the first thing that has really occurred in the church outside the old framework of the Christendom system and with roots in the common people. The Christendom system has been analyzed in much detail of late.[17] It represents a specific type of linkage between the church and civil society, effected through the state and the hegemonic sociocultural structures of a country. The church participates in the historical bloc and makes a deal with the ruling classes so that it can exercise its power and authority in civil society.

This whole effort reached the end of the line historically when changes took place within the historical bloc, a bloc subjected to multinational capitalism and its consequences of dependence and underdevelopment. Around 1960 there surfaced the historical preconditions for a church born of the common people and the dominated classes. We must realize clearly where the opposition evident today really lies. It is not between an official church and a people's church. It is between a people's church and the Christendom system (i.e., a church incarnate in the classes exercising hegemony). The people's church is linked up with the hierarchical church, but it is hostile to any New-Christendom project that would subordinate the church's pastoral activity to some sort of tieup with the classes exercising hegemony. Such a New-Christendom project was quite evident in the preliminary consultative document prepared for the 1979 Puebla Conference.

What we see realized by the grassroots ecclesial communities is a church within society (preferably in the oppressed classes) rather than society being within the church. They signify a Christian diaspora throughout the whole social fabric. Besides their theological or ecclesiological value, they possess eminent political value. For they are helping to reconstitute the cells of a civil society that is constantly being torn and pulverized by class divisions and anti-populist assaults from the hegemonic class. The grassroots ecclesial communities foster a spiritual mystique of mutual aid. They are concretely trying to implement a communitarian praxis of solidarity that anticipates and paves the way for a new form of social coexistence, one that is opposed to bourgeois society.

8. A Church of Liberation

Here I go back to what I said earlier about the link between the church and the oppressed lower classes. From the standpoint of the common people, the Christian community can represent the starting point for a politics in which commitment and practice seek to serve the common good and social justice. Christianity is the religion of the people, and all comprehension and organization flows from that fact. When Christianity links up with the expectations and demands of the oppressed, then it emerges as a force for liberty; and the ecclesial community becomes a community of liberation. In grassroots ecclesial communities the symbolic capital of the faith is practically the only source of motivation for political involvement and commitment. The life of Jesus leads to liberation from injustices.

But it should be noted that this is only a first step. After that comes analysis. Then the field of politics emerges as one with its own relative autonomy. Faith is not set aside. Instead it acquires its true dimensions as a spiritual mystique, a source of inspiration, and a signpost pointing toward liberation. That liberation transcends history, but it can be seen and anticipated in history through a process of liberation that generates less inequitable forms of social coexistence within society.

9. A Church that Sacramentalizes Concrete Liberations

The grassroots ecclesial community does not just celebrate the word of God, and the sacraments when that is feasible. In the light of faith it also celebrates its own life, the achievements and encounters of the whole group. It knows how to dramatize its own problems and its own solutions to them. It turns the liturgical sphere into a thing of the people, and it turns the people's reality into liturgy. It learns to discover God in its own life, struggles, and happenings.

In this way the grassroots ecclesial community recovers from the sacramental amnesia to which the whole church was subjected when the Council of Trent limited the whole sacramental structure to seven sacraments.[18]

10. A Church that Continues the Great Tradition

Jesus, the apostles, and the early Christian communities were people who came from the common people. They were poor people, members of the subjugated classes. The memory of those humble origins was never lost in the church. But with the construction of the Christendom regime, those humble origins were turned into myth. The liberative message of Jesus was taken hostage by the ruling groups and used to serve their own interests. The present-day CEBs feel that they are in close touch with the church of the Acts of the Apostles, with the church of martyrs, and with the various prophetic movements in the church that have repeatedly arisen. Those prophetic movements have consistently picked up the various dimensions of the gospel message: i.e., poverty, service, renunciation of pomp and domination, and committed involvement with the marginalized.

The church of the people, the church of the poor, has always existed, though its story was hardly ever told. The church is continued in the experience of today's grassroots ecclesial communities. They are not simply reproducing schemes of the past, however. They are creating fresh schemes to answer historical appeals. This grassroots church is not so much an institution with already established structures: i.e., sacraments, doctrines, hierarchical officials. Rather, it is a happening made up of people who come together for the sake of God's word. This is not to say that institutional structures are a matter of indifference or that they simply do not exist. But it means that they are not the pivotal axis of the grassroots ecclesial community as such. Its axis is the word of God read and interpreted in terms of its community problems, the performance of community tasks, mutual aid, and community celebrations.

11. A Church in Communion with the Great Church

We should not view the grassroots church as a church running parallel to that of the larger institution. As I indicated above, the antagonism does not lie between institution and community. It lies between a Christendom system (a church tied to the classes exercising hegemony in civil society) and a people's church. In Brazil, and in Latin America in general, one can see a noticeable convergence between the larger church, structured as a network of institutional services, and the church as a network of grassroots communities. From the larger church the latter gets the symbolic capital of the faith, its links with apostolic tradition, and the dimension of university. The larger church, in turn, benefits from the grassroots church. From the latter it gets concrete embodiment on the local and personal level, insertion among the common people, and links with the most urgent human causes revolving around justice, dignity, and participation.

The two are geared toward each other, in mutual consideration and acceptance. They are not two churches. They are one and the same church of the Fathers of the faith, made concrete at different levels of society and confronting specific problems. The grassroots level is not at all allergic to the presence of priests and bishops in its midst; indeed, it cries out for them. But it demands of them a new style in exercising their ministry of union and communion. It is to be simpler, more evangelical, more functional, and linked with the people's cause. Because of the grassroots communities, the whole church has presently adopted a firm option favoring the liberation of the oppressed,

the defense of human rights (of the poor in particular), and the overall transformation of society into more socialized forms.

12. A Church That Builds Unity on the Basis of a Mission of Liberation[19]

Theological tradition has seen church unity as something built on three
axes: the same faith *(vinculum symbolicum)*, the same sacraments *(vinculum
liturgicum)*, and the same hierarchical government *(vinculum sociale)*. The
Latin church stressed hierarchical government as the fundamental principle
of unity: *unus grex sub uno pastore—unum corpus sub uno capite* ("one
single people under one pastor—one body under one head"). There was an
extreme development of centralized authority (the theory of headship), to the
point where all forms of participation in decision-making were stripped away
from the Christian people. The Eastern Orthodox church placed the main
stress on the sacrament as the principle creating and expressing unity, and
particularly on the Eucharist (one Eucharist, one people). In our grassroots
ecclesial communities, unity is structured basically around the notion of mission. To be sure, they have the same faith, they administer and receive the
same sacraments, and they are in communion with the larger church and its
hierarchical structure. But this interior unity is created and nurtured by reference to something outside: i.e., the church's mission.

The conflict-ridden context of the grassroots people gives very concrete
configuration to the mission of the church. That mission is to ponder and live
the faith in a liberating way, to commit oneself to the oppressed, to fight for
their dignity, and to help build a societal life more in conformity with the
gospel standards. This option is becoming increasingly inevitable and obligatory among grassroots communities, be they rural or suburban. Usually divisions do not arise over the faith, sacraments, or hierarchical leadership. They
arise over the matter of involvement and commitment at the level of concrete
reality. The grassroots communities, it could be said, are fashioning unity on
the basis of one and the same option: *una optio, unus grex* ("one option, one
people").

13. A Church with a New Concrete Embodiment of Its Universality

Unity helps us to understand universality. The grassroots communities are
clearly marked in terms of social class. They are the poor and the exploited.
At the same time, however, they make explicit a universal vocation: justice
for all, rights for all, participation for all. The rights of all must come by way
of rights being regained by the poor and assured to them. The causes advocated by the grassroots communities are universal causes, and they become
universal to the extent that they assume the universality of those causes.

So these communities are not locked up in themselves and their own class
interests. All those who opt for justice and join in their struggles will find a
place in their midst, no matter what social class they may come from. Fight-

ing for economic, social, and political liberation, which opens one's eyes to the full liberation of God's kingdom, the grassroots church is in the service of a universal cause.

As a system of dissymmetrical societal life, capitalism stands as an obstacle to the universality of the church. For capitalism realizes only the interests of one class. A democratic, socialist society would offer better objective conditions for the fuller expression of the church's catholicity. In other words, under capitalism the catholicity of the church is in danger of remaining on the level of mere intention. The same set of symbols will be used, but their content will differ in accordance with one's class situation. Rich and poor receive Communion together in church, but they mutually excommunicate each other in the factory. If there was communion in the factory or workplace, then Eucharistic communion would not just be an expression of eschatological communion insofar as history is concerned; it would be real societal communion here and now.

14. A Church Wholly Apostolic

We are used to viewing apostolicity as a characteristic of the bishops, the successors of the apostles. This reduction of the notion to the topmost level of church leaders was a later development. Originally an apostle was simply "one sent out." That is how the term is used in the New Testament, even of Jesus himself (Heb. 3:1). Indeed it is highly probable that Jesus did not apply the term "apostle" to the Twelve who were his first followers.[20] The Twelve became apostles when they were sent out to the world to continue Jesus' mission of revelation and proclamation. But the term does not apply exclusively to the Twelve. Paul, too, is called an apostle. Everyone sent out—and every baptized person receives the task of proclaiming and bearing witness to the news of God in Jesus Christ—is an apostle who carries on the mission of the first Twelve. The Twelve remain the ones who deciphered the mystery of Jesus as the incarnate Son of God. We are bound to the faith of the apostles and their teaching, as it is preserved in the founding texts and in the living memory of their communities. By reason of their interpretive function, the apostles became coordinators of the communities. It is in this sense that we say that all those who exercise this service of coordination and unity are in the apostolic succession. Finally, tradition talks about the *apostolic life,* a life committed to the following of Jesus; in it one shares in the life of Jesus and his destiny.

The problem came when canonical and theological reflection began to view the twelve apostles in individual terms. It lost sight of the symbolic import of the Twelve as a designation for the messianic community (the new Israel), and of their collegiality. It is not that each one of the Twelve individually is sent out. It is the group, the college, the community of the Twelve, that first miniscule *ecclesia* around Jesus, that is sent out. So it is the community that is apostolic, not just a few bearers of sacred power and authority.

In that sense the grassroots ecclesial community recaptures the earliest sense of apostolicity insofar as it feels itself sent out as a community. It sees itself as the bearer of the orthodox doctrine of faith, as the trustee of the various services that the Spirit gives rise to within it. It lives an apostolic life by following Jesus. It shares his attitudes, his message, and the hope of the kingdom that lies buried in the hearts of the faithful.

Apostolic succession, then, is not reduced to hierarchical functions. There is not introduced, right from the start, a division between the haves and have-nots in the church. The division of services comes later, and it is based on a deeper, underlying fraternity and equality. All are the bearers of the correct teaching of the apostles, and all participate in the three basic services of Jesus Christ: bearing witness, sanctifying, and being responsible for the unity and proper functioning of the community. In our grassroots ecclesial communities we can note this equilibrium among the various elements; there is no fixed prejudice against a symmetrical division of different functions and responsibilities.

15. A Church Realizing a New Style of Holiness

The holy person or saint is not just the ascetic, not just the faithful observer of divine and ecclesiastical dispositions, not just the person who has explored and internalized the sacrosanct mystery of God and God's human appearance in Jesus Christ. All that retains its perennial value, which is irreplaceable. But the grassroots ecclesial communities are creating the conditions for another kind of holiness, that of the militant. Rather than concentrating on the fight against one's own passions, which remains a permanent struggle, one fights politically against the creation and use of exploitative mechanisms of accumulation; and one fights for the establishment of more well balanced, communitarian relationships. The new virtues find expression in class solidarity, participation in community decisions, mutual aid, criticism of abuses of power, endurance of slander and persecution for the sake of justice,[21] unjust imprisonment, loss of one's job, and aversion to private profit and accumulation that is devoid of social responsibility.

The grassroots communities find their points of reference in people who have suffered courageously because of their commitment to the community and the gospel message. Many communities are preserving and cherishing the names of their confessors and martyrs. They recall them in their celebrations, and celebrate their victories.

CONCLUSION: THE CREDIBILITY OF CHRISTIAN HOPE

All the above traits, and others could be added, characterize the new ecclesial experience that is taking place at the grassroots level of the church and society. Each trait could be debated, but taken together they point toward the same things: a new spirit, a greater fidelity to the liberating wellsprings of the gospel message, and also fidelity to the transcendent destiny of the earth with all its anxieties and yearnings. Faith does not alienate us from the world. It does not create a community set apart from the rest of humanity. It is a leaven of invincible hope and love, which stakes everything on the strength of the weak and on the infallibility of the cause of justice and community. Concern for heaven does not cause us to forget the earth. On the contrary, heaven depends on what we do on earth, what we do with the earth.

A church committed in this way to the cause of today's oppressed confers credibility on what faith proclaims and hope promises. It reveals a face of Christ that is still able to fascinate lively spirits dissatisfied with the existing order of this world. The grassroots communities are discovering that they can be Christian without being conservative; that they can be human beings of faith and, at the same time, deeply committed to the destiny of society; that they can hope against hope, and hope in eternity, while still keeping their feet on the ground and involving themselves in the struggle for a better tomorrow here within our present history.

NOTES

1. See Yves Congar, "Breve história da problemática das notas," *Mysterium Salutis* (Petrópolis: Vozes, 1976), IV/3, 6–9.

2. On this whole problem the basic work remains that of C. Thils, *Les notes de l'Église dans l'apologétique catholique depuis la Réforme* (Gembloux, 1937).

3. See F. Grivec, "De via empirica notarum Ecclesiae," *Antonianum,* 56 (1961): 395–400.

4. Kung's work is full of merit insofar as he uses historical and exegetical findings to rework the view of the church. But his work is very inadequate when it comes to the relationship between the church and the world. The church is studied in itself as if it subsisted in and by itself. He prescinds completely from an examination of the church in the sociopolitical and economic history of society with its specific mode of production. See, for example, *The Church,* Eng. trans. (New York: Sheed and Ward, 1967); *Structures of the Church,* Eng. trans. (South Bend: University of Notre Dame Press, 1968).

5. For this whole section I am indebted to the following authors. Clodovis Boff, "Igreja e política," *Comunidade eclesial—comunidade política* (Petrópolis: Vozes, 1978), pp. 64–84; P. Bourdieu, *A economia das trocas simbólicas* (São Paulo: Perspectiva, 1974); and, in particular, O. Maduro, "Campo religioso y conflictos sociales: Marco teórico para el análisis de sus interrelaciones en Latinoamérica," final thesis, Louvain, 1978.

6. See P. Bourdieu, section on "Gênese e estrutura do campo religioso," in *A economia das trocas simbólicas,* pp. 27–78; O. Maduro, "Campo religioso," pp. 47, 111, and passim.

7. See O. Maduro, "Campo religioso," pp. 51–54; A. Touraine, *Production de la société* (Paris, 1973), p. 145f.

8. On this point see the reflections of E. Hoornaert in SEDOC, Volume 11, January–February 1979; also in REB, 1978, 474–502, "Comunidades de base: dez anos de experiência," especially pp. 475–79.

9. See H. Portelli, *Gramsci y el bloque histórico* (Mexico City: Siglo Veintiuno, 1977), pp. 65–92.

10. See A. Faivre, "Naissance d'une hierarchie: les premières étapes du cursus clérical," *Theol. Hist.,* 40 (Paris: Beauchesne, 1977). His material is summed up by Hoornaert in the article cited in note 8. Also see the anthology edited by W. Weber, *Macht, Dienst, Herrschaft in Kirche und Gesellschaft* (Freiburg: Herder, 1973); and the anthology edited by J. Türk, *Autorität* (Mainz: Mathias Grünewald, 1973).

144 LEONARDO BOFF, O.F.M.

11. For this whole section see O. Maduro, "Campo religioso," pp. 104–22.

12. See the mimeographed study by P. Richard, "Mort des chrétientés et naissance de l'Église: Analyse historique et interprétation théologique de l'Église en Amérique Latine" (Paris: Lebret Center for Faith and Development, 1978), especially the first three parts.

13. See J. Guitton, *Diálogos con Paulo VI,* Spanish edition (Madrid: Ed. Cristiandad, 1967), p. 392.

14. I attempted to analyze this phenomenon and justify its theological and dogmatic possibility in my work entitled *Eclesiogênese: As comunidades eclesiais de base reinventam a Igreja* (Petrópolis: Vozes, 1977).

15. The work which does the best job of articulating this problem in terms of Catholic theology is *Pueblo de Dios y comunidad liberadora: Perspectivas eclesiológicas desde las comunidades religiosas que caminan con el pueblo,* Document 33 of the CLAR theology team, Bogotá, 1977.

16. J. Sobrino, "Resurreción de una Iglesia popular" (San Salvador, 1978), mimeographed.

17. See P. Richard, "Mort des chrétientés." This is the central thesis of his work.

18. See my study, *Minima Sacramentalia* (Petrópolis: Vozes, 1976). In it I tried to establish the theological foundation of grassroots sacramental teaching.

19. For more detail see my comments in the section, "Missão universal e libertação concreta," in *A fé na periferia do mundo* (Petrópolis: Vozes, 1978), pp. 76–94.

20. See J. Dupont, *Le nom d'Apôtres a-t-il été donne aux Douze par Jésus?* (Louvain, 1957); Y. Congar, "A Igreja é apostolica," in *Mysterium Salutis,* Portuguese edition, IV/3:157–59. Classic and monumental is the work of F. Klostermann, *Das christliche Apostolat* (Innsbruck: Tyrolla-Verlag, 1962); on this point see pp. 119–28.

21. St. Augustine saw in persecution for the sake of justice a mark of the true church: *Epistula* 93:8; 185:9.

12

Fundamental Questions in Ecclesiology

José Míguez Bonino (Argentina)

At the present time in Latin America, Christian communities of the common people—or base-level ecclesial communities, as they are wont to be called—are basically a Roman Catholic phenomenon. They are a pastoral experience of the Roman Catholic church. This does not mean we do not find an analogous experience in Latin American Protestantism. We do, particularly in some Pentecostal communities and in some indigenous communities (on the Bolivian altiplano, for example). But their historical process and their features differ. They are minority phenomena, and somewhat marginalized. They arise from a break-away experience, from a conversion that often is dramatic in character. For this reason they often represent a dialectical stance vis-à-vis populist sectors and movements to which the members belong in terms of class. In some sense they have broken off their *natural* relationship with such movements, and they must recover it by a conscious *option*.

Granting this difference, I do not propose to offer a theological treatment of that Protestant experience here; it would probably distract us from our chief focus. Instead, starting off from a Protestant ecclesiological vision (but not in any confessional sense), I would like to comment on some of the questions and topics that have surfaced during our reflections. Rather than offering a systematic presentation, I will simply offer some pertinent reflections.[1]

THE HORIZON OF ECCLESIOLOGY:
THE RELATIVIZATION OF THE CHURCH

As I understand the term "relativizing" here, it does not mean slighting the reality and mission of the church; nor does it mean that the church's reality and mission are peripheral or optional. It means looking at the church in terms of its "relation to" its reason for being and its finality. The opposite course would be to "absolutize" the church, to regard it as the ultimate point of reference, as the total, overall horizon. But the global horizon and the ultimate point of reference for the Christian faith is not the church but the Kingdom of God. The church is *relative* to that horizon; it must be seen in that perspective. In that sense the church is relativized.

That sort of relativization is obvious in the Bible. It is not a "church" but a "humanity" that God creates. It is in humanity that God's image is reflected. It is to humanity that God entrusts a mission. It is with humanity that God makes a covenant of commitment; and that covenant is renewed even after sin enters the picture (Gen. 9). The central focus of Jesus' mission is the proclamation of the Kingdom, whose coming is initiated in his words and deeds. The summons and mission of his disciples is framed in this perspective; and only in this perspective can we adequately frame the few references to the "church" that we find in the Gospels. Finally, the New Testament expands its vision to a total fulfillment that has to do with a new "humanity"—not a temple but a new city.

None of that detracts from the reality of a particular election, of the creation of a "special" people. Nor does it detract from the indestructible continuity that exists between the election of Israel and what happens in the New Testament. In the latter we have the re-construction of the "assembly," the "church," which Jesus Christ establishes and brings together, and in which he is present through his Spirit. The important thing to note is that this "particular" election is not absolute or "self-contained"; it is subordinate to the ultimate, overall objective—the Kingdom. In that sense we can say that the church is one of the precincts in which God carries out the proposal to re-create humanity and the human being, to consummate the Kingdom.

Note that I said the church is *one* of the precincts. It is not the only one because the Bible consistently bears witness to the universal operation of the Spirit in all of creation and to Jesus Christ's universal mediation in all of history; this universal operation and mediation is not confined within the church. And I use the term "precinct" [*ámbito*] rather than "means" because the church has its own proper dignity, a certain proper autonomy, and even its own eschatological import. The conflict-ridden process through which God asserts the sovereignty of divine love, justice, and peace in the world is carried out in the church in a way that is specific and peculiar to the church, even though it is related to the overall horizon.

Now, in connection with the topic that concerns us here (base-level ecclesial communities), this biblical-dogmatic reflection enables us to interpret two important facts. The first has to do with the legitimacy of the *populist* character of those communities. If what was said above is true, then we can indeed say that the church "does not have its center in itself." It is "decentered."

The center of the church is God's universal proposal and work. The church "finds itself again" when it takes shape in the very life of the people. There the church finds its meaning. Hence the church is renewed when it serves the people, when it carries out its evangelical mission within the people. Moreover, this same perspective enables us to point up the *specificity* of the church:

i.e., the fact that the church is not simply supposed to lose itself or dissolve in the people, that it serves the people truly only when it respects its own identity.

A frequently used analogy, that of the church as the "sacrament of humanity," brings out both aspects well. A sacrament re-presents (makes present) to faith a reality that is not yet fully present to all. But it does not substitute for that reality or replace it. Rather than bottling up hope in its realization, a sacrament stimulates it. The new humanity of the Kingdom—where human divisions have been truly reconciled in authentic peace and justice—is not yet visible; it is on the way towards realization. Hence we need an efficacious sign of the reality for which we are hoping and struggling. We need a place where faith can "discern" God's universal proposal. That is the point of the church. To confuse the sacrament with the reality, the church with the Kingdom, would be to commit idolatry; it would be to forget that the church is *only a sacrament*. Then we get the errors of ecclesiastical clericalism and religious imperialism. Ecclesiastical clericalism seeks to reabsorb the people into the church, and religious imperialism restricts the work of God to the church. But it is equally dangerous to overlook the specificity of the sacrament. Then we may erroneously sacralize the notion of "the people," cut out the eschatological perspective, and confusedly equate some historical achievement with the new humanity of the Kingdom.

But we must take one further step. It is easy enough, at least in theory, to recognize these two aspects and the dialectical tension between them. The concrete experience of populist Christian communities has enabled us to see more clearly the indissoluble *unity* at the heart of that tension. The fact is that we often hear talk about the tension existing between the "identity" of the church and its "identification" with the people (or with the poor). The implication seems to be that the two realities are inversely proportional. Greater identification supposedly jeopardizes the identity of the church, whereas greater stress on the specific nature of the church's identity necessarily poses obstacles to identification with the people. This antinomy is one of the many antinomies that afflicts theological thinking. It results from the application of a formal schema that does not pose the fundamental question: Wherein lies the "identity" of the church? The New Testament answer is unequivocal: in Jesus Christ. The church finds its identity when it "con-forms" to Jesus Christ, that is to say, when it assumes his "spiritual structure," his way of being.

And what is his way of being? Here again the writings of the New Testament are unanimous. It is to be found in his identification with humanity and, in particular, with the poor and lowly.[2] The logical conclusion is clear: the greater the church's identification with Jesus Christ, the more the church will be driven to an identification with the common people; the more the church is identified with the people, the more it will be in a position to reflect the identity of its Lord. Identity pushes towards identification, and identification is the matrix of authentic identity.

When this relationship is not found in the life of the church, we have a right to ask whether Jesus Christ himself has not been misunderstood. In other words, has he been given an identity separate or separable from his identification with the poor, or has the nature of that identification been misconstrued? The fact is that Jesus Christ was not the "champion of the poor," the powerful Messiah who comes to free the poor with "legions of angels." He himself "became poor" in order to bring to birth, in the very womb of humanity, the seed of the Kingdom that is to grow to consummate fullness. The church that knows its true identity and its true identification will not go off by itself and then summon all to come to it. It will not try to absorb the people into it, nor will it proclaim itself to be the "leader" of the people. Instead it will structure itself as a community of faith and incarnate itself in the very midst of the people, giving impetus to the quest of the Kingdom from there. It is precisely this praxis that measures the *ecclesial density* of populist or base-level Christian communities.

THE CHURCH: ONE AND MULTIPLE

In general, Protestantism has had a "modest" ecclesiology. It has been not so much a virtue as a necessity. Protestant ecclesiology has been protected to some extent from the danger of inflation by the fragmentary and ambiguous way in which it experiences its own reality as church—which is to say, as "churches." These churches cannot see themselves as *parts*, as if the church were a puzzle to be put together with different pieces; but neither can they see themselves as the *totality*, because they recognize the ecclesial reality of the other churches. This situation may be of some help to us today when we ask such questions as the following: Where is the church? Who is the church? The hierarchy? The people? Committed Christians? And these different answers are not easily integrated in practice.

Perhaps here we are helped by thinking of the church, not as a univocal term but as an "analogical" term. The "ecclesial realm" or "ecclesiality" is the precinct in which witness to God's liberating activity in Christ within the world is made explicit. But this ecclesial reality has different "condensations," so to speak. It had different ways of manifesting itself. They are not to be viewed as isolated or mutually extrinsic; but neither should they be reduced to one single form of manifestation as the one that is absolute or normative in every sense. In my opinion, this view corresponds with the conception of the New Testament itself. There the term "church" is used both for the first reality, the ecclesial totality, and for the second, the local churches and those of a region. And this is not due to imprecision or semantic confusion, nor does it merely signify two uses of one and the same term. Rather, the church is viewed as totally present in its local realizations and, at the same time, as a reality that transcends them.[3] This vision should not be understood in static terms. It should be seen as a process in operation, or better still, as a dialectical process in operation. In different ways and in differing institutional forms the Spirit is realizing this witness to Jesus Christ amid the circumstances and movements of history.

This formulation, which is rather abstract, has a specific application to our theme which seems important to me. The Protestant experience can prove to be instructive. In general, Protestantism tends to locate the ecclesial reality basically in the congregation. That has fostered a certain vitality, a capacity for incarnation in historical reality, which we could call "localizaton." It has been the secret of its growth. If I am not mistaken, these are the very possibilities which the base-level ecclesial communities are realizing: authentic incarnation in the populist classes, community initiative, and integration into the struggles of the people.

But it would be unwise to overlook some of the hazards to which Protestanism has been exposed. One is sectarianism: the isolation of congregations or denominations that absolutize themselves, lose all sense of transcendence vis-à-vis their own culture and social milieu, and keep dividing up further because of the tensions in the social milieu where they are incarnated. Another hazard is the loss of any sense of historical continuity, of union with our own past; and the result is a lack of perspective that prevents us from locating ourselves within a historical process. For Protestantism in particular, ecumenism has entailed the need to get beyond such historical and geographic narrowness, to make an effort to link up the vitality and localization of a congregation or a denomination with concrete structures fostering universal ties and the recovery of tradition. To be sure, the form employed has been the conciliar one. It dovetails with the ecclesiological perspective that I have indicated, and that differs from the hierarchical structuring of universality that characterizes Roman Catholicism. So there is no question of taking over the Protestant experience. But I do think that we may very well call attention to a real problem facing the new ecclesial realities that are emerging in Latin America, and that represent the initial beginnings and prospects for a "church of the people." These new ecclesial realities must find concrete ways and forms for ecumenical ties, both within their own confessions and across their boundaries, that will not undermine their incarnation in the people or their dynamism and creativity, but that will nevertheless enable them to overcome the dangers of sectarianism, isolation, and a loss of any historical sense.

NOTES

1. The present exposition was part of a panel discussion on the topic indicated. It should be viewed in connection with the other expositions which complement it and which are to be found in this work.

2. It is neither possible nor necessary to try to prove this point here. It has been dealt with extensively in the reflections and investigations of Latin American theology. Indeed it has come to be a universally recognized datum, though it is not always interpreted and valued in exactly the same way.

3. I am thinking in particular of the well-known article "Ekklesia," by K.L. Schmidt in the *Theologisches Wörterbuch zum N.T.* It established clearly, for the first time, the vocabulary usage of the New Testament with respect to this term. One of the definitive conclusions of that study refers precisely to this aspect. We are familiar with the image that Schmidt used to illustrate it: water, one and the same, is in every river, lake, or sea; but none of the latter particular realities exhausts it.

13

Ecclesiology in Latin America

Ronaldo Muñoz (Chile)

Now we face the task, as theologians, of bringing together and shedding light on the rich experiences of the grassroots church that have been exchanged and analyzed during this conference. This experience has been one of sharing the journey of the poor people, who are enduring suffering and fighting hopefully. Living amid these poor people and trying to aid their struggle, the grassroots church has been trying to open up areas for fraternal encounter and contemplation where it can proclaim in truth the liberating name of Jesus Christ.

What I propose to offer here is a systematic presentation of the major convictions about the church that have been affirmed at this conference. I will do it from my own standpoint as a Catholic, Latin American, and Chilean. My standpoint is obviously and inevitably limited, of course. As my frame of reference I shall use the Puebla Final Document.[1] I shall use not only its section on "The Truth About the Church" (PFD, nos. 220–303) but also the major ecclesiological lines of the whole Final Document. I focus on the Final Document, not only in itself insofar as it has special authority for us Latin American Catholics, but also insofar as it brings together, interprets, and gives further impetus to the whole course of our Latin American church as involved with the life and practices of our people's communities.

And so we get three major convictions about the church or, if you prefer, three outstanding "notes" of this church. It is an evangelizing church, a church of the poor, and a church as community.

AN EVANGELIZING CHURCH[2]

Let us start off from the perspective of *mission*. What is the church for? What is its most proper and essential business? Here we find that three points stand out.

150

The church exists to evangelize.

The church's life and reason for being is the proclamation of the living gospel message of Jesus Christ to human beings and concrete peoples.

This implies, first of all, that the church has its center outside itself. The church is essentially *eccentric,* in the sense that it does not exist for itself; it is not geared to self-expansion and living its own life. The church exists for the world, for service to human beings. More specifically, the church exists to serve human beings for the sake of the kingdom of God. It is meant to reveal and give impetus to the liberating thrust of the kingdom which runs through the history of peoples.

There is a second implication in the fact that the church exists to evangelize. It is that the church is continually summoned to *conversion* and reform. The church must be continually going out of itself, letting itself be summoned by its Lord, who speaks to it from others. In this committed dialogue the church is simultaneously supposed to be learning and proclaiming the ever new gospel of Jesus Christ. This conversion is not just required of persons and human groups in the church. It is also required of the church's structures. Conversion must apply to its institutions, its dominant criteria, and its practices.

Authentic evangelization is liberative.

Authentic evangelization is a proclamation of, and a radical impetus to, liberation for human beings and concrete peoples. This liberation is not just within each individual or aimed solely at the salvation of the individual's soul. It is meant to cover the totality of human and societal life. It is not solely aimed at complete fulfillment and happiness in the eschatological future; it is to be operative right now, generating a new human being and a new society in history.

This implies, first of all, that the church is supposed to proclaim the gospel message in deeds and words. These *words* are to proclaim God's love and the power of God's reign amid human beings, to reveal the presence of Jesus Christ the Liberator in human life and collective history. Hence these words must also denounce the personal and social sinfulness that stand in opposition to the kingdom and deny God in practice. To give expression and concrete truth to these words, *deeds* are also required. They are to be acts of effective service in the promotion of human dignity and in our peoples' process of historical liberation. Thus the words and deeds confirm and explain each other.

Thus liberative evangelization also implies that we Christians and the church itself must continually strive to effect a living synthesis of faith, justice, and witness. *Faith* (confident adhesion to the Father and hope in his kingdom) must be joined with *justice* (commitment to a solidary struggle for a more egalitarian and fraternal society) and with *witness* (to a more humane lifestyle and social coexistence that is to be exemplified and lived even now).

The fonts of the living gospel and the place to hear it.

I have already indicated that the Church must constantly be going out of itself, not only to bring to those outside the gospel message it already knows, but also to rediscover and explore more deeply that very gospel in meeting others. Now we must make an even more concrete assertion: we cannot know the God of Jesus Christ, seek out God's countenance, and do God's will, if we turn our backs on what is happening in *our history* and a deaf ear to the clamor of our oppressed people. Here we are dealing with an experience as old as biblical faith. It is the fact that our God is found to be present and operative in the situations and events of history. It is the evangelical experience that the God of Jesus Christ is the living God, the God of the poor, the liberator God who travels along with the people today. So here we have one of the "two fonts" of the living gospel message: lived history, the challenges of societal reality, committed praxis in our people's journey toward liberation.

But this history and praxis do not "speak" to us of God and God's liberative activity in and of themselves. They do so under the illumination of the prophetic *word,* which we recognize as inspired by God. To recognize and acknowledge God, we must pay attention to reality and reflect upon it in the light of the word of God that has been set down in Scripture and handed down to us by the tradition of faith. By the same token our clear-eyed presence and involvement in historical reality calls into question our preconceptions about the faith and enables us to gain a new grasp and understanding of the Scriptures as the living word that God addresses to us.

So neither lived history by itself nor traditional Scripture by itself gives us the living gospel message. They provide us with that message insofar as they interact and shed light on each other. And the place where this interaction takes place is precisely the church. For the church is *the community of believers,* historically involved with its own prophetic word. It is the ecclesial community to which all make their contribution, and in which brothers and sisters share a common quest. The church is the body of Christ in history, which is animated by his Spirit. It benefits from the differing contributions of all its members and from the specific contribution of the ministers of the word.

A CHURCH OF THE POOR[3]

Having traced the main outlines of the church's mission, let us now consider the matter of *the people.* Whence arises the church? In what sectors does it have its social basis? From what context, historically speaking, is the liberating gospel of Jesus Christ proclaimed? Here we can focus on four points.

The church is born of Jesus Christ and it is to be incarnated in the poor as a people.

The church is the product of God's love for humanity. It is born of Jesus Christ and animated by his Spirit. It was born *once* from the ministry and historical destiny of Jesus of Nazareth. In Galilee and in his journey to Jerusalem he gathered together his first disciples and gave them training. Later, as the resurrected Messiah, he sent them out with the power of his Spirit. He made them the initial nucleus and foundation of the new people of God, a universal and eschatological people. In its faith the church of the Risen One must recall the historical career of Jesus, who was the Messiah of the poor and the crucified Prophet; and in its practice the church must follow in the footsteps of that career. Jesus Christ does not simply stand at the historical origin of the church as its founder and normative model. Today, as the resurrected Christ, he stands as its living center, the inexhaustible wellspring of its love and its hope amid the sufferings and struggles of history.

Because Jesus is its historical origin and its living center, the church strives to incarnate itself among the common people, *among the poor* and marginalized of the earth; for that is where Jesus Christ himself once became incarnate and fulfilled his ministry. So *today in Latin America* the church arises from the faith-response of the poor as a people to their Messiah and Lord.

The church is sent out and encouraged to be Jesus Christ's visible body and liberating sacrament in history. The poor play the same role. As needy persons and as a people with its collective history of passion and liberation, they are the visible body and a sacrament of Jesus Christ according to the gospel faith. Hence we are called upon to profess that today "Jesus Christ [is] living in his church and particularly among the poorest" (PFD: 330). Hence he is alive where the poor "have begun to organize themselves to live their faith in an integral way, and hence to reclaim their rights" (PFD: 1137).

In Latin America the church must continue to move from the side of the powerful to the side of the poor.

While that is the christological essence and the spiritual dynamism of the church, its historical work has not been consistent with that essence in all times and places. Today in Latin America our concrete churches are being prodded by evangelical fidelity to be more effective in shifting their social center from the side of the powerful to the side of the poor. They are being prodded to move from more or less inadvertent assimilation to, and complicity with, the dominant sectors to committed involvement with the oppressed majorities. And this assimilation to the latter is a decision deriving from the gospel message.

Today the church is being summoned to undergo a *conversion to the poor* of the land. It is being called upon to let itself be "domesticated" by the poor, to share their sufferings and struggles in its own body, and to assimilate their culture and their way of living the faith. This means that the church must thoroughly revise its structures, its viewpoints, its practices, and the concrete life of its members—of its most representative agents in particular. The aim of all this is to ensure that the poor will be able to find in the church *their own true home* as an oppressed, believing people, *the expression of their own faith* and hope, and the anticipated realization of their own yearnings for liberty, community, and participation.

The social siding of the church with the poor and its commitment to their historical cause confer a more concrete perspective and content on its *mission as liberating evangelization.*

As proclamation and denunciation, *the word* of the gospel message is "Good News" for the poor. *The poor* are declared blessed because God is a just King and a kindly Father who is tired of seeing them suffer. In the future there will be no poor and oppressed because God is to establish his kingdom (the Synoptic Gospels), because he is going to establish true communion among his children (John's Gospel). Among us, therefore, proclamation of the gospel message should liberate the common people's faith and culture, which have often been inhibited by traces of pagan fatalism. Or, to put it more truly, they find themselves captured and alienated by the imposition of the culture and ideology of the dominant classes. The gospel message is to liberate the faith and culture of our people so that a fresh encounter with Jesus Christ the Liberator will awaken critical awareness and inspire solidarity in their struggles for liberation.

For the gospel message is not just to be proclaimed *to* the poor. They are not just the primary addressees of liberative evangelization. They are also the natural subjects and bearers of it. Among us Latin Americans "commitment to the poor and oppressed and the rise of grassroots communities have helped the church to discover the evangelizing potential of the poor" (PFD:1147). Thus it is *from the poor and by the poor* that the gospel is announced to all human beings: to the poor themselves, first of all, but also to human beings of every class and social condition. The saving love of the Father does not exclude the powerful, nor does the justice of God's kingdom require the destruction of the oppressors. It is simply that for the ruling sectors of our society, as was true with Jesus' preaching in his own day, the words of the gospel message ring out primarily as "serious and timely warnings" (Puebla Message: 3): "Woe to you rich people. . . . Woe to you, scribes and Pharisees. . . . How difficult it will be for the wealthy to enter the kingdom of God!"

The kingdom does not exclude oppressors and wealthy people, but only on the condition that they detach themselves from their wealth, stop oppressing their fellow human beings, and "accept and take up the cause of the poor as if they were accepting and taking up their own cause, the cause of Christ himself" (Puebla Message: 3). It is in that sense that "the witness of a poor Church can evangelize the rich whose hearts are attached to wealth, thus converting and freeing them from this bondage and their own egotism" (PFD: 1156).

Finally, we come to the *deeds* with which the church is to make its message creditable and concretely visible. At present our people are suffering from marginalization, exploitation, and frequently cruel repression. If the church does not want its word to be a lie in such a situation, it must take an active part in the defense and promotion of human rights. More concretely, it must undertake the defense and promotion of *the rights of the poor,* rights which are being systematically disregarded and trampled. The church must invest all its social power in the defense of those rights: the rights of persons and also the rights of poor groups (e.g., oppressed classes and ethnic groups) with their own values and organizations. All that entails the denunciation of social sinfulness, which is interiorized by idolatrous ideologies and institutionalized in oppressive structures.

This entails persecution and internal conflicts.

When the church undergoes conversion to the poor, shoulders the cause of their liberation, and joins them in their passion and struggle, it inevitably must face persecution and internal conflicts.

It must face *persecution* because it must share in the repression being suffered by all the organizations and movements of the people and, in particular, because its evangelical witness calls into question the good conscience of the dominant groups and jeopardizes the security of the system of domination.

It must face *internal conflicts* because the church finds itself on two sides as an institution. On the one hand it is assimilated to, and established among, the dominant groups. On the other hand it is becoming increasingly incarnate among the poor majorities and taking up their cause. Historically speaking, then, our churches suffer from persecution and internal conflicts as two inseparable dimensions of one and the same *Way of the Cross* as they try to follow Jesus Christ. Here, too, we are learning the painful lesson that "the disciple is not greater than the master."

Grassroots ecclesial communities of the common people are wont to suffer repression and even martyrdom from the same type of authorities—socioeconomic, political, and religious—that brought Jesus to death on the cross. And they do so for the very same reasons. Among us, too, the powerful act in this way in order to defend the established social order and "traditional" religion. However, like Jesus of Nazareth, the church born of the oppressed people bears witness to a different justice and, more radically, to a different God. It is the God of the poor, the lowly, and the oppressed; the God who "puts down the mighty from their thrones and exalts those of low degree";

the Father who raised Jesus from the dead. The same pathway of conflict, persecution, and martyrdom prompts our churches to reaffirm their commitment and to radicalize their faith in life and their hope in the resurrection of the dead. For Jesus told them: "Do not be afraid. I have overcome the world."

A CHURCH AS COMMUNITY[4]

We now come to the third aspect: *community.* What is the deepest secret of the church's life? How is it lived and expressed in the church's own shared existence? How important is it for the church to exemplify this form of social existence in the midst of the people? Here we must focus on five points.

The church is a mystery of communion between God and human beings, and among human beings themselves.

The church proclaims the kingdom of God, and it does so by setting up its tent among the poor of the earth as Jesus did. But its own communities—like the group of disciples around Jesus and, even more, like the community transformed by the Spirit of the Risen One—already constitute a *dense and significant realization of the kingdom itself,* living amid the people and seeking to move their history toward the definitive, universal kingdom.

The church is not the only scene or instrument of the kingdom in history. But its communities are already living the new communion between God and human beings, and between human beings themselves, that constitutes the most essential content of the kingdom. They are living it imperfectly in the chiaroscuro of faith and with sinful defects, but they are living it in a real way. This is the deepest underlying secret of the church's life. It is the very life of the risen Jesus Christ communicated to us through the Spirit. It enables us to share Jesus' own communication as *Son* with the Father, and hence it makes us *brothers and sisters* down to the very core. From its deepest roots, therefore, the church is a grace. It is a gift of the Father, who shares his own joy with his children and gathers them as brothers and sisters around his own table.

By deeds we must turn this grace into truth *in the concrete life* of the church and every single Christian community, through communal encounter and sharing, prayer, and solidary service. There the mass of human beings can continually fashion themselves into a people of brothers and sisters; there the people can continually move toward encounter with their God. It happens in a special way when the community comes together for *prayer:* prayers of petition or gratuitous praise, moments of talk and silence, and rituals of gesture and song. These are the moments when the people consciously meet their God, take repose in God, enjoy God's presence, and share the food and drink they need to keep moving on in hope.

The church must be a sign and instrument
of the transformation of society.

As we noted above, the Christian community is a locale for encounter with God and human fraternity. But it is not an island or refuge in the world. As a local community, and as an organized complex of communities, the church must be a sign and instrument fostering the transformation of human society.

Sign and instrument: these are the the two dimensions inseparable from the vocation of the church as a *sacrament* of God's kingdom in history, and as a sacrament of encounter and communion between God and human beings, and human beings themselves, through the Spirit of Christ. For the church and each Christian community, being a *sign* means fleshing out visibly and concretely in its own societal life and in the face of humanity the liberty and new life of the kingdom that it proclaims with the gospel message. Hence in the church "human dignity is to be expressed and realized . . . in a communitarian way" (PFD: 333). Here we are referring to the human dignity that constitutes the inalienable vocation and right of every human person and every people as children of God and fellow members of one family.

This entails a serious responsibility for the church. In its teaching the church proclaims certain values to be exigencies of nature and part of the vocation of the human being: e.g., fundamental equality and liberty, corresponsibility and participation. The church calls for their realization in human society. With all the more reason, then, and in a striking way, all those values must be realized and verified in the societal life and the institutional structures of the church itself. The church is a historical sign of the kingdom, an alluring model and hope-giving "utopia" for the transformation of human society, to the extent that the church itself, embodied in its representative groups and its institutional structures, can concretely exemplify those values. In other words, the church fulfills this role to the extent that it does not let itself be "secularized," to the extent that it does not take over the ideology, mechanisms, and behavior patterns of the sinful world in which we live: e.g., power confined to closed groups; vertical authority; servility and the career mentality; one-sided information or secrecy; the denial of participation on the pretext of unity and discipline; the repression of critical thinking and liberative solidarity on the pretext of institutional security or for the sake of maintaining the established order.

We recall what Jesus had to say. Heads of nations lord it over people and those in power make their authority felt. He criticized the scribes and Pharisees for wanting first place and recognition. His disciples were not to act like that. One who wanted to be first was to take the last place and be the servant of all. They had only one teacher, and they were brothers.

In the case of the church, being an *instrument* at its various institutional levels and in its concrete communities means being truly in the service of the *kingdom's* liberty and new life within the history of peoples. It means serving and abetting, through acts of commitment and concrete programs, the struggle of our poor peoples for life and dignity, justice and a new society. Active in that struggle, we know, is the Spirit of Christ. It is the Spirit who directs the struggle toward the fullness of justice and shared life that we expect in the definitive kingdom, where we will find the city of God-with-human beings, the Father's banquet with all his children.

I have already pointed out that this sort of service basically makes up the evangelizing task of the church. It is a task to be carried out with words and deeds. And in its own life and open-ended societal operation, the church is to be the signifying datum *par excellence:* "You are the salt of the earth, . . . the light of the world. . . . But if the salt loses its savor, how shall its saltiness be restored?"

The church must be socially embodied in communities.

"Christians ought to find the living of the communion to which they have been called in their 'base communities,' " as Medellín put it.[5] And the Christian people should find it in a web of Christian communities that are woven together institutionally into a church that is truly communitarian.

The base-level or grassroots communities are truly "the first and fundamental ecclesiastical nucleus."[6] There the people's faith and their love for Jesus Christ is to be nourished and exemplified week after week. In all their various forms these communities are centers of evangelization and liberation in the midst of the people: "The CEBs embody the Church's preferential love for the common people. In them their religiosity is expressed, valued, and purified; and they are given a concrete opportunity to share in the task of the Church and to work committedly for the transformation of the world" (PFD:643).

But the communitarian dimension of the church is not exhausted in its grassroots communities of the people. The vitality of the individual communities and their organization into broader, more complete ecclesial units require the support and the coordinating work of the *larger ecclesial institutions,* along with the corresponding pastoral ministries. The institution and ministries, in turn, are rooted in those communities and continually learn more from their ongoing course.

A people, as a more universal collective unit with its own land, culture, history, and hopes, needs the authorized word and the visible sign of a prophetic ministry and an ecclesial institution tailored to its measure. The same holds true on an even wider level, when we are talking about the peoples of a given region or the whole world. They need the same thing for their common problems, in order to combat the growing injustice on the international front and to foster the vocation of all peoples to form one single family of God. So at every level the church should express communion through a style that embodies fraternity and participation, mutual respect and collegial collaboration. This means that at every level, including that of universal communion, there should exist effective instances and channels for communitarian deliberation and corresponsibility. All this is ultimately served by the ministry of Peter: "And you, when you have come back, confirm your brethren."

There must be pastoral ministries serving the local communities and learning from them.

The importance of pastoral ministries at every level should now be obvious. Within the life of each community, and on broader fronts, there must be pastoral ministers to serve the local communities and learn from them.

All the ecclesial ministries—hierarchical, lay, and religious—are urged by the Puebla Conference to great *commitment to the poor and oppressed as a people.* Those who come from outside are to make a real option for the poor and incarnate themselves in the sociocultural reality of the poor. Within the ranks of the poor themselves, we are to recognize and promote truly autochthonous ministers who will more deliberately shoulder the cause of their own oppressed class or ethnic group.

All these ministries and ministers are also asked to display a greater *consecration to the mission.* They are to do so by living witness to, and revitalized proclamation of, the liberating gospel of Jesus Christ.

Each and all of these ministries are asked to exercise *communitarian leadership* in their own proper way and in the spirit of the gospel message. They are to trust in the power of the gospel message, not in worldly power and possessiveness. They are to exemplify fraternity in human relationships and helpful reciprocity. They are to humbly serve the community, helping it to become more clear-eyed and consistent in its practice as it obediently seeks to follow the one and only Lord of the church and history.

In line with their position and their charisms, each and all are asked to help keep the community open-ended, to foster ties with neighboring communities, and to nurture ecclesial communion in the broadest terms of geographical and ecumenical universality. This *service to universal communion* should contribute to the real, effective catholicity of the church in time and space, a catholicity reconstructed from the poor of the earth. It would be catholicity in space by virtue of communion with all the churches of the world and participation at every level of the universal church. It would be catholicity in time by virtue of communion with the faith and holiness of all the generations of Christians, with a living tradition going back to the witness of the apostles to the once-for-all-time manifestation of the Word of life in the flesh and in the history of the poor.

Finally, there must be committed involvement with the organizations and movements of the common people.

One final point will make this commitment to the poor as a people even more concrete. All of us are urged and compelled to committed involvement with the organizations and movements stemming from the common people.

For *Christian communities themselves,* this necessary relationship and collaboration poses different challenges insofar as various peoples are living in different historical circumstances. However varied the forms of collaboration may be, the basic fact of collaboration represents an important step forward in liberative solidarity and gospel witness. Moreover, aside from the kinds of support and assistance that often prove to be indispensable, we must always try to preserve the proper autonomy and identity of each particular body, be it a local church community or some organization fighting for the rights of the people. Such autonomy is indispensable to the process of integral liberation.

Lay christians, in particular, are compellingly urged to solidary participation in people's organizations and movements. Moreover, stress is laid on the fact that this is the most proper locale for their own militant involvement as persons of the people *(laikoi)* and as Christians. The Christian community itself must stimulate and encourage such commitment, allowing itself to be stimulated and challenged in turn by the witness of involved lay people. In this way the ecclesial community will truly be in the service of the people and the ongoing thrust of the kingdom. Christians will be able to flesh out in history the force of solidary love and sure hope of liberation that are part of their faith.

NOTES

1. The Puebla Final Document is abbreviated PFD in citations here. Puebla's Message to the Peoples of Latin America is cited as Puebla Message. For a complete English version of these texts, related papal homilies and addresses, and commentaries, see John Eagleson and Philip Scharper, eds., *Puebla and Beyond* (Maryknoll, N.Y.: Orbis Books, 1979).

2. For this theme, see the following sections of the Puebla Final Document: 84–85; 267, 270, 274; 333, 338–39; 347–51; 476–77; 552, 562; 679, 692–93; 725–27, 747; 777, 796–99; 971–75; 1297–1305.

3. For this theme, see the following sections of the Puebla Final Document: 6, 8, 10; 83, 92; 141–49; 226–28, 267–68; 413–15, 419–20, 433, 436–38; 448, 452, 457–58; 622–24; 696–97, 706–7, 711; 733–35; 965–66, 974–75; 1129–32; 1134–44, 1147, 1156–58. Also see Puebla Message: 3.

4. For this theme, see the following sections of the Puebla Final Document: 96–99, 104–7, 110–11, 113–18, 125; 150–56; 227–30, 243, 260–62, 272–74; 618–27, 629–35, 638–51; 664–68, 701–5; 752–55, 771–73; 780–85, 800–5, 811–17, 827–28; 1184–85, 1199, 1203.

5. Medellín Conference Conclusions, "Joint Pastoral Planning," no. 10.

6. Ibid. For the papers of the Medellín Conference see the official English edition: Louis Michael Colonnese, ed., *The Church in the Present-Day Transformation of Latin America in the Light of the Council,* 2 vols. (Washington, D.C.: United States Catholic Conference, 1968–69).

14

The Witness of the Church
in Latin America

Jon Sobrino, S.J. (El Salvador)

In this paper I would like to offer a theoretical and theological analysis of the church's witness in Latin America. Thus I am not offering a simple description of this witness, even though my effort seeks to take into account the concrete witness that local churches have offered over the last ten years or more in their desire to be faithful to the Medellín Conference.[1]

In trying to talk about the witness, or testimony, of the church, we must begin by attempting to clarify a basic question. Witness is normally regarded as the subjective holiness of the church, which helps to lend credibility and efficacy to its practice. In short, it is viewed more in terms of the subjectivity of the church than in terms of the objectivity of church practice.

This understanding of church witness is not adequate, however, if we wish to track down the roots of its historical activity or even to grasp the very essence of witness. The objective aspect of the church's witness should be the most basic, because it is witness to something, a stand for or against something. It is that objective something that should require logical and historical credibility from the witnessing subject. The subjective aspect of witness derives its meaning and necessity from the objective aspect of witness. The more important the objective content of the witness is, the more necessary the subjective credibility on the part of the one who offers that witness becomes.

Insofar as the church is concerned, this means that we must begin with this first basic question: to *what* is the church bearing witness in its practice of evangelization? That will lead us into the second question: *how* is the church bearing witness?

To answer the basic point of these questions in general terms, I would say that on the objective level the church is bearing witness to life, and on the subjective level its witness and holiness consist in offering up its own life. To put a little more historical flesh on this bareboned answer, I would say that

161

the church in Latin America is bearing witness to a *just* life, and the form of its offering is specifically *martyrdom*.

I think this way of presenting the witness of the church is important for three reasons. On the *formal, systematic level* it brings both aspects of witness together, and even though it does so dialectically, it brings them together on the basis of the objective side. Subjective witness loses its autonomy and arbitrariness; as is only right, it can be understood only in terms of the content to which one is supposed to bear witness. This is important if we are to avoid viewing the subjective witness of the church in idealistic and voluntaristic terms, if we are to see it correctly as a response to an objective exigency of history that mediates the will of God. In that case the content of the church's holiness will not simply be the stamp of credibility on any and every type of ecclesial practice; it will also be that content which objectively dovetails with the demands of reality.

On the *historical level* this way of presenting the witness of the church brings together the two items of data that, in my opinion, are historically the most novel and fundamental in the practice of the church. One item is the active participation of the church in the processes of liberation; the other is the persecution that this participation is bringing down upon the church. There can be no serious reflection on ecclesial witness if we do not bring together those two items and regard them as central to the historical witness of the church.

On the *theological level* this way of presenting the witness of the church sums up what is presently constituting the concrete experience of faith in Latin America. The content of our *fides quae creditur* (what is believed) is the God of life, made concrete and familiar in God's various aspects as God the Creator, God the Crucified One, and God the Liberator. Our *fides qua creditur* (the form belief takes in practice) is taking shape in line with that God. It involves the wholehearted surrender of the human being to God in faith, and it takes the form of following Jesus. For Jesus was "the pioneer and perfecter of our faith, who for the joy that was set before him endured the cross, despising the same . . ." (Heb. 12:2).

In the following pages I shall offer a theological analysis of these basic points. I shall try to make clear what it means to say that the church is bearing witness to life, to a life of justice and fulfillment. And I shall also try to consider how it is bearing this witness by giving of its own life, and indeed by giving its very life at times.

THE OBJECTIVE WITNESS OF THE CHURCH
ON BEHALF OF A JUST LIFE IN THE PRESENCE OF DEATH

The New Testament frequently makes it clear that the disciples of Jesus must bear witness as an essential part of their faith. There is no Christian faith unless there is something to which Christians must bear public, unconditional witness. Witnessing will obviously require a certain configuration of the believing subject; but it derives its meaning first and foremost from something objective to which the Christian must bear witness.

In many different ways the New Testament gives christological expression to this object content. Christians must bear witness to Jesus Christ, to his whole historical life and, above all, to his resurrection.[2] To put it in strictly theo-logical terms, Christians must bear witness to Jesus Christ as the definitive "mediator" of the Father.

A more rigorous analysis of this witness, as the New Testament views it, tells us that its content is not just the person of Jesus Christ. It is also the historical "mediation" that Jesus serves, or that makes its presence felt in him. As far as the historical Jesus is concerned, it is clear that he did not bear witness to himself; he bore witness to the kingdom of God. As far as we consider the Christian community and its reflection on Jesus, it is clear that it associates the mediator Jesus with a mediation that makes its presence felt in him; that mediation is broader than Jesus himself. Christians can bear witness to Jesus only by bearing witness to the divine mediation that Jesus himself proclaims or expresses.

In the New Testament, witness to the mediator Jesus is bound up with witness to the mediation of God: "This Jesus God raised up, and of that we all are witnesses" (Acts 2:32). Witness does not remain on the christological level. It moves on to the strictly theo-logical level, becoming witness to the God who "raised from the dead Jesus" (Rom. 4:24). In systematic terms this God is now defined as the God "who gives life to the dead and calls into existence the things that do not exist" (Rom. 4:17). Life and resurrection are the mediation of God to which Christians must bear witness.

The Johannine theology also links up witness to Jesus with witness to the divine mediation that Jesus serves: "I came that they may have life, and have it abundantly" (John 10:10). It is on that basis that Christians understand exactly what they are supposed to bear witness to: "That which was from the beginning, which we have heard, which we have seen with our eyes, which we have looked upon and touched with our hands, concerning the word of life— the life was made manifest, and we saw it, and testify to it . . ." (1 John 1:1-2).

Let me spell out the importance of these few brief references. Whatever further exegetical study may tell us about the exact meaning of such terms as "the kingdom of God," "resurrection," and "life," it is clear that in the New Testament witness to the mediator Jesus cannot be separated from witness to the mediation he serves. And the content of that mediation is not some compartmentalized section of human life or some strictly "religious" sphere; it is what we can call life in its totality.

Witness on behalf of life, I believe, constitutes the deepest root of the church's activity in Latin America. It is life viewed as life in all its fullness, activity touching every level of life. That is why the church wants full and complete—integral—liberation. I shall say more about this fullness of life in the last section of this paper.

Right now I want to focus on the first basic historical embodiment (or, historicization) of life as it is being lived in Latin America and served by the church. The most fundamental datum in this connection is the fact that life is being threatened and annihilated by structural injustice and institutionalized violence. I refer to the life of the vast majority of people, and to life on the most basic levels. That is why the witness of the church on behalf of life has devoted more serious attention to the basic levels of life and advocated a life of "justice" as opposed to one of injustice.

The reason why the church can give this form of historical embodiment to life right now is the irruption, the breaking-in, of the poor.[3] Both on the Latin American continent and in the church the poor have made their presence felt. The church's preferential option for the poor was its response to this irruption. This concrete option for the poor means that the church's witness on behalf of life can find correct historical embodiment, that it need not degenerate into abstract, idealistic witness. Its option for the poor gives historical stress to the fact that when it is talking about life, it is talking about the life of the majority of the people, about life that is being threatened and crushed at its most basic levels. Such an option ensures that the witness of the church will not hasten on too quickly to the "fullness" of life, ignoring its basic levels in practice and devaluating them theologically. Instead the church will take serious note of those basic levels as an object of its testimony and as a mediation of the spiritual experience of a God of life.

Wittingly or unwittingly, then, the church is in the process of giving renewed value to an authentic theology of creation. It is not a matter of offering one of those simplistic theologies of creation that ignore the sinfulness pervading objective creation and that plump for a straight-line historical development out of the dynamic seeds contained in creation. To offer such a simplistic theology would be to give theological endorsement to developmentalist types of socioeconomic theory. In this case we choose rather to see in creation the first—logical—mediation of the reality of God. We choose to see creation as the first manifestation of the God of life. And in so doing, we look where theology has all too often failed to look, i.e., at the very fact of living and managing to stay alive, at work, and at the use of nature and its resources in the service of human beings. Instead of falling into the lure of an overhasty eschatology, we want to get back to the sober first steps of protology. For the real problem in Latin America is not that eschatology has not arrived but that the values and realities present at the beginning have not yet come to be.

This means that we are rejecting another view, which is evident in practice if not in theory. According to this other view, the basic, primary levels of life and the very fact of being alive are merely natural, socioeconomic data. As such they are worthy of study by anthropology, sociology, and economics; and they may serve indirectly as the basis for understanding and practicing a more circumscribed or regionalized Christian ethics. But in themselves they are not data that need be integrated into theo-logy in the strict sense. Theology, according to this view, begins at a different level. It has to do with "authentic" life, with "Christian" living, or with "eternal" life.

Such a view is thoroughly mistaken, in my opinion, and it has the most disastrous consequences. Indeed it was denounced by Bartolomé de Las Casas when Latin America was first being evangelized. With profound theological insight he saw first the creaturely reality of the native Indians. He described the Indian as a poor and oppressed creature rather than as an infidel. And so he drew his famous conclusion: "Better a live non-believing Indian than a dead Christian Indian."[4] Las Casas was denouncing a method of evangelization that made destruction and death a necessary precondition for the conversion of the Indians. He was denouncing the ethical falsification involved in a particular type of evangelization practice. On a deeper level, however, on a theo-logical level, he was denouncing a false conception of God. A living infidel is a sacrament of the God of life whereas a murdered Christian Indian is merely a sacrament of idols. We cannot bear witness to God at the price of negating the basic levels of life, even if we go on to say that this God offers a fuller life than any merely natural one and that the fullness of this God is mediated to us through the fullness of the Christian life.

This recovery of the basic, primary aspect of life may seem to be a rather minimal attainment; but it is fundamental if we are to comprehend the activity of the church and the experiencing of God through that activity. It is a minimal attainment because life is not exhausted on those basic levels. But it is fundamental because there lies the foundation of all life; without it there is no chance of truly bearing witness to a God of life. A creation in which life is ignored, threatened, or crushed is a vitiated creation. It would be illusory, useless, and even blasphemous to claim to bear witness to God without engaging in practical activity to repair creation. Faced with the basic primary needs evident on our continent, all experience of God and all witnessing by the church must *logically* start there.

These considerations regarding witness in favor of life at its most basic and primary levels take on all their radicalness when we consider the concrete reality of our continent. If the Johannine Gospel testifies that in Christ there appeared the Word of Life, then what we see on our continent is the anti-Christ and its word of anti-life. On this point we find agreement among Medellín, Puebla, and many pastoral letters.

But the manifestation of anti-life is not a reality of nature—the mere absence of life on the primary levels because creation is not able to provide. It is the historical result of the will of human beings, crystallized in unjust structures. Anti-life is not a natural product; it has its anti-Christ. What manifests itself is the absence of life as injustice, and hence the essence of sin. Sin finds its basic embodiment in history in the death that some human beings inflict on other human beings. Unjust structures foment and inflict death daily; and to defend those structures people kill all those who attack them. God's creation is vitiated, not only because there is a de facto absence of life on primary levels but also because life is actively oppressed and quashed by injustice.

Witness in favor of the primacy of life thus becomes witness in favor of justice, and this entails involvement in the struggle against injustice. Witness to God the creator necessarily becomes witness to God the liberator.

The relationship between experience of God and witness to a life of justice is all the more clear in Latin America because structural injustice is given implicit or explicit theo-logical sanction. The reigning structures—capitalism and national security in their many forms—operate as true deities with divine characteristics and their own cult. They are deities because they claim characteristics that belong to God also: ultimateness, definitiveness, and untouchability. They have their own cult because they demand the daily sacrificing of the majority and the violent sacrificing of those who oppose them. These deities need victims to survive, and they produce them of necessity. What prevails on our continent, then, is an injustice that is sanctioned theologically in the name of deities that are deities of death.[5]

Conviction about the nature of the true God, God's true mediation, and God's true cult arises from considering the opposites of false gods and their death-dealing mediations. If sin reveals itself as the death of human beings, then grace reveals itself first and foremost as the life of human beings—the first and most basic divine gift to human beings. If doing injustice reveals itself as the worship of false gods, then the practice of justice is seen to be worship of the true God. If capitalism and national security reveal themselves as idols, as deities of death, then the true God is seen to be the God who produces life and wills liberation.

Since the reality of our continent makes it abundantly clear that there is no middle ground between life and death, grace and sin, justice and injustice, it is clear that in this matter the objective witness of the church cannot be any sort of third-way compromise (*tercerismo*). Negatively speaking, this means that no witness to God can in practice relativize the life and death of human beings in the name of some eschatological reservation; or relativize the basic, primary needs of human beings in the name of the fullness of life. Positively speaking, it means that any and all correct witness to God must include the practice of justice as an essential element.

But let us remember one important point at this juncture. Why precisely has the practice of justice become so historically necessary and so theologically basic for the witness of the church? It is because anti-life, the generalized repression of life, is to be found at basic, primary levels that cannot be concealed. Thus we are not talking about a vague, general demand for justice, as there will always be some limitation and oppression in any and every historical configuration. We are talking about a demand for justice on those primary levels where the first roots of ethical awareness and the experience of God are to be found. It is not a matter of calling for "human rights" in general, for example. This approach generally does not foster much ecclesial life or practice, nor does it alter the self-awareness of the church. Instead it is a matter of calling for "the rights of the poor"; for this approach and practice is capable of converting the church and giving depth to its practice.

The outcries of the Latin American people are primary, and God heeds them. Only by listening to those cries and converting them into liberation hope and practice will the church be in tune with the primary reality of God and bear witness to it.

The two facts mentioned above—the absence of life on basic, primary levels and injustice as the cause of this absence—are well known. The point to be underlined here is that both facts are central to any understanding of the church's activity. The novel nature of its activity can be appreciated only in terms of those facts. In incarnating itself in the authentic reality of our continent, the first thing it has experienced is the unjust death of the majority of the people. And starting out from the very opposite of life, it has undertaken an ecclesial and pastoral task designed to overcome death and to implant justice.

At the level of programmatic formulations the church has affirmed its preferential option for the poor. To be sure, this option is rooted in Sacred Scripture and, more concretely, in the mission of Jesus. But this option was not taken merely for the sake of formal fidelity to the biblical text, nor for the sake of mechanical, voluntaristic imitation of Jesus. Instead this option was taken because the poor—as people with very concrete faces and unsatisfied basic needs, and as a collective body that is the product of injustice (see Puebla Final Document, nos. 31–39 and 63–69)—are the mediation of the primary summons to conscience. It was also taken because in such an option for the poor we find something ultimate that is justified in and of itself. Indeed that is what the Puebla Conference affirmed in its own sober but no less profound way:

> For this reason alone, the poor merit preferential attention, whatever may be the moral or personal situation in which they find themselves. Made in the image and likeness of God (Gen. 1:26–28) to be his children, this image is dimmed and even defiled. That is why God takes on their defense and loves them . . . [no. 1142].

That statement points up the ultimateness of the church's conviction and hence it is a profoundly theo-logical statement. It is not a deductive statement based upon some already established faith in God. Rather, it expresses a concrete experience which is constitutive of the ultimate, and hence of God. The option for the poor is not optional, or necessary only in a given set of circumstances. It is the unconditional affirmation of life and the unconditional rejection of injustice.

Here, in the most minimal but also the deepest sense, lies the root of the church's practice. In recent years the church has engaged in the unwonted practice of prophetically denouncing injustice on a large scale; and it has assumed the risks entailed. Its defense of human rights has not been a defense of the liberal version of human rights—human rights as "civil" rights. It has been a defense of human rights in the most basic sense of the right to live and the right to the basic necessities of life. That is why the church has renamed them the "rights of the poor." Insofar as it could, it has demanded and advocated necessary structural changes on the social, economic, and political levels. It has fought for the organization of labor and of the common masses as a way of breaking oppressive centers of power and achieving a more humane and humanizing kind of power. And instead of merely offering doctrines about these problems, it has often injected itself into the struggle to make the solutions a part of real life.

This whole range of activity cannot be viewed merely as a response to localized ethical exigencies, or as applications of a ready-made, completed social doctrine. It must be viewed as the basic response to a demand posed by reality itself, and hence to a demand posed by God. It is, therefore, the most basic way to bear witness on behalf of life.

The radical nature of this conviction can be seen in the historical novelty of the church's way of acting in certain instances. For example, the church has sometimes supported projects for "popular unity" that have been socialist in tenor; and it has even accorded legitimacy to insurrection by the people.[6] This is not the place to explore in detail the complex specifics of such situations or the exact nature of the church's support. The point is that neither ideologies normally viewed with suspicion by the church nor the seriousness of the conflicts, which may end up being armed conflicts, can set limits to the witness of the church on behalf of a just way of life.

There is no question here of naiveté or of losing the Christian substance and its specificity. The underlying basis is the conviction that the church cannot stand forever outside the processes going on, that it cannot rest content with proposing conciliatory, third-way options, when it is a matter of life and death for human beings. There is no other standpoint of supposedly greater importance from which it could relativize life and death as if they were not matters of ultimate truth in the final analysis. However necessary and primordial may be its obligation to criticize the limited and dehumanizing features in these borderline-limit processes, the church feels that the demand for the establishment of life on a just basis is even more primordial. Criticism of these processes and all others is indeed necessary. But the church can indulge in such criticism only within the framework of a basic option for furthering life, even though such an option may entail ambiguity and strains of conflict. The church cannot operate on the basis of some vague general truth that allegedly enables it to pass better judgment on life.

This manner of bearing witness to life exemplifies a new ecclesial awareness. Its origins lie in the ecclesiology of Vatican II, but its radicalness goes beyond that insofar as the church has incarnated itself in the injustice and death on our continent and in our people's yearnings for liberation. Vatican II told us that ultimately the church is not meant to be a self-serving reality; that it is supposed to serve the world; that it is to bear witness, not to itself, but to something distinct from, and greater than, itself.

This has become quite evident in Latin America, where the church is not bearing witness to itself. Indeed it is not even bearing witness to "Jesus" or "God." It would be more correct to say that it is bearing witness to Jesus as he is the Word of Life, and to God as he is the God of the kingdom and of life.

Something profound is involved here, and we are now beginning to see the first consequences of it all. Indeed it could shape the future of the church, and indirectly that of the whole Latin American continent. The church is moving away from itself, and is even apparently moving away from a certain notion of Christ—absolutized as a person and separated from the Word of Life—and away from a certain notion of God—formally absolutized as the ultimate reality and separated from the mediation of the kingdom. But by so doing the church is recovering its most profound identity and its faith in Christ and the true God.

This work of recovery is being done on the most basic, primary levels, but that does not make them any less theological. The church is theologically recovering the characteristics of Jesus as he faced up to the primary needs of human beings. For Jesus, it should be noted, had pity on the crowd (Mark 6:34), asked his disciples to feed them (Mark 6:37), asked his Father for our daily bread (Matt. 6:11; Luke 11:3), and healed the sick. The church is also recovering the logic used by Jesus in his controversies (Mark 2:1–3:6, for example), his work of unmasking hypocrisy (Mark 7:1–23), and his denunciations (Luke 6: 24–26; 11: 37–53)—all part of his effort to defend the life of the poor and to fight against injustice. And the church is recovering the significance of the meals in which Jesus participated; they were signs of the fullness of personal, social, and transcendent life, but they operated by way of the basic, primary sign of life. This does not entail any reductionism in the following of Jesus. It is merely a way of concentrating on that which gives foundation and direction to our following of him.[7]

This is also a way of recovering that which gives foundation and direction to faith in the mystery of God. As Paul tells us (Rom. 1: 18–22), those who shackle truth with injustice or do violence to the truth of created things by their lies cannot know God. Their minds are darkened, and they prevent creatures from serving as sacraments of the Creator. By contrast, God can be known by those who respect the deeper truth of created things and allow reality to manifest itself as it really is. The church is not manipulating God when it shows respect for the reality of Latin America, when it does not manipulate the reality of anti-life on our continent, and when it does not turn a deaf ear to the people's cry for life and liberation. Instead it is letting God be revealed through a reality that is not falsely manipulated; it is letting God be God. So the church can then make its first great act of faith in a God of life and justice.[8]

Now I can briefly sum up what I have called the objective witness of the church. The church is bearing witness on behalf of life. Given the real conditions existing on our continent, this life must be historically fleshed out in terms of its basic economic, social, and political levels. And the church's witness must be fleshed out historically as a struggle to win through to those basic levels and to oppose the injustice that crushes them. This line of testimony, which in itself does not exhaust the fullness of life, is an integral and fundamental part of the witness that the church is obliged to bear to a God of life. It is a precondition for any faith in God to exist. And it seems to me that this line of testimony is becoming an irreversible one for many ecclesial groups.

THE SUBJECTIVE WITNESS OF THE CHURCH
IN PERSECUTION LEADING TO MARTYRDOM

Here I want to discuss what I have called the subjective aspect of the church's witness in its objective promotion of a life of justice. This subjective witness is nothing else but the holiness of the church. However, I am not interested in analyzing holiness in the abstract, as if we already knew what holiness is prior to objective witness. Instead I am interested in analyzing the type of holiness, the attitudes and Christian virtues, which are generated in the process described above. To put it more concretely, I want to show that when the church does bear the aforementioned kind of objective witness, then the historical result is the kind of holiness that the New Testament regards as the very epitome of holiness, i.e., giving up one's life for others as the highest proof of love.

Little need be said here about the fact that the church has been persecuted and has produced martyrs in trying to bear witness on behalf of life. Thousands of peasants, workers, catechists, and intellectuals have suffered persecution and death. More novel and newsworthy is the fact that hundreds of priests, religious, and bishops have been insulted, threatened, attacked, tortured, expelled, and killed.[9] My aim here is to offer a theological analysis of persecution and martyrdom. I propose to present persecution and martyrdom as the most typical and perfect form of holiness for the church precisely because it entails bearing witness on behalf of a just life.

Vatican II accords importance to witness as a way of living that calls attention to faith and spiritual values amid the prevailing materialism. The novel feature in its statements is the stress it lays on the fact that lay people, too, must bear witness in the world. However, Vatican II does not offer any theological analysis of the importance of persecution and martyrdom; it merely makes some general remarks about them. It tells us that persecution of the church is part of its mission (*Lumen gentium*, no. 8). When it does touch upon history, it tends to think of persecution as it has occurred in mission lands (*Ad gentes*, no. 42) or in lands where religious liberty does not exist (*Apostolicam actuositatem*, no. 17). It makes only vague references to the excellence of martyrdom (*Lumen gentium*, no. 42) and the history of martyrs (*Dignitatis humanae*, no. 11).

Thus Vatican II did not devote any special theological reflection to the realities of persecution and martyrdom. Nor did it relate them historically to the church's witness, which was spelled out in different terms as far as the present day is concerned. Certainly no thought was given to the possibility that these realities might be widespread in traditionally Catholic countries such as those of Latin America.

Neither *Evangelii nuntiandi* nor Medellín placed any stress on persecution and martyrdom either. They both re-emphasize the need for subjective witness in the evangelization process. Both, Medellín in particular, stress the need for poverty and the necessity of becoming poor in order to be in solidarity with the poor. But the essential nature of witness is not viewed in terms of persecution and martyrdom.

In noting this absence in such basic and fruitful ecclesial documents I am not trying to offer any anachronistic criticism of them. I am merely trying to show how novel persecution and martyrdom are in the Latin American church. That fact becomes patent in the Puebla documents. Despite the reticence of the early working draft, and efforts to suppress the topic at the conference meeting, the Puebla Final Document alludes several times to the situation of persecution in which the church now finds itself. Here as elsewhere reality forced itself on people's attention.

More important than the mere mention of the fact of persecution at Puebla is the incipient theology of persecution to be found in the Final Document. First, it reflects on the causes of persecution today that are rooted in a praxis designed to respond to "the cry of a suffering people who demand justice . . ." (no. 87). This response is embodied in "the church's prophetic denunciations and its concrete commitments to the poor" (no. 1138; see no. 92). Second, the Final Document goes on to suggest that facing persecution and death is the culminating stage in the witness of holiness performed in "the spirit of sacrifice and abnegation, . . . in the face of loneliness, isolation, incomprehension, and sometimes persecution and death" (no. 668).

Thus Puebla affirms that persecution is a widespread phenomenon and that it is the consummate form of bearing witness. But it also goes on to say that this persecution cannot be understood in terms of older models, e.g., the classic model of persecution in the early church, persecution in mission lands where other religions dominate, or persecution in lands that have an official ideology or that are officially atheistic. In other words, this persecution must be explained theologicallly in terms different from the traditional approaches.

The reason for this persecution does not lie directly on the level of the ideological superstructure but rather on the level of the infrastructure. The church is being persecuted when it defends the life of the poor masses, denounces the unjust crushing of life, and advocates the historical practice of justice. This is all the more obvious because those who are now persecuting the church often support their position "with a subjective profession of Christian faith" (no. 49). Persecution, then, cannot be understood in terms of the explicitly religious level; it must be viewed in terms of the truly human level. It must be understood as the response of the church's objective witness on behalf of a just life.

Puebla's incipient theology of persecution recovers one of the fundamental dimensions of New Testament ecclesiology, though it in turn may need to be theologically deepened and made more concretely historical. In the New Testament we find that de facto persecution of the church soon enters the picture, and that this persecution is quickly declared a de jure characteristic of the authentic church. The nascent church soon was subjected to persecution by Jewish and Roman authorities. Very quickly it formulated a declaration of principles regarding the necessity of persecution where Christians are concerned. In one of the earliest New Testament writings Paul states: "You yourselves know that this is to be our lot. For when we were with you, we told you beforehand that we were to suffer affliction; just as it has come to pass, and as you know" (1 Thess. 3:3-4). And when the early Christian communities attempt to express the underlying reason for this necessity in theological terms, they do so in terms of the destiny of Jesus (John 15:18,20; Matt. 10:24f.) and the prophets (Matt. 5:11f.).

The persecution of Jesus is to be understood theologically in terms of the Father's will. In historical terms, however, it has a clear cause. The cause is Jesus' activity of unmasking, opposing, denouncing, and anathematizing the powerful, the rich, the Pharisees, the scribes, and the ruling classes. Jesus fought against every type of oppressive and unjust power in order to defend and promote a just life for the poor. The fight is not merely a personal conflict between Jesus and other persons; it is not just a fight between "mediators." Instead it is a fight between different "mediations." On one side we have the defense of the just life of the poor; on the other side we have the defense of the unjust life of the powerful. This is very clearly typified in the death of Jesus. The *pax romana* and Jewish society, symbolized by the Temple, are unjust socio-political configurations that oppress the poor masses. Jesus is persecuted and condemned to death because he objectively attacked both in the name of the kingdom of God.

In the gospel narratives the persecution of Jesus is clearly brought out and presented on a religious level. But underlying the religious level is the truly human level. On the surface it seems that the religious orthodoxy of Jesus is what is at stake in the persecution of Jesus; but what is really at stake is the very *doxa* of God, which is manifested in the just life of the poor.[10]

These brief remarks are important if we wish to have an adequate theological conception of what church persecution means and hence what its practical consequences are. The starting point for understanding the import of church persecution is something other than the church itself. It is what we call the kingdom of God, the *doxa* of God as the life of human beings. Now the relationship of the church to the kingdom of God is twofold. First, the church is a servant, instrument of the kingdom; it is to ensure the kingdom's arrival. Second, the church, insofar as it gathers together many men and women, is an expression of the fact that the kingdom has or has not yet arrived. The concept of persecution must be elaborated in terms of this twofold relationship existing between the church and the kingdom of God.[11]

On this basis we can describe two ways in which the church is persecuted. First of all, the church can be persecuted *formally* in its explicit pastoral mission to serve justice and integral liberation. This happens when its bishops, priests, religious, catechists, authorized emissaries of the word, and members are threatened, harassed, or killed in attempting to carry out this mission. In this case persecution means rendering the church useless as a servant of the kingdom who is to help in its establishment and growth.

Note that in this context the church is not persecuted formally insofar as its church or religious character is concerned. The institutional nature of the church is not attacked, nor is there any explicit *odium fidei* ("hatred of the faith") involved. Instead the church is persecuted because it is a community that does in fact defend life and justice. In short, an *odium justitiae* ("hatred of justice") is what lies behind the persecution. In practice it is obvious that not all Christians, priests, or bishops are being persecuted; some, in fact, are praised, or used, or given privileges. Those being persecuted are those who have opted, like Jesus, for the kingdom—for the life and just existence of the poor. But it is equally obvious that behind this *odium justitiae* lies a real, if indirect, *odium fidei*.

Secondly, the church can also be persecuted in a *material* sense. It is no less real, and indeed it can be far more ferocious. In this case we must view the church as "world," that is to say, as a community of human beings whose real life is threatened and negated. In other words, the church is being persecuted when the people in real life are being oppressed and repressed. The point I am trying to make here is that when the people are structurally oppressed, and still more when they are repressed in their struggle for their lives, then it is not simply a matter of persecuting those who are furthering the kingdom of God; it comes down to annihilating the kingdom of God itself.

Some may rightly debate whether it is theoretically appropriate to apply the term "persecution of the church" to both situations, even granting their similarity. What cannot be denied, however, is the fact that the second type of persecution does exist and that it affects the very essence of the church. By virtue of its faith in the God of life, the church has to see itself as the guardian and custodian of life. If the life of human beings as creatures is being persecuted, then this is a direct persecution of God and an indirect persecution of the church that is grounded on faith in God. Even though it may not take the explicit form of persecution of Christians, the ongoing persecution of the life of human beings, of the kingdom of God, constitutes the greatest outrage against the church because its very reason for being is to realize this kingdom.

This theoretical specification of the theological concept of persecution is important, it seems to me, because of its practical implications for the church. For if the church understands persecution in these terms, then it will act in a different way, and ultimately in a more Christian way.

   a. If the two senses of persecution are accepted, then it is easier to understand the origin of formal persecution of the church. To the extent that the church makes its own the material persecution of the people, it will raise its voice in protest and hence be subjected to formal persecution itself. If it regards the oppression and repression of the people as persecution of itself, then it will not be able to ignore this persecution because it affects the church's very essence. Historically this explains why many churches have been formally persecuted while others are tolerated or even showered with praise. For the former have made the persecution of the people their own, while the latter have not felt affected as churches when the people were being persecuted.

   b. If the two senses of persecution are accepted, then the church will comprehend the essence of formal persecution of itself. It does not consist in depriving it of privileges, or even of certain civil rights. It consists in disabling or squelching it when it tries to defend life. As some bishops have already put it, we can say that persecution of the church and repression of the people are one and the same thing, though with different formalities. If the church accepts and understands the two, then it will continue to gain a dialectical appreciation of what persecution involves. When it experiences in its own flesh the persecution of its leaders and the reason for it, then it will understand more deeply what the oppression and repression of the people means. By the same token, when it comes to regard what is happening to the people as real persecution, then it will understand what formal persecution of the church itself means.

   c. This dialectic, lived out in reality, is one of the ways in which the church may learn some important things. Indeed it is an important and effective way. For persecution in the two senses described above concretizes truths that the church maintains in a general way. For example, the church learns who the poor really are. They are seen, no longer in their peaceful aspect as individuals, but rather in their reality as a group caught in a conflict situation that evokes repression. The church learns what it means to immerse itself in the world of the poor, to shoulder their cause and their destiny. It learns about the ex-centricity that constitutes its essence. For persecution comes precisely when the church goes out of itself, ceases to defend its own rights, and turns outward to defend the rights of the people. Persecution and repression help the church to recover its own essence. It is in that sense, not just in some purely eschatological sense, that it can consider itself fortunate and blessed in persecution.

   Persecution as described above can and indeed does generate a series of Christian attitudes and virtues that would be hard to come by otherwise. The most notable are choosing to become poor, solidarity with the poor, courage in suffering, and hoping against hope. All that is a very important part of the church's subjective witness. It culminates in what has traditionally been re-garded as the greatest form of witness: martyrdom.

Martyrdom, I would say, is the most perfect and most complete form of holiness. This is true, not only for general theological reasons, but also for current historical reasons. The latter make martyrdom a real, proximate pos-sibility and clearly reveal it to be the proof of greater love. I would also maintain that martyrdom, even though it is obviously not the destiny of all Christians, is theologically and historically the *analogatum princeps*, the touchstone, for trying to understand the holiness of the church and what I have called its subjective witness.[12]

In theory this has always been true in the church. The important thing in this case, as in others, is to spell out in historical terms what martyrdom means or should mean in current circumstances. The usual definition of mar-tyrdom is "the free and patient acceptance of death for the sake of the faith (including its moral teaching) in its totality or in relation to some concrete doctrine (the latter always being viewed in terms of the totality of the faith)."[13] This definition takes in the fundamental features of martyrdom: bearing witness to Christ—this is already indicated in the New Testament—and bearing witness with one's very life, as this was understood from the middle of the second century on. Implicitly it also includes another New Testament tradition: i.e., that giving one's life for others embodies the greatest love (see John 15:13; 1 John 3:16), the greatest holiness.

To see the death of numerous Christians in Latin America today as martyr-dom, we must historicize, give historical concreteness to, some of the ele-ments in the above definition of martyrdom. Three points need to be stressed:

1. The "profession of faith" inherent in martyrdom must be spelled out historically as a profession on behalf of a just life. In terms of the usual definition, then, it would be a matter of bearing witness with one's life to a fundamental moral teaching: the obligation to lead a just life. And this fun-damental moral teaching would be viewed in association with faith in the God of life.

2. Today we must give different historical expression to the "patient" as-pect of accepting death for the faith. The traditional view, also evident in the Working Draft for the Puebla Conference, sees it as death "not provoked by acts of physical or moral violence."[14] As I have already indicated above, per-secution and death normally come now precisely because people are strug-gling for justice; and all struggle objectively generates some type of violence. Today martyrdom cannot be understood without this element of "violence," just as the Christian life in general cannot be understood without it; but of course we will have to decide what type of violence is just.[15] Without the element of violence, however, we cannot possibly understand martyrdom. Indeed we cannot possibly understand the death of Jesus without it since Jesus used moral violence—objectively at least. It would be ironic if ques-

tions of mere terminology were to prevent us from talking about "martyr-dom" in Latin America today; for countless Christians are suffering the same fate as Jesus, and many of them at least are using the same type of violence that Jesus himself used.

3. Finally, and here we come to the most important element, we must give historical expression to the notion of dying out of love for others. We must concretize it as love for a whole people and for their liberation. It is quite clear, as Thomas Aquinas shows us,[16] that love is the formal element of mar-tyrdom, which accounts for its excellence. But there is no reason why this love need be exclusively directed toward one individual person or another rather than toward the people in general.

This reality of martyrdom is abundantly evident in Latin America. It takes many different forms, and I want to analyze two of them. First of all, there is the kind of martyrdom that more clearly reproduces the concrete features and characteristics of Jesus' own martyrdom. Many Christians, ranging from lay people to bishops, have denounced the sinfulness of the world, fought for the advance of justice, entered into conflict with those in power, done violence to them in the name of God, and been assassinated as a result. They have been killed because they loved their people, because they wanted a just life for the poor masses, out of fidelity to Jesus and God. To cite but three names, this is the kind of martyrdom suffered by Héctor Gallegos, Rutilio Grande, and Hermógenes López. On the basis of what was said above, they are undoubtedly martyrs. They are celebrated as such by the people and recognized as such by some members of the hierarchy, though there is no lack of people who raise doubts about them.

There is a second kind of martyrdom, of sacrificing one's life, that is some-what similar to the first type but also has distinctive characteristics of its own. I am referring to what we might call the martyrdom of the people qua peo-ple.[17] Consider the situation in many Latin American countries. Consider, for example, the still recent sufferings and struggles of the people of Nicaragua and the situation in El Salvador and Guatemala. Given that situation, it would be truly scandalous for us to overlook those deaths and the type of holiness they reflect, whether it be called martyrdom or not.

These processes of martyrdom might be sketchily described as follows. Vast masses of people are daily giving their lives on account of unjust struc-tures. Genocide and massacres are frequent among the people. Here we can talk about a "material" martyrdom, since in many cases the victims die without consciously realizing why they are dying or to what they are bearing witness by their death. But the basic, oppressive fact stands: countless num-bers of people are dying, are being massacred, daily.

In many instances these oppressed majorities are shouldering their situa-tion of misery and despoilment in a Christian spirit.[18] This leads them to take conscious note of their poverty and death, and to undertake a praxis of liber-ation. Their own privation and death is turned into love for others, into a real, effective desire to achieve a just life.

In seeking to be effective, this love for the poor masses tends to lead to the social organization of the people, to political organization, and in extreme cases even to politico-military organization. During this process many suffer despoilment and total abandonment, torture and murder. Sometimes it is for the mere fact of being organized as a people or demonstrating peaceably. When the conflict takes on the dimensions of an armed struggle, as it did recently in Nicaragua, people die by the hundreds of thousands.

These are the bare facts about events occurring repeatedly on our continent. Now we want to know what type of holiness they manifest. And we also want to know, though this is not the most important thing, whether this kind of dying can be called martyrdom and ecclesial witness.

With regard to the death of the common people, of the common people organizing themselves politically and socially, it is obvious that they are giving up their lives with great freedom. From historical experience they know that death will necessarily overtake the organized people. The likelihood is even greater here than in the case of the first type or model of martyrdom, since normally the common people are more defenseless than church leaders. And even though the sacrifice of their lives is not "patient," we cannot disregard the many massacres of defenseless populations or the inequality of forces in these social conflicts. Even if the imbalance does not turn the people into totally defenseless victims, it does force upon them the "historical patience" of a self-defense that is disproportionately meager. It is also clear that in general the deaths that occur are due to love for the common people and their attainment of real liberation.

These reflections must be extended even to the borderline-limit case of armed insurrection by the people. Two things must be distinguished here. The first is the ethical legitimacy of insurrection under the conditions provided for by moral law. The bishops of Nicaragua did in fact accord this legitimacy to their own concrete situation, and Bishop Romero spoke realistically about the possible legitimacy of an insurrection in El Salvador. The second thing is more directly of interest to us here, because it concerns the kind of holiness that might be displayed even in and through an armed insurrection. On the one hand it is clear that by its very nature an insurrection can produce dehumanizing, sinful forces, e.g., hatred, vengefulness, disproportionate violence, or sheer terrorism. If, on the other hand, people can get beyond the mad cravings typical of armed struggle, the struggle itself can give rise to a series of Christian values, e.g., fortitude, generosity, forgiveness, and magnanimity in victory. Thus it is very possible that armed struggle itself, when it is inevitable and just, can be a vehicle of holiness; life sacrificed in it can also be regarded as witness to love in fuller measure. Thomas Aquinas, at least, saw no difficulty in regarding the death of a soldier as potential martyrdom because "the good of the commonwealth is the highest of human goods," and "any human good can be a reason for martyrdom insofar as it is referred to God."[19]

On the theoretical level it is a moot question whether the deaths of the people, forced upon them historically as they are trying to organize, constitute martyrdom or not. In the last analysis only God can judge where the greatest measure of love exists. My reflections are not meant to disregard the failings and sins of these Christians. I am not trying to idealize them in every respect, nor am I saying that every Christian who fights for the people possesses "all" the Christian virtues. I simply do not want to ignore the pervasive and surprising fact that many Christians are freely giving up their lives so that the people may live. They are doing so with a generosity that compels them to abandon everything, to face persecution bravely, and to endure cruel torture and death. We cannot ignore the fact that here we have one type of that full measure of love mentioned by the gospel message, even though each individual case may contain failings and weaknesses. At bottom I am trying not to ignore the greater thing, even though we may rightfully criticize lesser failings.

Now if we bring together the two models, the two ways of giving up one's life for others, then the church's situation of martyrdom in Latin America is strikingly similar to its situation in the first three centuries of its history. It is so both in terms of its dimensions and its novelty. On the level of pure theological theory we could go on debating whether what we have here is martyrdom in the strict sense or not. We might be more conceptually correct if we spoke about the "analogy of martyrdom." But none of that should allow us to ignore the pervasive situation. Nor can we overlook the important fact that various Christian communities, and sometimes the church hierarchy itself, do regard those who have given up their lives in countless ways to ensure the life of the people as martyrs and true Christians. Without going into lengthy theological expositions, the bishops of Nicaragua recognized and acknowledged the Christian value of the blood spilled in Nicaragua:

> Our people fought heroically to defend their right to live with dignity, in peace and justice. This was the deeper significance of their action undertaken against a regime that was violating and repressing human rights on the personal and social level. . . . We assume the underlying motivation for this fight on behalf of justice and life.
>
> The blood of those who gave their lives in this prolonged struggle . . . signifies the unleashing of new forces in the construction of a new Nicaragua.
>
> The hopes of this revolution rest first and foremost on the young people of Nicaragua. They have lavishly displayed a generosity and courage that has astounded the world. And they now will be the chief architects of the new "civilization of love" (see Puebla Final Document, no. 1188) that we are seeking to fashion.

This kind of martyrial holiness, the subjective witness of the church, is related to its objective witness. Analyzing this relationship is not merely a conceptual or academic exercise, it seems to me. Indeed I think that exploring the relationship between believing in life and giving one's life is the way to go deeper into the essence and practice of the Christian faith.

a. Historically it is clear that the witness of martyrdom is a consequence of objective witness on behalf of life. Only if we realize that witnessing to God and Jesus must be witness on behalf of life can we appreciate the necessity of persecution and martyrdom. To put it more concretely, only when we have witness on behalf of the primary levels of life in a world of injustice do persecution and martyrdom become explicable. In other regions of the world there will be other kinds of injustice, other violations of human rights. But when they have to do with the primary levels of life, then the defense of life provokes persecution and martyrdom. It is the defense of life that forces the church's witness of holiness to take such a radical form, not just in isolated cases but in general.

b. Theologically the relationship between the object of faith, God, and the way to approach God appears more clearly. Even though it might seem to be a transcendental, a priori question, and hence an academic one, there is good reason to ask what objective content of faith could require giving up even one's life. The formal answer is easy: the will of God. Nothing created, including one's own life, can be an obstacle to the fulfillment of God's will. But we do well to ask ourselves what exactly is to be found in God's will that prevents such a demand from being arbitrary. If giving up one's life is something ultimate in the subject, we must ask ourselves what exactly is ultimate in the will of God that makes such a sacrifice credible and comprehensible. I say "credible" and "comprehensible" since words fail us here.

In line with everything I have said so far, I would suggest that the ultimate factor in the will of God is the life of human beings—more concretely, a just life for human beings. It is this ultimate which, precisely because it is ultimate, gives credibility and reasonableness to the ultimateness demanded in the witness of martyrdom. And, by the same token, dying so that others may have life is a profound experiencing of God, of the fact that life is something absolutely ultimate. In giving up one's life so that others may live, one affirms *in actu* the God of life.

Of course there is a paradox here. A person gives up his or her life so that others may have life. This paradox is real because creation and history are shot through with sin, which produces anti-life. In a sinless creation it would not be necessary to give up one's life for the life of others. But in the real creation the sin of anti-life can only be overcome by letting oneself be overcome by it at first. Since the experience of God, too, takes in the experience of sin, giving up one's own life is the way to profess faith in the God of life.

On the purely notional level there may well be nothing more to say. Nor can we search for some rational synthesis that would unify the ultimateness of the God of life and the ultimateness of giving up one's life. The experience is more in the nature of negative theology. In martyrdom, as in all dying, there is a non-knowing. Some quota of non-knowing is a necessary mediation so that the mystery of God may be maintained. But in and through this supreme form of non-knowing there is manifested the deeper knowledge of the supremacy of life. Witness is borne to it in practice, even though it may not be fully grasped conceptually.

Historically I think that this is the way in which the two aspects of faith—*fides quae creditur* and *fides qua creditur*—are related to each other. The content of faith is not simply "God," nor does the act of faith consist simply of the human being's "surrender" to God. "God" and "surrender" are mutually concretized and clarified from within, not just through formal, abstract concepts, when we know we are dealing with a God who wants a just life for human beings and when we are talking about a total self-surrender so that such a just life might be.

c. Salvifically we see the mysterious relationship between sacrificing one's own life and human beings having life in full measure. As I indicated earlier, the relationship is mysterious because we cannot prove a priori that life will ensue from martyrdom. At this level our observation is ambiguous. But within the mystery of faith we recover the efficacy of martyrdom as something salvific. We see it, not just as an expression of subjective holiness, but as something productive of human life. We recover the mystery of the Servant of Yahweh and of Jesus' cross.

In the last analysis the subjective witness of martyrdom is in the service of historical salvation. It is not a matter of choosing suffering for suffering's sake. It is not that suffering in itself is good in some way, or that sacrifice is the first and most essential thing in trying to gain access to God. The witness here is that of the Servant of Yahweh, whose direct aim is historical liberation (Isa. 42:4) and whose cursed destiny makes many righteous (Isa. 53:11). This mystery of the suffering servant is being lived all the more intensely in Latin America because it is the whole people who are seeking liberation and sharing in the cursed fate of the Servant of Yahweh. Or, to put it in christological terms, it is the whole people who are offering a historical body to Jesus so that in it may be completed what is lacking in his sufferings (Col. 1:24).[20] Because persecution and martyrdom are being lived in the spirit of the suffering servant, the hope and struggle for liberation are being maintained. Hence, even in historical terms, the persecution and martyrdom are salvific.

The church's witness of martyrdom derives from a primordial option for life, justice, and liberation. It accepts the historical inevitability of suffering overtaking this witness; and, accepting it with the same faith as the Servant of Yahweh, it believes that this witness is salvific and effective. Here again we cannot add a rational postscript. The important thing is to realize that this is what is happening to the church, and that the church is growing as church because of it. Its historical response to the historical situation of our continent is enabling it to deepen and unify its faith in the God of life and the giving up of its life in imitation of the suffering servant. So its practice and hope are not languishing.

WITNESS TO LIFE IN ALL ITS FULLNESS:
THE CHRISTIANIZATION OF THE HUMAN

In talking about martyrdom I have already indicated the central nucleus, if not the full measure, of the church's witness. Now I should like to offer some reflections on the objective witness of the church on behalf of the fullness of life. These reflections are important if we are to be faithful to God, who is not only the creator and liberator but also the perfecter who grants completion and fulfillment. They are also important for understanding what I have already said about witness to a just life on the basic levels as a moment within the overall witness of the church, and for answering the often self-serving accusation that the church is reducing its activity to nothing more than the sociopolitical realm.

As a basic thesis, I would say that the service of the church on behalf of the fullness of life consists in the ongoing humanization of the human realm at every level and in every situation. The presupposition behind this assertion is that the human realm is always capable of growth and deepening. And the positive reason for this assertion lies in the fact that the Christian faith is capable of humanizing, in its own specific way that may be called "christianization."

The human realm to be christianized unfolds on three levels: (1) on the historical level, which takes in the basic fact that the human being is a material and spiritual being, a personal and social being, partly the product of history and partly a positive shaper of history; (2) on the transcendental level, which takes in the fact that the human being is referred to something prior and greater than itself, in whom it finds its fulfillment; and (3) on the symbolic or liturgical level, which takes in the fact that the human being expresses the inner depths of the historical realm and, in Christian terms, does so from the standpoint and for the sake of the transcendent.

To a certain extent these three levels are independent and relatively autonomous. They correspond to different areas of human life and so the humanization of one level—in a conscious and explicit form at least—does not automatically ensue from the realization of another level. This has a practical consequence for the witness to life in its fullness that the church is supposed to provide. It means that it must explicitly cultivate each of the three levels.

On the other hand the three levels are interrelated as well. This follows, not just from some a priori transcendental anthropology, but also from the Christian understanding of the human being and God. In the concrete, then, this means that even the proclamation of the fullness of transcendent life is related to witness to the fullness of historical life.

The basic, general conclusion from this first assertion is that the church has an obligation to humanize *all* the levels of the historical realm, and to do so in *any and every* historical situation. In so doing, it will also be bearing witness to the fullness of transcendent life that is celebrated and anticipated in the liturgy.

In order to appreciate what is being positively affirmed here, let us first consider the negative side. In other words, let us consider the temptation facing the church not to act in this way. The first manifestation of this temptation would be for the church to concentrate on the liturgical and transcendent levels in expressing its witness on behalf of the fullness of life. It would abandon the historical level, as if the other levels were more typically its own. This might happen for theoretical reasons stemming from an unsound theology, or for very concrete, practical reasons. For example, other ideologies purporting to "humanize" the historical realm might be in competition with the church, and it might not know what to do in that situation. The mistake would be in seeking to directly tackle the transcendent fulfillment independently of the "less complete" historical fulfillment. It would be a temptation, not just a mistake, because in so doing the church would be subtly abandoning faith in the God of life as I have already described it.

The temptation can also occur even when the church admits that it must bear witness to the fullness of life on the historical level. In this case it might make a distinction between certain historical areas that are suitable for fulfillment and others that are not. The former might be the spiritual and moral areas, for example; the latter might be the material, economic, and social levels. Or the church might say that in certain situations it can promote the fullness of historical life whereas in others it cannot. A peaceful social context or a situation of formal democracy might be regarded as acceptable, for example, whereas a conflict-ridden situation or a socialist society might not.

The mistake here is not in saying that certain situations and levels (e.g., the level of basic needs or conflict-ridden situations) intrinsically need to be surpassed and raised to "better" levels. The mistake would be in abandoning those levels as untypical ones for church witness or in considering the church's activity on those levels as transitory and provisional. At bottom it is the temptation, frequently evident in the church, of wanting to bear witness to the fullness of life "in itself" without being willing to go through the prior levels that should be fulfilled in turn and that make it historically possible to gain access to more fully human levels.

In positive terms the church is obliged to christianize what I have called the historical level. This means that it must humanize the structures in which human beings live as well as the human beings who make those structures, who are changed in the process, and who are to some extent shaped by those structures in turn.

In Christian terms this means that the church must humanize structures in the direction of the kingdom of God. It must try to ensure that they foster the satisfaction of primary needs, the basic equality of human beings, inter-human solidarity, and a fair sharing of power.

It must also humanize human beings themselves in the direction of the "new human being," to use the New Testament term. The ideal itself is quite familiar. New human beings are those wise enough to learn, to change, to undergo conversion, and to be honest with themselves. They are human beings whose values are those of the Sermon on the Mount. New human beings are clear of eye and pure of heart, a thirst for justice and willing to run the risks entailed. They prefer peace to unnecessary elements of strife. They are like Jesus, finding more joy in giving than receiving and prepared to offer the greatest proof of love. Generous in victory, new human beings are ready to forgive an enemy and offer still another chance to a foe. Finally, they are ready to celebrate life gratefully, for they believe in life and keep up hope.

These realities, though formulated in New Testament terms, are historical in themselves. There is no reason why the liturgical and transcendent level should surface explicitly in them. Yet herein lies the primary task of the church when it wishes to bear witness to the fullness of historical life. It is also evident that in themselves these realities, being historical, are limited; so they are not the fullness of life in the absolute sense. But these limited realities do bear within them the need for something "more," for an ever-increasing approximation to the ideal of the kingdom of God and the new human being. The witness of the church specifically consists in encouraging and furthering this "more" continually. The church must continue to go deeper into the historical order so that the latter may extend itself "more" in the desired direction.

The fullness of life to which the church is to bear witness should not consist right off in a fullness borrowed from the liturgical and transcendent level. Fullness is not achieved by mere quantitative addition, by adding something more of transcendence to the limited realm. At bottom that is the temptation already evident in the early history of the church and condemned in the Johannine and Pauline theologies. It is the temptation to be found in docetism, gnosticism, and enthusiasm, the temptation to look for salvation and fulfillment outside of history rather than by immersion in it.

The church must also bear witness to the fullness of historical life in every sort of situation. Depending on the kind of situation, of course, fullness will have to be understood analogously. But the church should not assert or hint that certain occasions are not favorable for its witness. It should not suggest that its witness is not suitable because the situation is one of obvious conflict, or because the current task is one of reconstruction in which the most basic levels of life take priority. I mention these two specific examples because they are topical today and because they pose a new challenge to the witness of the church.

Insofar as the first example is concerned, the church should humanize the two most important aspects of the situation: the emergence of profound human values and the emergence of serious conflicts, even armed conflicts. With respect to the first aspect, the church should promote the popular values that are emerging, e.g., consciousness-raising, organization, solidarity, the ethical dimensions of the people's struggles, and generosity in commitment. At the same time it must employ constructive criticism to rule out or minimize the anti-values that arise historically as negative by-products, e.g., disunity, excessive protagonism, vengeful tendencies, and the abuse of power.

With respect to the second aspect, the church must try to humanize the conflict itself when it becomes unavoidable and serious. This effort would include an overall ethical judgment about the conflict and an indication of where the fundamental truth in it lies. In extreme cases this would include a declaration about the legitimacy of an insurrection and reminders about the conditions surrounding a just war. The latter basically suggest that the result of the conflict should produce more rather than less life. Besides this basic judgment about the conflict, however, the church must try to humanize the conflict itself. The statement of Paul VI finds frequent confirmation in Latin America, i.e., that conflict itself "frequently finds its ultimate motivation in noble impulses for justice and solidarity."[21] In the process of humanization, then, the church has an obligation to see to it that these "noble impulses" are used as rationally as possible so that they may be turned into effective forces that are as humane as possible.

Without going into the complexities of all the various cases in Latin America, I want to suggest that these considerations lead us to a basic conclusion. It is that the church must bear witness to life even in situations of conflict, including serious conflict. It cannot act as if the situation is not suitable for its witness, hinting that it should wait for better times. Even in a situation of conflict, which is a human and historical reality, it must bear witness to life and try to ensure that a fuller measure of life comes from it. Here, I think, we have a new point which might be theoretically formulated in the following terms. In conflict situations the church's role is not just to pass judgment on the conflict and decide which side is right; its role is also to humanize the conflict from within so that life-fostering values are generated and more life results from the resolution of the conflict. Witness on behalf of the fullness of historical life must take on history as it is; such witness cannot be realized from outside history.

Now let me say a few words about the second example, or model, mentioned above: a situation of reconstruction. Here I am thinking of a situation of national reconstruction along anti-capitalist, socialist lines, such as the process now going on in Nicaragua. Here again the church should take the situation as it is, bearing witness to the fullness of historical life in and through the situation. To begin with, the church should be cognizant of the new historical context in which it is living, and it should make its novelty an object of profound theo-logical reflection. Understandably, the novel situation will create a certain amount of confusion and feelings of ignorance in church circles. But it is important to distinguish between a fruitful form of non-knowing and a paralyzing one. The latter could result from the fact that the revolution now occupies the place once held by the humanism advocated by the church. It could result from wondering how the church should operate in a new regime organized along socialist lines. Or it could result from the more immediate fact that the church was losing its importance as an institution.

But a highly fruitful form of non-knowing is equally possible. Put theologically, it would mean paying serious attention to the following question: What word is God voicing today about the history of Nicaragua? In this question there is a basic theological non-knowing imbedded, precisely because historical newness is involved. But it is a fruitful non-knowing because it forces the church to exercise judgment and discernment with regard to the questions that remain basic and fundamental for it: What sort of life is it supposed to bear witness to? How is it to bear this witness? How can and should it foster the fullness of life in this new situation?

In my opinion the church must bear witness to life by supporting structural changes on the economic, social, and political levels that will enhance life on the level of basic needs and on the level of power-sharing. It must also bear witness to life by encouraging the emerging human values that need to be carefully cultivated: solidarity, generosity, austerity, popular rejoicing, magnanimity in victory, the practice of reconciliation, and what the bishops have called revolutionary creativity. By doing all this the church will be bearing witness to the fullness of historical life.

I have been talking about the church's way of bearing witness to the fullness of historical life. But even though it is aimed at the historical level, this form of testimony is still carried out within the framework of the church's particular identity and specificity. It is carried out, in other words, within the context of the Christian faith. That is why I referred to this process of humanizing the historical realm as christianization. For it dovetails objectively with the values of the Christian faith, even though these values are not made explicit as Christian ones.

To humanize fully, however, the church believes that it must also bear witness to the fullness of life on the transcendent and liturgical level. Where the church itself is concerned, this is obviously an obligation; it offers it to others for their free acceptance. On the transcendent level the church offers people the explicit cultivation of faith in an eschatological life where God will be all in all. And it offers faith in Jesus. He is already the first fruit of the new creation, and the following of Jesus brings us to it.

On the liturgical level the church offers us the celebration of historical life, but with the depth that the church's transcendent faith confers on this life. For the church believes that the Word of God consistently discloses the inner depths of the human realm and points out how the human realm can become more human.

The church believes in the necessity and importance of historical life for the celebration of its liturgy and the formulation of its transcendent faith. Let us not forget that in the last analysis such realities as the "resurrection," the "new heaven," and the "new earth," are described as fulfillments of the historical realm. And let us not forget that it is only by "incarnation," by assuming the flesh of history, that we can share in the fullness of divine filiation.

By the same token, however, the church believes that we are not alienated from history by the explicit nurturing of transcendent faith and its celebration in the liturgy, or by the explicit remembrance of Jesus and the celebration of his perilous legacy. It believes quite the contrary, in fact. It feels that they are a spur, goading us on to fuller incarnation in history and to greater pursuit of historical fullness. In its transcendent faith the church finds a strong inducement to transfigure history and also the basic direction such transfiguration should take. So witness to the fullness of life is just as necessary for the church on the level of faith. Why? Because it must be faithful to its own essential nature and because its explicit proclamation does have humanizing potential. The church believes in God and in Christ, and it also believes more humanization is available to human beings with them than without them.

Thus the church is obliged to maintain its own specificity in bearing witness to the fullness of life. At bottom, this means that it must unite the historical and the transcendent, and do so in its own distinctive way. Here I think we must bring in the "utopian" character of the church's witness and its obligation to enunciate utopian principles. In general, the church must maintain the utopian principle of the kingdom of God. That principle spurs us on to carry out historical projects on the one hand, but not to absolutize them on the other. It inspires us to be effective in the liberation process and at the same time to keep on humanizing the human beings who are the movers behind this process.

We call these principles "utopian" because they cannot be adequately historicized, and because it is sometimes difficult to flesh them out in history at all. Herein lies the note of transcendence that the church contributes through its specific witness. But these utopian principles can get something positive started in history. In any case the mission of the church is to make them historical. This is the historical contribution in the church's witness. Thus the witness of the church on behalf of the fullness of life comes down to helping history to move toward God's utopia and make it partially real in history.[22]

In conclusion, I would like to emphasize the serious obligation facing the church to incarnate itself in its own specific way in the new processes that are surfacing throughout our continent. Witness on behalf of life in all its fullness, humanization, and christianization are possible for the church only if it involves itself in these processes, however much novelty, ambiguousness, and conflict they may contain. Declaratory proclamations about humanization from the outside would constitute a formal negation of the Christian scheme of incarnation. Such an approach would mark a reversion to the early temptations of docetism and gnosticism. Today that temptation can be formulated in more attractive and sophisticated terms. Its proponents can appeal to the transcendent and distinctive aspects of the Christian faith, claiming that it cannot be equated or identified with any concrete historical achievement. But in the last analysis that is still gnosticism and docetism. It is salvation based on idea rather than on incarnation, on some alleged truth rather than on concrete historical love.

Given the present situation on our continent, I think the church has a serious responsibility to bear witness in the manner outlined above. There are various reasons why this is true: ethical reasons, ecclesial and institutional reasons, and theological reasons. In *ethical* terms the church, like any other social organism in Latin America, cannot ignore the task of humanizing and doing justice that faces our continent. In *ecclesial* and even *institutional* terms, humanization is a decisive element with regard to the credibility of the church and the possibility of its being accepted by non-ecclesial groups that are promoting projects of humanization. In *theological* terms, it is only through humanization carried out in the radical way described above that the church will be able to bear witness to God and to believe in God. It would be tragic if the church were not to take seriously this responsibility to engage in humanization. For then the church itself would languish, particularly in areas and processes of liberation; it would also deprive those processes of the potential contained in its faith.

In many areas of Latin America the church, it seems to me, is meeting or trying to meet this grave responsibility. Herein lies the most original and novel aspect of its witness. Needless to say, there are many limitations, fears, mistakes, and sins in the activity of the church and that of other, non-ecclesial groups with which it is associating itself. Nevertheless the church is coming to realize that its witness can be carried out only where the stakes at issue are the life or death, the humanization or dehumanization, of the men and women on our continent. It is coming to realize that its duty is to bear witness to life, to life in all its fullness, even though it may have to give up its own life in the process. And hence the church is being granted the grace to maintain and grow in its faith in God as well as its following of Jesus.

NOTES

1. More specifically the following reflections are based on the activity of ecclesial groups in El Salvador, Nicaragua, and Guatemala. Since this is a theoretical rather than a descriptive essay, I focus here on the basic lines of this Christian activity insofar as it furthers theological reflection. I do not analyze their concrete activities. The latter are much more complex, of course.

2. The apostles are to bear witness to Jesus' resurrection (see Luke 24:28; Acts 2:32; 3:15; 4:33; 5:32; 13:31; 22:15) and to his whole public life (see Luke 1:2; John 15:27; Acts 1:22; 10:39).

3. See Gustavo Gutiérrez, *La fuerza histórica de los pobres* (Lima: CEP, 1979).

4. Ibid., p. 357.

5. See the anthology entitled *La lucha de los dioses* (San José: Departamento Ecuménico de Investigaciones; Managua: Centro Antonio Valdivieso, 1980).

6. Many episcopal documents deal with these new problems. See, for example, *La justicia en el mundo*, the Peruvian bishops' Episcopal Commission for Social Action, 1971; *He oído los clamores de mi pueblo*, the bishops and religious superiors of Northeast Brazil, 1973; and the excellent commentary on both documents by J. Hernández Pico, "El episcopado católico latinoamericano ¿Esperanza de los oprimidos?" *ECA*, October–November 1977, pp. 749–70.

For more recent messages see: *Mensaje al pueblo nicaraguense*, June 2, 1979, and *Compromiso cristiano para una Nicaragua Nueva*, both by the Nicaraguan Episcopal Conference; also see the Sunday homilies of the late Archbishop Oscar Romero of San Salvador from January 20, 1980, on.

7. See Jon Sobrino, "La aparición del Dios de vida en Jesús de Nazaret," in *La lucha de los dioses*, pp. 84-100.

8. See Jon Sobrino, "Espiritualidad de Jesús y espiritualidad de la liberación. Reflexiones sistemáticas," *Diálogo* (Guatemala), 49 (1979), pp. 24-31.

9. Among the many documentary contributions see: *Persecución de la Iglesia en El Salvador* (San Salvador, 1977); *Signos de lucha y esperanza. Testimonios de la Iglesia en América Latina 1973-1978* (Lima: CEP, 1978); *El Salvador: Un pueblo perseguido* (Lima, 1980).

10. See Jon Sobrino, "La aparición del Dios de vida," pp. 100-08.

11. In my analysis here I talk about the church and Christians. Something similar should be said about those who are not explicitly Christian, who work anonymously but truly for the kingdom, and who make it present or not in their own reality.

12. On the new conception of the holiness of the church as one of its distinctive notes see: L. Boff, *Eclesiogénesis* (Santander, 1979); J. Sobrino, "Resurrección de una Iglesia popular," *Cruz y Resurrección* (Mexico City, 1978), pp. 110-16. The same line of thought can be seen in J. Moltmann, *Kirche in der Kraft des Geistes* (Munich, 1975), pp. 378-83.

13. That is how Karl Rahner formulates the usual concept of martyrdom from the standpoint of dogmatic and fundamental theology in *Lexicon für Theologie und Kirche,* VII, 136.

14. Note on martyrdom, no. 223.

15. For a theological treatment of violence see Ignacio Ellacuría, *Freedom Made Flesh: The Mission of Christ and His Church*, Eng. trans. (Maryknoll, N.Y.: Orbis Books, 1976), Part Three.

16. *Summa Theologica*, II/II, q. 124, a.2, ad 2.

17. My observation in note 11 is even more pertinent here.

18. See I. Ellacuría, "Las bienaventuranzas como la carta fundacional de la Iglesia de los pobres," *Iglesia de los pobres y organizaciones populares* (San Salvador, 1979), pp. 105-18.

19. *Summa Theologica*, II/II, q. 124, a.4, ad 3.

20. See I. Ellacuría, "El pueblo crucificado. Ensayo de soteriologia histórica," *Cruz y Resurrección*, pp. 49-82.

21. Address at the Development Day Mass, Bogotá, August 23, 1968; included in the Medellín Final Document on Peace, no. 19.

22. For the situation of the church in El Salvador I have worked out this idea in "La Iglesia en el actual proceso del país," *ECA*, October-November 1979, pp. 918-20.

15

The Church Born of the People in Nicaragua

Miguel d'Escoto, M.M. (Nicaragua)

This is a *theology* congress. Even though I feel very close to your experiences, to your work and reflections, I am not a professional theologian. I am a Christian and a priest who tries to live his faith in Christ the Liberator. We all know that it is impossible to live something without translating it to the level of reflection, to a certain type of reflection. Personally, just as with many of you, my experience has led me to live and reflect on this faith in the midst of a poor people who struggle for their liberation, and also among companions who, theoretically, do not consider themselves Christians, but who in practice have lived out the evangelical demands to their ultimate consequences.

I am not a professional theologian, but is theology not a reflection on the Christian life? If it is, then it is the task of every Christian. Someone once said that theology is too important to be left to the theologians alone! So I would like to speak to you from an experience, share it with you, reflect together with you.

This is a theological congress in the context of the *Third World*. The experience that I would like to share with you is from that perspective of a poor country, of people who, like many others of this Third World, have suffered a prolonged period of exploitation and despoliation, but who also have learned to fight and die for their liberation.

I would like to be able to translate something of the experience of the Nicaraguan people, who have given their life's blood in order to combat that death which is caused by hunger, sickness, and repression. We have lived, and are actually living, difficult moments, but ones that are also filled with hope; painful moments, but ones that are also a source of deep joy; moments of rupture, but ones that are also of reconstruction. I want to be very clear on one point: we are not dealing here with the experience of a few outstanding persons, but rather with the work of an entire people. It is this popular dimension, this collective dimension—the mass dimension—that marks the Nicaraguan experience.

The theme of this meeting is theological reflection on the church, that is, *ecclesiology.*

The experience of the Nicaraguan people is that of an exploited people who fight for their liberation, but also of a Christian people who, at the very heart of this struggle, live and sing (in the *misa campesina*) their faith in the God of the poor.

And I ask myself, is not this in fact the proclamation of the kingdom of God, the kingdom of love and justice and of life? Is not this to begin to build, by means of Christian communities, a church that is a sign of the presence of this kingdom in history?

It appears to me that here we have an orientation for an ecclesiology that does not limit itself to saying what the church of Jesus Christ should be, but rather is the result of reflection on that which the church is actually doing in history. It is thus not an abstract and ingenuous "should be," but a demanding and realistic "this is."

FROM THE EXPERIENCE OF A PEOPLE

It is impossible to sum up in a few short phrases the richness of the life experience of an entire people, an experience marked by the special character of a process, a movement, a historical breakthrough. Nevertheless, permit me to underline a few points that seem to me to be interesting with respect to our topic.

A Pascal Joy

One of the most impressive characteristics of the Nicaraguan people is their joy in living: yesterday in the struggle, today in the reconstruction. This is not merely a subjective opinion. This joy is profoundly etched on the faces of the people. It expresses itself in song, and especially in the energy to put a country totally ravaged by tyranny back on its feet again. It is not a superficial joy, since it is the fruit of having passed through suffering and death. It is also the fruit of the awareness that all this suffering and pain, and death, products of an unjust social system, of exploitation and repression, have begun to be conquered.

This joy manifests a hope that permits us to look straight in the eyes of the future. Only the oppressors have a past to defend; thus they kill, trying to hold back the process of history. The poor alone have a future. The rich shall be sent away empty-handed; the hands of the poor contain history.

The church, the assembly of Jesus Christ, cannot turn its back on this joy of the poor of Latin America. Further, the church should be nourished by this joy and vibrate with this joyful people.

This is more exacting than may appear at first sight. How many times has the church been impeded from recognizing the subversive joy of a people who struggle for their dignity because of its complicity with the oppressor! This church, all the same, professes its hope in the resurrection, in a life that conquers death and confounds those who sow death. How many times in these past years the church has kept a safe distance from the forces of liberation of the oppressed, has not known how to share with them their struggles and their hopes!

We might ask ourselves if the church, when it acts like this, is not really denying itself as the church of Christ present in the poor of this world. It thus lives, or perhaps dies, at the margin of the gospel that it should announce, and that at the same is its judge.

But we also know that all over the continent communities of Christians are multiplying in the struggle and are celebrating—starting from the joy of the poor—the passage from death to life. Many Nicaraguan Christians have learned that one cannot really believe without fighting for justice. Thus there is constantly being born a church that rises up from its faith and hope in the poor. You are here reflecting on these experiences and being enriched by this hope.

Forgers of History

Throughout its history the poor of Nicaragua, like the people of Latin America, have been robbed not only of the fruit of their work, but also of their lives, their freedom, and their homeland. But in this history we also find important breaks, ruptures events in which the oppressed reveal themselves and demand their rights. In Nicaragua nothing better expresses this protest than the example of the extraordinary figure of the General of Free People: Augusto César Sandino. Sandino and others, such as Carlos Fonseca Amador, opened deep furrows in the history of my country and sowed a seed that the tyranny of Somoza tried to destroy. However, this was buried in fertile soil, nourished by the blood of the poor. It took root and began to live. It developed, and today we are reaping the fruits. An entire people repeated the cry of its vanguard, the Sandinista Front: "Free Homeland or Death." They achieved this freedom by giving their lives. For the first time in history this people felt that it was the master of its own destiny, not because anyone conceded it, but because they knew how to win it for themselves, with gun in hand and with hope in the heart.

The struggle to assume their own history is one of the characteristic traits of the experience of the Nicaraguan people, and also of the poor of our continent. It is a prolonged struggle with premature sunsets at times, but also with radiant sunrises that call us to work in full daylight.

This people, forging its own history, challenges and enriches our way of understanding the church. The People of God will henceforth be constituted by men and women ever more conscious of their right to life, to freedom, and to justice.

If the proclamation of the Christian message does not take into account this increasing maturity, it will be reduced to the restricted area of a private concern. It will remain on the fringe of history. Let us speak frankly. The church does not really feel comfortable in relation to these efforts to achieve national liberation. Its ties to the world against which the poor are struggling are stronger than it thinks. This makes the church feel out of place, foreign, vacillating and at times even hostile to such historical processes. We are aware of concrete cases in which the church, and here I speak of those who represent it in an institutional way, has had and continues to have the same reflexes as the dominant sectors of society and has contributed to the defense of their interests. There are cases in which the church echoes all the fears and lamentations of the bourgeoisie as their privileges are affected by the victorious popular processes. The bourgeoisie considers these privileges as rights, as if one could have the right to exploit, to cheat, and to despoil the poor.

I do not think we are confronted simply with errors in the analysis of the real situation or with personal limitations, but rather with a way of understanding the church and its mission in history in which the poor, their lives, their struggles, and their aspirations are not present. In order that this presence become a reality, the church has to set out toward a country that is still foreign to it: the homeland of the poor. To accept this challenge is to be converted to the tremendous masses of the poor and oppressed of the world, to those with whom we want to organically unite our reflection on the faith in Jesus Christ the Liberator.

Puebla has called the Latin American church to this type of conversion, and if it has been able to do this, it is because the process has already begun on the continent. There are, in effect, an ever-increasing number of Christians and Christian communities that have tied their fate to that of the popular sectors of society, that have broken their ties with the Old Human Being and have set out on untrodden paths toward the creation of the New Human Being.

Here we have put our finger in an open wound. Basically we are dealing with a question of spirituality. The term is a classical one and perhaps poorly understood at the present time. To speak of spirituality is to speak of a way of being Christian. It is necessary to understand that fidelity to the gospel today passes through the rupture with our familiar world in which privileges for the church are gained at the cost of forgetting the exigencies of the gospel. We cannot, as Christians who announce and constitute the kingdom, not rebel against this situation. But the rupture is only one side of the coin; the other is the audacious and valiant self-giving to the cause of the people, with the confidence that it is the cause of Christ.

Solidarity in the Struggle

The oppressors try to divide and fragment the poor, to make them believe that they are merely individuals, isolated from one another, and not a social class, a culture, a race. They try to make them believe that each one can and should overcome their situation of poverty individually, even by stepping on their brothers and sisters of the same class or race. The individualist mentality is the hallmark of the dominant class, or the bourgeoisie. It does not recognize friends; it only wants tactical allies in order to maintain its privileges.

One of the most impressive aspects of the Nicaraguan revolution is the increase of solidarity and unity—unity of the people; unity of the workers, campesinos, village people, and students; unity of the masses forged by the "People United Movement"; unity of the people with the vanguard, the FSLN; unity of all the tendencies within the front; unity of the people whose power was able to touch even important sectors of the anti-Somoza bourgeoisie; unity that integrated large groups of young people into the mainstream of the popular movement; unity in which women played an exceptional part; unity that generated international solidarity and that made even the OAS and regional groups on the continent tremble. Nicaragua was able, at the peak moment of the struggle, to unify the majority of the Latin American countries against Somoza, and in this way isolate North American imperialism.

This unity and solidarity constituted the dynamic force of the revolutionary process that has made a people of Nicaraguans; a people who have decided to make themselves present in history, in that very history from which the oppressor tried to make them disappear; people proud of their own values.

This solidarity is at the same time a cause and effect of the revolutionary struggle. We are also witnessing it as a reality of the oppressed peoples of the Third World and throughout the Latin American continent. We have lived it in the war; we continue living it in the reconstruction.

The generosity in the struggle, the blood shed by this exploited and Christian people, have made possible a qualitative leap in humanness. This advance was made in concrete action that cannot produce a preaching bereft of concrete gestures of solidarity.

The church cannot be the assembly called together by the word of Jesus if it does not possess, like the Samaritan on the road to Jericho, the courage to leave the beaten path, to care for the agonizing, the people who are robbed and beaten. This will be the occasion for the church to comprehend that only by drawing closer to and by entering into solidarity with the poor and the oppressed will it make itself their neighbor, and make neighbors of these people.

Here I would like to cite the text of the important pastoral letter of the Nicaraguan bishops, written in November 1979:

Today we are in our country facing an exceptional occasion to witness and announce the kingdom of God. It would be a serious act of infidelity to let this moment pass by, because of fears and anxieties, because of the insecurity that every radical process of social change creates in some people, because of the defense of small or large individual interests— this demanding moment in which this preferential option for the poor can be concretized. It is precisely this option which Pope John Paul II and Puebla call us to make.

And they add an evident consequence of this for the life of the church:

This option has presupposed the giving up of old ways of thinking and acting, the profound conversion of all of us as church. In effect, the day that the church fails to present itself to the world as poor and as an ally of the poor, it will betray its divine founder and also the proclamation of the kingdom of God. Now more than ever before in the Nicaraguan situation, it is urgent to ratify convincingly this preferential option for the poor.

And so that there may be no mistake concerning which poor we are speaking about, the bishops affirm:

The poor about whom Jesus speaks, with whom he was always surrounded, are real, authentic, hungry, afflicted, oppressed poor people; they are all those not foreseen in the organization of society and who are rejected by it. It is from this solidarity with the poor that Jesus announced the love of the Father for every human being; it is from that starting point that he encountered suffering, persecution, and death.

To be a disciple of Jesus today is—as the Nicaraguan experience demonstrates and that of so many other peoples confirms—to face up to death in order to give life to those whom the exploiting system robs and kills.

SOME CONSEQUENCES

By sketching these traits—the joy of a people, forgers of their history, solidarity in the struggle—I have tried to record simply that it is not possible to separate the building of church from the making of history, a history of freedom and justice. Such a separation would imply an inability to see the relation between church and kingdom, between the poor and the God of the Bible.

By the same token, these traits are not only historical realities that we can regard with interest and sympathy. They are also ecclesiological questions. They are challenges to build and to be the church. How in effect do we construct "the sign and instrument of the communion between God and human beings and human beings among themselves" without taking into account and denouncing all that destroys that communion? How can we be followers of Jesus without making our own the efforts of the poor to make this communion a historical reality.

To understand the kingdom of God and believe in the God of the kingdom means to live in solidarity with the poor and oppressed of this world. This is the practical and theoretical "locus" of an ecclesiology. In this relationship the church is reflected on and lived. The kingdom that it announces is made present in a history in which the poor fight for their most fundamental rights. The historical locus in which we meet Christ is in our insertion in the process of liberation.

But at the same time this kingdom-poor relation questions the church and judges its presence in the world. The church is at the service of Christ, who tells us that we will encounter him in our needy brothers and sisters. Therefore, for the church, to be born constantly from the poor and oppressed is to be born from what is deepest and most substantial in it—its faith in the Lord.

CONCLUSION

In the first place, I wanted to make a modest contribution, from the perspective of our revolutionary experience, to the construction of an ecclesiology that gives reason for the hope of the popular Christian communities. We want to discuss our experience and our reflection with you. Our revolutionary victory has helped us move forward, but this is not to say that we have the truth. We want our reflection to be the reflection of the entire Latin American church. We also want to benefit from your struggles and reflections. Let us not isolate Nicaragua from the liberation movements nor from the ecclesial reflection and renovation in Latin America and the Third World. We have something to give, and much to learn.

Our communion in liberation and our hope, lived and celebrated in a church born from the struggles of the people under the impulse of the Holy Spirit, must nevertheless be translated into concrete terms. We have defeated Somoza, but we have still not completely defeated "somozismo." Furthermore, the reconstruction of our homeland, destroyed by the forces of tyranny, remains as a challenge ahead of us. This is a gigantic task, even more difficult than winning the war. North American imperialism is just waiting for the chance to destroy us. We need the solidarity of all the Latin American peoples—economic and political solidarity, solidarity to combat the counter-revolution, solidarity to break the blockade and the isolation that they want to impose on us. We have complete confidence in the solidarity of the poor and the exploited, and we believe that the action of committed Christians will be decisive in the bringing about of this broad movement of continental solidarity. From these struggles, we Christians up and down the continent are proclaiming our faith and hope in the God who liberates. For us the celebration of this faith and this hope is not the result of inertia, the inertia of our religious formation. This celebration of the death and resurrection of Christ is of a permanent newness, and is nourished today by the generosity of those dead who never die, as we say in Nicaragua, because like Christ, they died out of love and for the liberation of the people.

The victory of July 19, 1979, is only the beginning. I want to make an appeal to all of you: that each one in his or her own place of struggle and all together at the continental level finish our process of liberation—today in Nicaragua and, sooner or later, in our great Latin American homeland!

Free Homeland or Death!

—Translated by the EATWOT staff

16

The Use of the Bible in Christian Communities of the Common People

Carlos Mesters (Brazil)

PRELIMINARY OBSERVATIONS

Limitations of This Report

The information I am going to pass along to you is limited for several reasons. First of all, I am going to talk to you only about Brazil because I am not that familiar with the rest of Latin America. Second, I am going to talk only about the Catholic church in Brazil because I know relatively little about other Christian churches. I am just now beginning to make an acquaintance with them. Third, my report is limited by the fact that there is this "opening-up" process now going on in Brazil. That may well force me to rethink a lot of the things I am going to say about the past twelve years or so in Brazil. Finally, my report is limited by my own eyesight. Even though I wear glasses and have good intentions, I find it hard to grasp certain sides of reality—the political side in particular. That may be due to the fact that when I got my education the social sciences and their findings were not a part of the picture.

The Importance of the Bible in Grassroots Christian Communities

The Bible is very important in the life and growth of grassroots communities. But its importance must be put in the right place. It's something like the motor of an automobile. Generally the motor is under the hood, out of sight. It is not the steering wheel. The history of the use of the Bible in grassroots communities is a bit like the history of car motors. Way back when the first cars came out, the motor was huge. It was quite obvious and made a lot of noise. It also wasted a lot of gasoline and left little room for passengers. Today the motors are getting smaller and smaller. They are more powerful,

197

but they are also quieter and better hidden. There's a lot more leg room and luggage room in the car. Much the same is true about the Bible and its function in the life of Christian communities. The Bible is supposed to start things off, to get them going; but it is not the steering wheel. You have to use it correctly. You can't expect it to do what it is not meant to do.

My Relative Optimism

Perhaps what I am going to say to you may seem a trifle optimistic. If so, it is something like the optimism of a farmer watching the grain surface above ground. A storm may come later and wipe out the whole crop. But there is room for optimism, and it's good to be optimistic.

INTRODUCING THE ISSUE: THREE BASIC SITUATIONS

First Situation

In Brazil there are many groups meeting to focus on the Bible. In this case the motivating occasion for the group is some pious exercise or special event: a feast day, a novena, a brotherhood week, or what have you. The people meet on the parish level. There is no real community context involved. The word of God is the only thing that brings them together. They want to reflect on God's word and put it into practice.

Second Situation

In Brazil some groups are meeting within a broader context. They are meeting on the level of the community and its life. I once went to give a course to the people in such a community. In the evening the people got together to organize the course and establish basic guidelines. In such groups you generally get questions such as these: "How do you explain the Apocalypse? What does the serpent stand for? What about the fight between David and Goliath?"

The questions, you see, are limited to the Bible as such. No hint of their own concerns, no hint of real-life problems, no hint of reality, no hint of problems dealing with economic, social, and political life. Even though they are meeting as a community, the real-life problems of the people are not brought up.

Third Situation

To introduce the third situation, I am going to tell you a typical story about my experience in this area. I was invited to give a course in Ceará, in northeast Brazil. The group was made up of about ninety farmers from the backlands and the riverbanks. Most of them couldn't read. In the evening we met to get things organized. They asked me about a dozen basic questions, but these are the ones I remember:

1. What about these community activities we are engaged in? Are they just the priest's idea? Are they communism? Or do they come from the word of God?

2. What about our fight for land? (Most of them had no land. But they had plenty of problems and fights on their hands.) What about our labor struggles and our attempts to learn something about politics? What does the word of God have to say about all that?

3. What about the gospel message? Does it have to do just with prayer, or is it something more than that?

4. The other day, in a place where there was a big fight going on between the landlord and his tenants, this priest came, said Mass, and explained the gospel in a way that made the landlord right. Then the local priest of the parish read the same gospel and explained it in a way that made the tenant farmers right. So who really is right?

5. The landlord gives catechism lessons that teach subservience and bondage. In our community we have a catechetics of liberation, and the landlord persecutes us for it. So how do we settle the matter and figure it all out? We want to know whether the Bible is on our side or not!

Here we have three basic situations. In the first situation the group involved comes together solely for the sake of discussing the Bible; the Bible is the only thing that unites them and they stick to it. In the second situation the people focus on the Bible, too, but they come together as a community. In the third situation we have a community of people meeting around the Bible who inject concrete reality and their own situation into the discussion. Their struggle as a people enters the picture. So we can formulate the following basic picture:

We find three elements in the common people's interpretation of the Bible: the Bible itself, the community, and reality (i.e., the real-life situation of the people and the surrounding world). With these three elements they seek to hear what the word of God is saying. And for them the word of God is not just the Bible. The word of God is within reality and it can be discovered there with the help of the Bible. When one of the three elements is missing, however, interpretation of the Bible makes no progress and enters into crisis. The Bible loses its function.

When the three elements are present and enter the process of interpretation, then you get the situation that I encountered when I gave a course in Ceará. The people asked me to tell them the stories of Abraham, Moses, Jeremiah, and Jesus. That is what I did. But in their group discussions and full meetings, the Bible disappeared. They hardly ever talked about the Bible. Instead they talked about real life and their concrete struggles. So at the nightly review the local priest asked them what they had learned that day. They quickly got to talking about real life. No one said anything about the Bible. Ye gods, I thought to myself, where did I go wrong? This is supposed to be a course on the Bible and all they talk about is real life. Should I feel upset and frustrated, or should I be satisfied? Well, I decided to take it easy and feel satisfied because the Bible had achieved its purpose. Like salt, it had disappeared into the pot and spiced the whole meal.

It's like what happens when you take a sponge and dip it in a little bowl of water. The water is soaked up and disappears inside the sponge. At the end of the nightly review the people were asked what they had learned from the biblical explanations. They squeezed the sponge a bit and let a few drops of water out. I could see that the sponge was filled with water. At the final ceremony for the week, which lasted four hours, they squeezed the sponge completely and everything inside came out. I realized that when the three elements are integrated—Bible, community, real-life situation—then the word of God becomes a reinforcement, a stimulus for hope and courage. Bit by bit it helps people to overcome their fears.

Conclusions

1. When the community takes shape on the basis of the real-life problems of the people, then the discovery of the Bible is an enormous reinforcement.

2. When the community takes shape only around the reading of the Bible, then it faces a crisis as soon as it must move on to social and political issues.

3. When the group closes itself up in the letter of the biblical text and does not bring in the life of the community or the reality of the people's struggles, then it has no future and will eventually die.

4. These three factors or situations characterize the use of the Bible by the common people and reveal the complexity involved. The three situations can be successive stages in a single ongoing process, or they can be antagonistic situations that obstruct and exclude each other. It all depends on how the process is conducted.

5. It doesn't matter much where you start. You can start with the Bible, or with the given community, or with the real-life situation of the people and their problems. The important thing is to do all you can to include all three factors.

SOME OBSTACLES AND HOW THE PEOPLE
ARE SURMOUNTING THEM

It is not always easy to integrate all three factors in the interpretation of the Bible. There are many obstacles along the way that the people are trying to surmount in various ways.

Many Don't Know How to Read

Many people don't know how to read, and the Bible is a book! Sometimes no one in the group knows how to read. They are inventing ways to get around this problem. They are using song and story, pictures and little plays. They are thus making up their own version of the "Bible of the poor." Thanks to songs, for example, many people who have never read the Bible know almost every story in it.

Slavish Literalism

Another obstacle is slavery to the letter or fundamentalism. This usually occurs when the Bible is read in dissociation from a real-life community and concrete situation. The circle closes and the letter becomes a source of further oppression rather than of liberation.

The Bible is ambiguous. It can be a force for liberation or a force for oppression. If it is treated like a finished monument that cannot be touched, that must be taken literally as it is, then it will be an oppressive force.

Three things can help to overcome this obstacle. The first is the good sense of the people. In one community composed of blacks and other farmers the people were reading the Old Testament text that forbade the eating of pork. The people raised the question: "What is God telling us today through this text?" Their conclusion was: "Through this text God today is ordering us to eat the flesh of pork." How did they arrive at such a contrary conclusion? They explained: "God is concerned first and foremost with life and health. In those times eating the flesh of pork was very dangerous to people's health. It was prohibited in God's name because people's lives had to be protected. Today we know how to take care of pork meat, and the only thing we have to feed our children are the piglets in our yards. So in this text God is bidding us to eat the flesh of pork."

A second thing of great importance in breaking through enslavement to the letter is the ongoing action of a local church that takes sides with the poor. The ongoing movement of the church in this direction is helping to ensure that questions focused exclusively on the letter of the biblical text gradually give way to others. Literalist questions are falling from the tree like dry leaves to make room for new buds. The larger complex of a local church that sides with the poor and joins their fight for justice is very important in correctly channelling the people's interpretation of the Bible.

The third thing has to do with various devices of a fairly simple kind. For example, we can show people that many of the things we talk about in words cannot be taken literally. Symbolism is an integral part of human language. In many instances the first step towards liberation comes for people when they realize that they need not always take the biblical text literally. They discover that "the letter kills, the Spirit gives life." This realization unlocks the lid and lets new creativity out.

The Conception of Time

Another problem or obstacle is the people's conception of time. Often folks will ask questions like these: "Did Abraham come before or after Jesus Christ? Did David live before or after Cabral discovered America? Was it Jesus Christ who created the world?" Such questions may seem to indicate a great deal of confusion to us, but I think not. Apart from a certain amount of ignorance about the content of the Bible, I don't think it is a matter of confusion at all. Instead it is an expression of their circular conception of time. In such a conception you don't know exactly what comes at the beginning and what comes at the end. A simple explanation will not suffice to change this view of time, because it is a cultural problem rather than a problem of mere ignorance. In their minds the people simply don't have a peg on which to hang a concept of linear time.

How do we help them to overcome this obstacle? How do we unroll the carpet of time in their consciousness? Perhaps the best way we can help is to help them discover their own ongoing journey in their lives today. We can help them to recover the memory of their own history, of struggles lost and forgotten. We can help them to begin to recount their own history. In Goiás a group of farmworkers was asked: "How did the Bible come about?" An old farmer gave this reply: "I know. It was something like this. Suppose fifty years from now someone asks how our community arose. The people will reply: In the beginning there was nothing here. . . ." Thanks to his own concrete journey in life, the old farmworker perceived that the Bible had arisen from narrative accounts, from stories people told to others about their history. He realized that the Bible was the collective memory that gave a people its identity.

Dependence on Informational Knowledge and the Learned Expert

You often hear people say something like this: "I don't know anything. You or Father should do the talking. You're the ones who know things. We folks don't know anything." In the past we members of the clergy expropriated the Bible and got a monopoly on its interpretation. We took the Bible out of the hands of the common people, locked it with a key, and then threw the key away. But the people have found the key and are beginning again to interpret the Bible. And they are using the only tool they have at hand: their own lives, experiences, and struggles.

Biblical exegetes, using their heads and their studies, can come fairly close to Abraham; but their feet are a long way from Abraham. The common people are very close to Abraham with their feet. They are living the same sort of situation. Their life-process is of the same nature and they can identify with him. When they read his history in the Bible, it becomes a mirror for them. They look in that mirror, see their own faces, and say: "We are Abraham!" In a real sense they are reading their own history, and this becomes a source of much inspiration and encouragement. One time a farmworker said this to me: "Now I get it. We are Abraham, and if he got there then we will too!" From the history of Abraham he and his people are drawing the motives for their courage today.

Now here is where the danger comes in. Some teacher or learned expert may come along. It might be a pastoral minister, a catechist, or an exegete. This expert may arrive with his or her more learned and sophisticated approach and once again expropriate the gains won by the people. Once again they grow silent and dependent in the presence of the teacher or expert. Our method is logical. It involves a reasoning process, a careful line of argument. We say it is scientific. When the people get together to interpret the Bible, they do not proceed by logical reasoning but by the association of ideas. One person says one thing; somebody else says another thing. We tend to think this approach has little value, but actually it is just as scientific as our approach! What approach do psychoanalysts use when they settle their patients into a chair or couch? They use the free association of ideas. And this method is actually better than our "logical" method. Our method is one for teaching information; the other is one for helping people to discover things themselves.

Lack of Tact on the Part of Pastoral Agents

Another obstacle that crops up at times is the lack of tact on the part of pastoral workers among the people. They are in a hurry and have no patience. They ride roughshod over some of the natural resistance that people have to our interpretations of the Bible. One time a nun went to give a course on the Old Testament. Halfway through she had to close down the course because no one was showing up. The people said: "Sister is destroying the Bible!" A certain priest offered an explanation of the Exodus. Many people never came back. "He is putting an end to miracles," they complained.

Meddling with the faith of the people is very serious business. You must have deep respect and a delicate touch. You must try to feel as they would and intuit their possible reaction to what you are going to say. The people should be allowed to grow from the soil of their own faith and their own character. They should not be dragged along by our aggressive questions.

Erudite Language

Another obstacle is erudite language, abstruse words. We talk a difficult idiom, and the language of translations is difficult. Today, thank God, various efforts are being made to translate the Bible into more popular terms. Nothing could be more desirable. People now feel that they are getting the point at least. The first and most basic requirement is that people talk in such a way that their listeners can understand them. It sounds simple enough, but often it is very hard to do.

Another important point is that we must not lose the poetry of the Bible. We must not reduce it to concepts. The Bible is full of poetry, and poetry is more than a matter of words. It is the whole way of seeing and grasping life.

From Confrontation to Practical Ecumenism

Another problem crops up on the grassroots level with "fundamentalist" groups. They head for people's homes with the Bible in their hands and make it clear that they have the only right answer. This leads to a defensive reaction and sectarian apologetics. It is hard to foster any ecumenism around the Bible in such an atmosphere.

In some areas, however, practical biblical ecumenism is growing from other starting points. Roman Catholics and Protestants are meeting each other and working together in labor unions, in fights for land ownership, and in other real-life struggles. Gradually other sectarian issues are taking a back seat to practical ecumenism.

CHARACTERISTICS OF THE PEOPLE'S INTERPRETATION OF THE BIBLE

In a sense we can say that the tabernacle of the church is to be found where the people come together around the word of God. That could be called the church's "holy of holies." Remember that no one was allowed to enter the holy of holies except the high priest, and he was allowed in only once a year! In this holy of holies no one is master—except God and the people. It is there that the Holy Spirit is at work; and where the Spirit is at work, there is freedom. The deepest and ultimate roots of the freedom sought by all are to be found there, in those small community groups where the people meet around the word of God. One song in Ceará has this line: "It is the tabernacle of the people. Don't anyone touch it!" Certain characteristics are surfacing in this tabernacle, and I should like to point them out here.

The things I am going to mention now are not fully developed and widespread. They are more like the first traces of dawn in the night sky. We are dipping our finger into the batter to savor how the cake will taste when it is baked and ready. The following characteristics are just beginning to surface here and there in the ongoing journey of various communities. I think they are very important.

The Scope of the Biblical Message

In the eyes of the common people the word of God, the gospel message, is much broader than just the text itself. The gospel message is a bit of everything: Bible, community, reality. For the common people the word of God is not just in the Bible; it is also in the community and in their real-life situation. The function of the Bible, read in a community context, is to help them to discover where God is calling them in the hubbub of real life. It is as if the word of God were hidden within history, within their struggles. When they discover it, it is big news. It's like a light flicking on in their brains. When one leper in Acre made this discovery, he exclaimed: "I have been raised from the dead!" He used the idea of resurrection to express the discovery he had made.

Theologians say that reality is a *locus theologicus*. The common people say: "God speaks, mixed into things." A tinker defined the church this way: "The church is us exchanging ideas with each other to discover the idea of the Holy Spirit in the people." If it hadn't come from Antonio Pascal, I would have said it came from St. Augustine. But it came from Antonio Pascal. It is us exchanging ideas with each other to discover the idea of the Holy Spirit in the people. Not in the church, in the people!

So you see, when they read the Bible, basically they are not trying to interpret the Bible; they are trying to interpret life with the help of the Bible. They are altering the whole business. They are shifting the axis of interpretation.

The Unity of Creation and Salvation

The common people are recovering the unity or oneness of creation and salvation, which is certainly true in the Bible itself. The Bible doesn't begin with Abraham. It begins with creation. Abraham is not called to form some separated group apart. Abraham is called to recover for all peoples the blessing lost by the sin of Adam. This is the oneness between life and faith, between transforming (political) activity and evangelization, that the people are concretely achieving in their praxis.

The Reappropriation of the Bible

The Bible was taken out of the people's hands. Now they are taking it back. They are expropriating the expropriators: "It is our book! It was written for us!" It had always been "Father's book," it seemed. Now it is the people's book again.

That gives them a new way of seeing, new eyes. They feel at home with the Bible and they begin to link it with their lives. So we get something very interesting. They are mixing life in with the Bible, and the Bible in with life. One helps them to interpret the other. And often the Bible is what starts them developing a more critical awareness of reality. They say, for example: "*We* are Abraham! *We* are in Egypt! *We* are in bondage! *We* are David!" With the biblical data they begin to reflect on their real-life situation. The process gradually prompts them to seek a more objective knowledge of reality and to look for a more suitable tool of analysis elsewhere. But it is often the word of God that starts them moving.

The rediscovery of the Bible as "our book" gives rise to a sense of commitment and a militancy that can overcome the world. Once they discover that God is with them in their struggles, no one can really stop them or deter them. One farmworker from Goiás concluded a letter this way: "When the time comes for me to bear my witness, I will do so without any fear of dying." That is the kind of strength that is surfacing. A sort of resurrection is taking place, as I suggested earlier.

We who have always had the Bible in hand find it difficult to imagine and comprehend the sense of novelty, the gratitude, the joy, and the commitment that goes with their reading of the Bible. But that is why these people generally read the Bible in the context of some liturgical celebration. Their reading is a prayer exercise. Rarely will you find a group that reads the Bible simply for better understanding. Almost always their reading is associated with reflection on God present here and now, and hence with prayer. They live in a spirit of gratefulness for God's gift.

History as a Mirror

Another characteristic which I hinted at already is the fact that the Bible is not just history for the people; it is also a mirror. Once upon a time we used to talk about the Bible as "letter" and "symbol." Today we might do well to talk about it as "history" and "mirror." The common people are using it as a mirror to comprehend their own lives as a people.

We who study a great deal have a lot more trouble trying to grasp the point of images and symbols. If we want to get a handle on symbolic language, we have to go through a whole process of "demythologizing." We have to go through a long process of study to get the point of the symbol. To us images are opaque glasses; we can't see through them at all. To see at all, we have to punch out the glass and smash it. To the common people in Brazil, an image or symbol is a pair of glasses with a little dust or frost on it. They just wipe them a bit and everything is as clear as day.

I don't think we pay enough attention to this educational item. We are awfully "Europeanized" in our training. Take the question of the historicity of a text. I think you have to approach it very differently, or worry about it differently, when you are dealing with ordinary people. Very often pastoral workers are talking about the Bible and they ask questions like these: "Did that really happen? Did Jesus walk on top of the water? Were there only five loaves and two fishes?" They think that this is the most important problem that the people have with the text in front of them. I don't think so. Once, in Goiás, we read the passage in the New Testament (Acts 17:19) where an angel of the Lord came and freed the apostles from jail. The pastoral worker asked his people: "Who was the angel?" One of the women present gave this answer: "Oh, I know. When Bishop Dom Pedro Casaldáliga was attacked in his house and the police surrounded it with machine guns, no one could get in or out and no one knew what was going on exactly. So this little girl sneaked in without being seen, got a little message from Pedro, ran to the airport, and hitched a ride to Goiana where the bishops were meeting. They got the message, set up a big fuss, and Dom Pedro was set free. So that little girl was the angel of the Lord. And it's really the same sort of thing."

The people don't always take things literally. They are far smarter than you would think. Our question simply will have to take more account of the way that ordinary people understand history. They are far more capable of understanding symbols than we assume.

DISLOCATIONS

Gustavo spoke earlier of the irruption of the poor [see Document 10 above]. When there are only five people in a room, then each one can be pretty much at ease. When fifty more people enter the room, then the original five find themselves a bit crowded and some moving around has to take place. Well, the common people have entered the precincts of biblical interpretation and they are causing much shifting and dislocation.

A Shift in Standpoint

First of all, the Bible itself has shifted its place and moved to the side of the poor. One could almost say that it has changed its class status. This is important. The place where the people read the Bible is a different place. We read the Bible something like the wealthy car owner who looks out over the top of his car and sees a nice chrome finish. The common people read the Bible something like the mechanic under the car who looks up and sees a very different view of the same car.

The common people are discovering things in the Bible that other readers don't find. At one session we were reading the following text: "I have heard the cries of my people." A woman who worked in a factory offered this commentary: "The Bible does not say that God has heard the praying of the people. It says that God has heard the cries of his people. I don't mean that people shouldn't pray. I mean that people should imitate God. Very often we work to get people to go to church and pray first; and only then will we pay heed to their cries." You just won't find that sort of interpretation in books.

The Bible has changed its place, and the place where the common people read the Bible is different. It is the place where one can appreciate the real import of Jesus' remark: "I thank thee, Father . . . that thou hast hidden these things from the wise and understanding and revealed them to babes; yea, Father, for such was thy gracious will" (Matt. 11:25–26). If you take sides with the poor, you will discern things in the Bible that an exegete does not see. All of us have a slight blind spot that prevents us from seeing certain things.

From Biblical Text to Real Life

Another shift mentioned earlier has to do with the fact that the word of God has moved in a certain sense from the Bible to real life. It is in the Bible but it is also in real life—especially in real life. So we come to the following conclusion: the Bible is not the one and only history of salvation; it is a kind of "model experience." Every single people has *its own* history of salvation.

Clement of Alexandria said: "God saved the Jews in a Jewish way, the barbarians in a barbarian way." We could go on to say: "God saves Brazilians in a Brazilian way, blacks in a black way, Indians in an Indian way, Nicaraguans in a Nicaraguan way, and so on." Each people has its own unique history. Within that history it must discover the presence of God the Liberator who journeys by its side. The scope of this particular dislocation is most important.

From Meaning in Itself to Meaning for Us

Another dislocation is to be found in the fact that emphasis is not placed on the text's meaning in itself but rather on the meaning the text has for the people reading it. At the start people tend to draw any and every sort of meaning, however well or ill founded, from the text. Only gradually, as they proceed on their course in life, do they begin to develop an interest in the historical import and intrinsic meaning of the text. It is at this point that they can benefit greatly from a study of the material conditions of the people in biblical times: i.e., their religious, political, and socio-economic situation. But they do so in order to give a better grounding to the text's meaning "for us." In this framework scientific exegesis can reclaim its proper role and function, placing itself in the service of the biblical text's meaning "for us."

From Abstract Understanding to a Community Sense

The common people are doing something else very important. They are reintroducing faith, community, and historical reality into the process of interpretation. When we studied the Bible back in the seminary in the old days, we didn't have to live as a real community or really know much about reality. We didn't even have to have faith. All we needed was enough brains to understand Greek and Hebrew and to follow the professor's line of reasoning.

Now the common people are helping us to realize that without faith, community, and reality we cannot possibly discover the meaning that God has put in that ancient tome for us today. Thus the common people are recovering something very important: the *sensus ecclesiae* ("sense of the church"). The community is the resonance chamber; the text is a violin string. When the people pluck the string (the biblical text), it resonates in the community and out comes the music. And that music sets the people dancing and singing. The community of faith is like a big pot in which Bible and community are cooked just right until they become one tasty dish.

From Neutrality to Taking Sides

The common people are also eliminating the alleged "neutrality" of scholarly exegesis. No such neutrality is possible. Technology is not neutral, and neither is exegesis.

Clearing up Overly Spiritualized Concepts

The common people are giving us a clearer picture of concepts that have been excessively spiritualized. Let me give just one example. Some time ago Pope Paul VI delivered an address in which he warned priests not to become overly preoccupied with material things. He urged them to show greater concern for spiritual things. One farmworker in Goiás had this comment: "Yes, the pope is quite right. Many priests concern themselves only with material things, such as building a church or decorating it. They forget spiritual things, such as food for the people!"

This is what the people are doing with such notions as grace, salvation, sin, and so forth. They are dusting them off and showing us that these notions have to do with solid, concrete realities of life.

Putting the Bible in Its Proper Place

Finally, the common people are putting the Bible in its proper place, the place where God intended it to be. They are putting it in second place. Life takes first place! In so doing, the people are showing us the enormous importance of the Bible and, at the same time, its relative value—relative to life.

PROBLEMS, CHALLENGES, REQUIREMENTS

There are many problems, difficulties, and failings associated with the interpretation of the Bible by the common people. But every good tree has a strong, solid limb that can be pruned when the time comes. The point is that its roots are okay. The common people are reading and interpreting the Bible as a new book that speaks to them here and now. And this basic view of the Bible is the view that the Church Fathers of the past had when they interpreted the Bible.

Here I simply want to enumerate a few further points that need greater attention.

1. There is the danger of subjectivistic interpretation. This can be combated in two ways: by more objective grounding in the literal sense of the Bible and by reading the Bible in community.

2. It is possible to read the Bible solely to find in it a confirmation of one's own ideas. In this case the biblical text loses its critical function. Community-based reading and interpretation help to overcome this tendentious use of the Bible. In addition, people must have a little humility and a little signal-light in their brains that calls them up short when they are tempted to absolutize their own ideas.

3. People may lack a critical sense in reading and interpreting the biblical text. They may be tempted to take the ancient text and apply it mechanically to today, without paying any serious attention to the difference in historical context.

4. The above three points underline the proper and necessary function of scientific exegesis. Exegesis is being called upon to concern itself, not with the questions it raises, but with the questions that the common people are raising. In many cases the exegete is like the person who had studied salt and knew all its chemical properties but didn't know how to cook with it. The common people don't know the properties of salt well, but they do know how to season a meal.

5. We need biblical interpretation that will reveal the material living conditions of the people in the Bible. We need a materialist reading and interpretation of the Bible, but not a narrow and confined reading. It must be broad and full.

6. We urgently need to give impetus to ecumenism on the grassroots level. It is a hard and challenging task, but a beginning has been made here and there.

7. The Bible is a book derived from a rural environment. Today we live in an urban environment. Re-reading the Bible today here in São Paulo, in this urban reality, presents no easy task of interpretation.

8. There is the matter of revolutionary effectiveness and gratitude for the Father's gift. This is another matter that needs further exploration.

9. Criticism can be derived from the word of God to foster transforming action.

PART III

PERSONAL EXPERIENCES AND LITURGIES

More than anything else the São Paulo Congress was an encounter, a celebration, a festival of solidarity, commitment, and hope. The papers presented at the Congress do not convey the whole wealth of experiences interchanged and the uninterrupted dialogue of living personal testimony. For this reason we chose to include in this volume some of the grassroots experiences narrated at the Congress as well as some texts from the liturgical celebrations held during it.

17

Personal Experiences

GUILLERMINA HERNÁNDEZ (Colombia)

My name is Guillermina Hernández de Badillo. I come from the southern part of the Department of Santander (Colombia) as a representative of the People's Women's Organization (Organización Femenina Popular).

I would like to tell you how I began and what I have done in the organization. I am of peasant origin. At the age of twenty-eight I came across the People's Women's Organization, which has provided me with technical, moral, and intellectual training.

I had no prior education. For this reason reading is difficult for me. As the old saw goes: "It's hard for an old parrot to learn to talk; it learns little, if anything at all."

What I really want to share with you is the life of our organization, the ideal we envision and the difficulties we are facing.

The chief objective of our organization is the technical and moral training of women. We are a women's organization, and our work is chiefly with women. We want to help women to learn how to make a living. But we also are interested in helping men, if they show an interest in our work.

In our work we meet many obstacles in trying to achieve the goal of social change in Colombia. Here are some of those difficulties.

First of all, we do not have the collaboration of the priests. In the diocese of Barranca Bermeja, where we live, there are many priests; but only three or four help us. We are worried because many priests do not seem to understand the gospel message. They preach from their churches, deceiving folks; but they do not mix with the people.

The majority of women in our organization do not have a personal acquaintance with the bishop. He doesn't put in an appearance, even to scold us. When we have undertaken some project of consciousness-raising that the bishop does not like, he calls in our priest advisor, bawls him out in private, and that makes the priest's work harder. We have reached the conclusion that we must work in secret, concealing ourselves from the bishop.

We get little collaboration from the men, from the laborers and their unions. When they need help, we try to help them as much as we can. For example, we help to distribute bulletins and leaflets among the inhabitants. We have also helped by hiding strike leaders, since they are persecuted by the government. But when we need help from the men—to take over some plot of ground in a neighborhood, for example—they won't help us. The women and wives say that the men won't help because they are afraid. They are afraid of being arrested, thrown into jail, interrogated, and tortured.

Another obstacle to our work is the opposition and persecution displayed by government authorities. There have been cases where some of our members were carrying our organization's anthem on a piece of paper and policemen forced them to eat the paper.

In other cases the situation can become extremely dangerous for us. We women want social change. But we have to work in secret, and recently we have encountered tremendous repression.

The people have urgent needs, but we don't know how to make further progress. There are so many people without work and without pay. I myself am in desperate need.

We have an aware organization and we have made much progress, but we don't have the wherewithal to confront a repressive government. How are we to fight a government that is so powerful, if all we can do is wield a kitchen knife? We can't fight with sticks and stones.

We are also worried by the fact that the very soldiers used by the government to repress us come from the common people. They are told that they must combat us and kill us because we are a threat to their lives. So they are setting our own sons against us women.

This is my personal experience, which I wanted to share with you. Excuse me for not being able to explain myself very well. I have had little formal study or intellectual training.

RANULFO PELOSO DA SILVA (BRAZIL)

My name is Ranulfo, and I come from Brazil. I have been active in base-level ecclesial communities for many years, and I would like to share my experience with you. First I would like to tell the story of those communities as I have experienced it personally, and then I would like to point out some of the dangers and ambiguities that I see.

I don't know for sure when these ecclesial communities began. I think it was around 1950. But I do know that they came into being because something was needed for survival. The number of these communities grew after 1964 and 1968, after the military coup and the increasing repression in our country. The people felt stripped of their dignity, their culture, and the fruits of their labor. They were facing disintegration.

The base-level communities represented survival space. They were a place for resisting domination. Moreover, the people realized that the organization of the church into dioceses, prelacies, and parishes did not suit their needs. As structures, they were too big. The base-level community solved this problem, becoming a place for reflection and debate, for religious celebrations, and for all sorts of activities by Christians.

A second point I would like to bring out with regard to these communities is that the people began to become aware of the fact of domination as they discussed and debated their problems. They came to realize more clearly that they were persons, that they ought to have a role in society, that they could make decisions, and that they had a right to make their presence felt.

A third aspect of this story is what I would call the start of political participation. It is one thing to know that my house is on fire. It is something else again to know how the fire started and, even more important, how to put the fire out. That is a step forward. It means knowing the causes and acquiring a critical-minded awareness. Taking some stand goes along with each new acquisition of awareness and knowledge. This is what I call the start of political participation.

Through their communities, the people took cognizance of their oppressed situation. They began to dream that they could get out of that situation. Then the repression became more severe. People went further with their reflection and discussion, increasing the level of their political awareness. They came to realize that the situation of oppression had no easy solution, that they would have to formulate middle-range and long-range plans.

When the people are maltreated and marginalized, they begin to develop a class consciousness. They also develop greater interest in labor unions and political parties. Workers begin to see that the unions organized by the government do not meet their real needs, and that the problems go much deeper. It is not simply a matter of improving the unions but of having to change a whole sociopolitical system.

Something similar happened with respect to the political parties. We who have participated in base-level communities are critical of the existing parties. We don't want to enter them as an inert mass, as a passive group joining an institution that is already complete and defined. The base-level communities have helped workers by offering them guidelines for participation in politics. In reality, however, only a minority within the communities have reached that level of reflection.

Now I would like to mention some of the problems we have encountered in the operation of these communities. The latter have helped people a great deal, but sometimes they don't achieve all we would like because we cannot overcome certain problems and ambiguities.

For example, in the name of co-responsibility the church has fabricated many mini-fathers, mini-priests. Lay people have been invited to distribute Communion and administer baptism. In this way the work of priests has been diminished while that of the laity has been increased. The only disadvantage is that the lay people do not receive a salary.

These lay people are turned into mere executors of what others want done.

From the outside it looks as if the people have responsibilities and are participating actively, but in reality they are being manipulated to serve clerical interests.

What I see here is an attempt to recapture people who have been lost. People have moved away from the church, so new forms are organized to win them back.

But we can succumb to the opposite danger as well. In trying to avoid orders and prefabricated solutions, to overcome paternalism, we may fall prey to sheer spontaneity for its own sake. In that case we fail to urge people to organize themselves in a disciplined way for the political tasks aimed at overcoming domination. I compare the situation of the people to that of a car stalled on some hillside road. We must know how to get it out of the mire and going again. Those who help to push it and get it going are those who are working for the laborers. Those who don't push the car are against us.

Sometimes people don't want to participate in the struggle for liberation. They give all sorts of reasons, sometimes contradictory ones. When workers want to drink *cachaza* (a liquor made from sugar cane), they can always find a reason for it: because they're cold, because they're hot, because they have worries, and so forth. There is always some reason. The same thing is true in our base-level communities. People don't want to participate in the struggle and they find all sorts of reasons for not doing so: because the members are Communists, because they don't have time, because it is too dangerous, and so forth.

I have seen a lot of naiveté in some communities. People are delighted when more people come to join the community. They readily share all their experiences and secrets with the newcomers, even though they may hardly know them. But in Brazil we must be very security-conscious because the repression has been very harsh. There have been sad instances where workers naively handed over other workers to the police.

Another difficulty we encounter at times is the lack of commitment among those who preach the message of Jesus Christ. It is not too common in Brazil, but in some areas the church still possesses big schools, property holdings, and buildings. In some places the church still owns large areas of land. This is a contradiction when viewed in terms of the huge number of landless peasants. We cannot preach the gospel of liberation if we are not consistent, if we do not give example within our own church.

These are some of the ambiguities that I have seen in my work within base-level ecclesial communities. They make the work of the church more difficult.

18

Worship

This is a meditation on our people's organizations and the martyrs among our people.

Today's theme is people's movements. In the church we often look upon them with mistrust because they do not bear the label "Christian," because they are no longer the "Christian" political organizations that characterized the earlier era of New Christendom in Latin America. Perhaps the words of Jesus will help us to meditate on this mistrust of ours and change it into trust. Our text is Luke 9:49–50:

John answered: "Master, we saw a man casting out demons in your name, and we forbade him, because he does not follow with us." But Jesus said to him, "Do not forbid him; for he that is not against you is for you."

Let us meditate in silence for a few moments.

In the church we sometimes want to enjoy a monopoly, not only over work in Jesus' name, but also over work on behalf of humanity. Organizations of the common people carry out their liberative practice in the name of humanity. Will we be able to accept their work as the work of love, as the practice of justice? Will we be able to sense that they are for us and not torture ourselves because they attract committed Christians?

Our martyrs are also the martyrs of our people. They belong to them. Sometimes we remember only the martyrs of our Christian communities. Today let us remember the martyrs of our base-level Christian communities and the other martyrs among our organized people. Let us unite them all in one single embrace of solidarity and motivation. Let us celebrate their presence as a stimulus to our own intention to continue their struggle. After each line, let us all say: PRESENT!

Thousands of martyrs among the people of Haiti	PRESENT
Thousands of martyrs in the liberation struggle of the Dominican people organized in 1965	PRESENT
Agrarian communities suppressed in Paraguay	PRESENT
The assassinated, imprisoned, or disappeared in Uruguay	PRESENT
The tortured, killed or disappeared from the School of Naval Mechanics in Buenos Aires	PRESENT
The tortured, assassinated, or disappeared from the National Stadium in Santiago, Chile, in 1973	PRESENT
Victor Jara, minstrel of the Latin American people	PRESENT
Those assassinated in the massacre at Tlatelolco, Mexico, in 1968	PRESENT
Those tortured and disappeared in Tiradentes Prison, Brazil, from 1968 to 1973	PRESENT
Hector Gallego, assassinated in Panama in 1971	PRESENT
Salvador Allende	PRESENT
Employees of Ingenio Astra assassinated in Ecuador	PRESENT
Two Deputies of MAS tortured in Venezuela	PRESENT
10,000, 20,000 perhaps 30,000 massacred in the peasant uprising in El Salvador in 1932	PRESENT
Twenty killed in the national teachers' strike in Peru in 1979	PRESENT
Those assassinated in the El Valle and Todos los Santos massacres in Bolivia.	PRESENT
Those crushed in the banana workers' strike in Limón, Costa Rica, in 1979	PRESENT
Rodolfo Aguilar and Rodolfo Escamillá, priests calumniated and assassinated in Mexico	PRESENT
The more than 30,000 Indian and Latin American people killed in the repression of the risen people in Guatemala from 1963 to 1980	PRESENT

Camilo Torres Restrepo and thousands of Colombian martyrs	PRESENT
Ernesto Che Guevara	PRESENT
Iván Betancourt, Casimiro, and twelve fellow martyrs in Olancho, Honduras, in 1975	PRESENT
The 3,252 people assassinated by the Death Squad in Guatemala, in 1979	PRESENT
The martyrs assassinated in the peaceful demonstration of Popular Unity on January 22, 1980, in El Salvador	PRESENT
The martyrs of the Ixil and Quiché people burned alive in the Spanish Embassy in Guatemala on January 31, 1980	PRESENT
The 40,000 martyrs in the struggle for liberation in Nicaragua	PRESENT

Lord, keep alive in us the subversive memory of the martyrs from our organized peoples.

Let us now read a passage from a homily delivered by Father Rutilio Grande, a martyr in El Salvador. The words were uttered less than a month before he was assassinated on March 12, 1977:

My brothers and sisters, some people want a God up in the clouds. They don't want the Jesus of Nazareth who is a scandal for the Jews and foolishness for the pagans. They want a God who won't question them, who will leave them settled and at peace, who will not speak the dreadful words: "Cain, where is Abel your brother? What have you done?" There is no call to take away the life of a people. There is no call to put one's foot on the neck of any human being, to humiliate or dominate others. In Christianity we must be ready to give our lives in the service of a just system, to save others and uphold the values of the gospel message.

In conclusion:

May the emerging church of the common people be in solidarity with our people's organizations!

May the subversive memory of the martyrs of our organized people stay alive in us!

GIVE US THIS DAY OUR DAILY BREAD
Samuel Rayan (India)

1.
an invitation
to prayer and quiet meditation:
an invitation to wake up to reality and explore its depths,
social, personal, cosmic;
the reality of a world of oppression and suffering;
the reality of people who struggle and hope.
an invitation to be where God is
with the oppressed in their struggle.

prayer is openness and sensitivity to reality,
issuing in commitment and action for fuller, freer, truer human beings.

the helps we offer are asian in origin, sensitivity, imagery, and concern.
thanks for being open to this asian reality,
to asian experience and spirituality.
we use asian stories and symbols
from a collection which you call the bible.
we center on the experience of a young asian
whom his mother called jeshua and you call jesus.
we shall listen also to other asians who are glad to be jesus' disciples
like kim chi ha, koyama, gandhi.

2.
music (filipino, indian, zen) meant to create
and enlarge spiritual space,
and to provide an atmosphere of peace and quiet reflection.

3.
there is a prayer that comes from jesus
and conveys to us in symbols some of jesus' dreams for our world
and his best wishes for the human race.
we call it the lord's prayer.
[read luke 11:1–4 and pause].

one father or mother, one human family;
one earth, one table laid out for all;

one forgiving love bonding all together in their rich variety of colors and cultures, sufferings and hopes.

[the lord's prayer is played from record or tape in tagalog, in tamil, in korean. . .]

4.
at the center of this prayer is the symbol of bread, food.
in it the other symbols become concrete, historical, tangible.
we make the bread-petition our refrain,
and say it and sing it each in one's own language:
give us this day our daily bread.

5.
for god, for jesus, for humankind, food is central.
food is, like god and along with god, the basis of life.
god is food, the sustainer and nourisher of our existence.
food stands for god and for people:
it is the place where they meet intimately and most meaningfully.
in bread numberless cosmic forces converge and touch our lives,
merge into it and become humanized.
food is the living focal point of the labor of many hands
and the concerns and loves of many hearts.
it expresses and promotes our social relationships
and carries our celebrations.
food is a rich human reality,
at once religious and political,
social and economic,
unitive and conflictual.
no wonder jesus places food, bread, rice,
at the heart of the prayer he gave us [pause].

6.
the voice of an asian celebrating food in song:
an asian whose body is broken,
but whose song and love remain unbroken;
who is held in solitary confinement,
but has the company of thousands of men and women to whom people and dignity and freedom matter more than profit, power, and capital.
a song of the korean christian poet and freedom fighter, kim chi ha:

   rice is heaven
   as we cannot go to heaven alone
   we should share rice with one another.

as all share the sight of the heavenly stars,
we should share and eat rice with one another.
rice is heaven
when we eat and swallow rice
heaven dwells in our body.
rice is heaven
yes, rice is the matter
we should eat together.

7.
let us pray:
give us this day our daily bread,
daily rice.

8.
in the bible food is the vehicle of salvation-history.
from genesis 1 through exodus and isaiah and proverbs,
through the story of jesus in the gospels
and of the first christians in the acts
on to the end of the book of revelation 22,
food plays a central role, decisive and critical;
and carries the story with its lights and its shadows.
the presence of food means god is present with a blessing.
its absence can mean his absence,
or the attempt to abolish him.
food is the sacrament of god.

9.
[read genesis 1:27,28a,29,30; pause]
let us pray:
give us this day our daily bread.

10.
[read exodus 16:10–12; pause]
let us pray:
give us this day our daily bread.

11.
shared bread is the experience of people as community,
and therefore the experience of god.
it is communion at once human and divine.
it is so all over the world,
it has been so all through the ages.
a central concern of jesus is to promote table fellowship
and get people to share bread and life.

[read mark 6:34–44; pause]
let us pray:
give us this day our daily bread.

12.
shared food is concerted action to build community.
community has its necessary material basis in community of wealth,
in the common possession of the one earth.
the cup we bless is a sharing in the outpoured life of jesus.
and the bread we break is a sharing in the given body of jesus.
"because the loaf of bread is one,
we, many though we are, are one body,
for we all partake of the one body."
if then in the church one goes hungry while another is sated and drunk,
the reality of the church is violated,
and what is eaten is no longer the supper of the lord.
without the fraternity founded on shared food and community of resources,
there is neither church nor its celebration in the eucharist.
"therefore, my brothers, when you assemble for the meal, wait for one
another."
[read 1 cor. 10:16b–17; 11:20–22a,b; 33; pause]
let us pray:
give us this day our daily bread.

13.
jesus continues to eat with us.
he may be our guest and we his any day
in our bastis, barrios, favelas, and inner-city slums.
kosuke koyama, japanese theologian, tells us of his experiences:

dear friends,
we had rice with jesus!
the place was tondo, cebu, central luzon.
our menu was dried fish, some strange soup, and rice.
he looked to us as though he was indignant.
he looked to us as though he was infinitely concerned.
he looked to us as though . . . [pause].

let us pray:
give us this day our daily bread.

14.
food and land unshared, hoarded and privatized,
grabbed from the people, denied to the needy, and degraded to vulgar
consumerism

is the destruction of the human community
and the destruction of authentic god-experience
and the construction of atheism.
"grain as weapon" is the special theme of one issue of *time* magazine.
a weapon with which the ruling classes kill people,
and kill god.
food comes from the land.
food is land transformed through love's labor.
the land is food, life, bread,
and basis of life in its basic form.
the earth is the great bowl of rice god has cooked for the human family;
it is the large loaf of bread god has baked for god's children.
the right of these to their portion is inviolable.
colonial, neocolonial, capitalist, agribusiness land-theft
violates god and insults god's people.
it litters the world with hunger and squalor,
conflicts and wars,
wretchedness and death.
with the gun and the bomb and computer technology,
with many smiles and much religious verbiage,
they have taken
and continue to take
the rice out of children's bowls,
and to seize the food from mothers' hands,
and to uproot from the land
and throw to the winds
the bread-earners of millions upon millions of peasant families.
they have striven to subvert people's faith in people and in god.

15.
therefore gandhi has rightly said that

    to the poor man god dare not appear
    except in the form of bread and the promise of work.
    grinding pauperism cannot lead to anything else than moral
    degradation.
    every human being has a right to live
    and therefore to find the wherewithal to feed him [pause].

let us pray:
give us this day our daily bread.

16.
there are landless people, resourceless people, rootless people.
what is their nationality?

to whom does brazil belong
if not to the people of brazil?
to whom does india belong
if not the masses of the indian people,
the harijans, workers, and poor peasants?
could any law or tradition to the contrary have any validity whatever?
once this land belonged to those now made landless or now marginated
through acts and institutions of cruelty, injustice, and oppression. whose
indeed is the land?
and whose is the earth? [pause]

17.
little child,
you, you are hungry.
you cry and reach out for the food in the shops and in the marketplace.
in the shops, in the marketplace, and in the land
there is an abundance of food.
but it is not for you, little child.
not for a million children like you.
you rage and ask,
whose is all this food,
for whom is it all meant,
and why do ships carry it away when we are hungry? . . .
do we understand children's questions?
do we understand the questions of simple people?
do we have answers for them?
let our answer at least be the prayer:
give us this day our daily bread.
bread is land.
bread is life.
bread is our brother and our sister.
bread is god.
give us this day our daily bread.

18.
food is different from fodder.
food is what we make and share in freedom.
it is what god gives in love and reverence.
satan the enemy and pharaoh the oppressor take our freedom and offer to
feed us.
but unfreedom's affluence can only spell death.
numbers 11 is an instructive passage,
modern in perspective.
there is first an account of the people's consumerist cravings
at the expense of freedom and dignity.

they are ready to return to egypt and its slavery
if only they can have more and finer food than was available in the desert.
god therefore proceeds to demonstrate that consumerism and the sale of
one's dignity to secure trinkets end in death to the human.
thousands eat and die.
in the third place, the people want to be mothered by moses,
and moses would have god mother the people.
god refuses.
god's own way of dealing with such a socio-economic and political-
cultural crisis
is to return the problem to the people,
to reorganize leadership,
to decentralize initiative,
to distribute spirit and power,
and make the entire people responsible.
true human food is the food of freedom and fraternity,
and responsible reorganization of the basis of life [read num. 11; pause].
let us pray:
give us this day our daily bread.

19.
it is we with god who make true bread,
the food that makes us free and human.
it is we with god who remake our earth
and build our future and shape our destiny.
in our toil and our struggle,
the new earth and the new person keep shaping up and emerging.
in our endeavor and suffering,
the new leaven is rising
and the resurrection is taking place.
for yahweh is faithful and true.
[read isaiah 25:2,4–6; pause]
let us pray:
give us this day our daily bread.

20.
the risen jesus continues to handle bread,
share food,
build up fellowship,
and make life's joy complete.
and it is always in the heart of shared food
that the face and mystery of the new hope and the new humanity
is discerned and gladly proclaimed.
[read luke 24:30–31a]
let us pray:

give us this day our daily bread.
[read john 21:9–13]
let us pray:
give us this day our daily bread.

21.
say,
sing,
dance
the lord's prayer together,
so that all of us may become a loaf of bread broken
and a bowl of rice shared
for the revelation of god
and the life of the world.

PART IV

FINAL DOCUMENTS

19

Final Document

International Ecumenical Congress of Theology, February 20–March 2, 1980, São Paulo, Brazil

INTRODUCTION

1. We, Christians from forty-two countries, meeting in the city of São Paulo from February 20 to March 2, 1980, held the Fourth International Ecumenical Congress of Theology, convoked by the Ecumenical Association of Third World Theologians.

At the same time we have shared our reflections with the Christian communities who have been meeting at the Theology Week each night at the Catholic University in São Paulo.

One hundred and eighty persons of various Christian churches, including laity, bishops, pastors, priests, religious, and theologians, participated in the Congress. We came from the popular Christian communities spread throughout Latin America and the Caribbean; we have also come from Africa and Asia and from the ethnic minorities of the United States; observers from Europe and North America were also present.

The Congresses of Dar es Salaam (Tanzania) in 1976, Accra (Ghana) in 1977, and Colombo (Sri Lanka) in 1979 preceded this fourth Congress.

2. The theme of our meeting was "Ecclesiology of the Popular Christian Communities." Our reflection took as its starting point the rich experience of these basic ecclesial communities, sign of the renewal of the churches of the Third World, and was concentrated particularly on Latin America. In this experience we find ourselves profoundly linked to our churches and pastors, faithful to the appeal of the Word of God as well as to the involvement of the Christian communities in the life of our peoples.

3. Catholics and Protestants from various churches, we admit to a common search in the establishment of the Kingdom of justice and peace. In reflecting on the practice of the popular Christian communities, we shared days of community prayer, praising the Lord for all the signs of liberation and pleading on behalf of those who still suffer the destitution of captivity.

4. Challenged by the Word of God, which comes to us through the Bible and the history of our peoples, and as members of the community of Jesus Christ, we now give witness to the results of our work.

5. But first we want to express our deep gratitude to Cardinal Paulo Evaristo Arns for the fraternal hospitality with which he received us in his archdiocese.

We also appreciate the messages of support received from Rev. Philip Potter, general secretary of the World Council of Churches, from Cardinal J. Willebrands, president of the Secretariat for Christian Unity, and from Bishop Federico Pagura, president of the Latin American Council of Churches.

I. THE IRRUPTION OF THE POOR INTO HISTORY

A. Popular Liberation Movements

6. The situation of suffering, misery, and exploitation of the great majority of human beings, concentrated especially but not exclusively in the so-called Third World, is as undeniable as it is unjust.

7. Nevertheless, the most important historical process of our times has begun to be led by these very peoples, the truly "wretched of the earth." Their oppression finds its roots in the colonial system of exploitation of which they were victims for centuries. Their struggle to defend their lives, to preserve their racial and cultural identity, denied by the foreign oppressor, is as widespread as this domination. But it is clear that their determination and their capacity for human liberation have today an outreach never before equaled, as we see in the recent case of Nicaragua.

8. In the context of the Third World, the emerging popular classes generate social movements; in their struggles is forged a more lucid consciousness of society as a whole as well as of themselves.

9. These popular social movements express much more than an economic grievance. They represent a phenomenon, new in our times: the massive irruption of the poor in every society. These are the exploited classes, the oppressed races, people who some would hope to keep anonymous or absent from human history, and who, with increasing determination, show their own faces, proclaim their word, and organize to win by their own efforts the power that will permit them to guarantee the satisfaction of their needs and the creation of authentic conditions of liberation.

10. In the case of Latin America, alongside the industrial workers' movement, whose strength has traditionally been recognized, and the peasants' union organization, which includes vast masses of the impoverished, new forms of workers' organizations are arising, broader opposition groups within the unions, as well as popular social movements originating at the local level, e.g., neighborhood associations, mothers' clubs, movements against the high cost of living, for better housing, for better health conditions, etc. From the deepest levels of our poor, the oppressed indigenous nations affirm their ancient identity and oppressed races fight to shake off their ethnic oppression within the popular movement as a whole. It is a complex and discontinuous process, with advances and setbacks; nevertheless, it shows an ever-ascending tendency that is a sign of hope.

11. To the degree that the popular movement develops, the fundamental question of formulating a broad historical project is posed. Today such a historical project is based on the critique of capitalism and of imperialist domination. It includes a radical demand for democratization in the construction of a political system in which popular control over those who govern as well as popular power are effective realities.

B. Structures of Domination

12. This historical journey of the people of the Third World takes place within the framework of dependent capitalism. In that system the sectors that hold economic, political, and cultural power exercise their domination over society by means of an enormous number of structures, institutions, and mechanisms, which are multiplied at the national and international levels, and which vary according to each country and region: unequal ownership of the land, concentration of wealth and of technico-scientific discoveries, the armament race with its production of weapons and destruction of life, transnationalization of the economy, etc. At the international level this is effected by means of monetary mechanisms, multinational corporations, political decision-making clubs for the rich nations (e.g., the Trilateral Commission), leading the nations of the Third World into an ever increasing foreign debt.

13. In the African, Asian, and Latin American societies, with specific characteristics in each region, the international structures in conjunction with the national structures of the capitalist system produce a process of development which is concentrated for the benefit of the few, with the consequent impoverishment of the masses, increase in the cost of living, inflation, unemployment, undernourishment, deterioration of the quality of life, super-exploitation of women and children, etc.

14. The dominant sectors exercise their power in society by means of the internalization of certain attitudes and behavior through formal education, the mass media, political parties, and even popular organizations. Thus, a certain type of society is being shaped with its materialistic and utilitarian values and lifestyles.

15. Furthermore, power is concentrated in authoritarian states which, from the top down, consider themselves as the protectors of society, penetrating even the private lives of the citizens. This procedure is justified in Latin America by models of restricted democracy, which are such only in form, or of National Security.

The political institutions, at every level, restrict and try to control the participation of the popular groups and classes in making decisions and in effecting social change.

16. It is also important to stress the implacability of a whole series of mechanisms of a more subtle domination, often underestimated in the analyses, which produce forms of inequality and discrimination among blacks, indigenous peoples, and women. It has to be noted that the different mechanisms are not opposed, nor even juxtaposed, one to the other, but on the contrary, are articulated in one and the same comprehensive structure of domination. The black populations, the indigenous peoples, and the women of the popular classes have been for centuries, and are still today, doubly oppressed; more than in the past, however, they are struggling for their liberation. These mechanisms respond neither in a deterministic nor a linear manner to the interests of domination, but rather give rise to contradictions that the popular sectors can use to their own benefit on their journey.

17. In reality, these structures and mechanisms of domination follow different rhythms according to the different nations and regions, especially according to the varied capacity for response—in terms of organization, awareness, and struggle—of the popular social forces that are emerging. Thus, these forces are constantly occupying more space in the various institutions of society.

18. Furthermore, it is clear that this system of domination has been in a permanent state of crisis from the very beginning, even though this crisis has become increasingly more acute in the last few decades with the strengthening of the popular sectors.

C. Popular Movement and Basic Ecclesial Communities

19. Today in Latin America there is at the heart of the popular movement a growing number of Christians who explicitly express and celebrate their faith in Christ and their hope in the Kingdom of God. A popular, ecclesial stream is emerging that expresses itself in various forms of Christian life and community.

20. The irruption of the poor also is occurring within the established church, producing a religious and ecclesial transformation. The church is experiencing the judgment of God, which breaks into the liberating history of the poor and exploited. It is a moment of ecclesial grace and conversion, an inexhaustible source of a new and demanding spiritual experience. In the people's struggle, the church continues to rediscover its own identity and mission.

21. This Christian stream within the popular movement and the renewal of the church from the standpoint of its option for the poor constitute a unique and specific movement in the church. This movement takes shape in different types of basic ecclesial communities, where the people find a space for resistance, struggle, and hope in the face of domination. There the poor celebrate their faith in the liberating Christ and discover the political dimension of love.

22. The basic ecclesial communities, or popular Christian communities, form an integral part of the people's march, but do not constitute a movement or political power parallel to the popular organizations, nor do they seek to legitimate them. The Christian communities—through consciousness-raising, popular education, and the development of ethical and cultural values—exercise among the poor a liberating ministry that is an integral part of their specific mission of evangelization, prophecy, pastoral care, and ministering the sacraments.

23. The church redeems the people's symbols of hope, manipulated for centuries by the system of domination. The church celebrates the presence of the God of life in the people's struggles for a more just and human life. The church encounters the God of the poor by confronting the idols of oppression. The church receives the Kingdom as a free gift of the Father in the building of brotherhood and the solidarity of all the oppressed classes and races, humiliated by this anti-Kingdom of discrimination, violence, and death that is the dominant capitalist system.

24. The historical manifestation of the poor who appropriate the Gospel as a source of inspiration and hope in their struggle for freedom is deeply rooted in the biblical tradition. It can, moreover, be easily verified over the course of the history of the Christian churches.

25. In the Old Testament the entire history of a people in the process of liberation is told from the standpoint of their exodus from a situation of oppression and toward a space and time of freedom, abundance, and brotherhood. The same occurs in the New Testament, where the teaching of Jesus, in Matthew, starts with the beatitudes of the poor (Matt. 5:2–11) and ends with the definitive affirmation that Christ can be encountered only in concrete actions that redeem the poor from their condition of exploitation, oppression, hunger, that is, of being stripped of their human dignity as children of God (Matt. 25:31–40).

26. The whole of the biblical record reveals that the struggles of the poor for their liberation are signs of God's action in history, and as such are experienced as imperfect and provisional seeds of the definitive Kingdom. Christians are responsible for discerning the action of the Spirit, who moves history forward and who creates a foretaste of the Kingdom in every part of the world of the poor.

II. CHALLENGE TO THE ECCLESIAL CONSCIENCE

27. This path of suffering, of a growing consciousness, and of the struggle of our people poses questions and challenges for us as Christians and as church. On the one hand, we must understand this journey in the light of God's revelation throughout history. On the other hand, our ways of living and understanding the faith are challenged by the vitality and creativity of the popular movements and the basic ecclesial communities. In a special way we need to bring up to date and deepen our ecclesiology, mainly along three lines: *(a)* the profound relationship between the Kingdom, human history, and the church; *(b)* evangelization and the basic ecclesial communities; and *(c)* the following of Jesus.

A. Kingdom, Human History, and Church

28. By our faith we know that the collective history that we live with our people, with its contradictions of domination and liberation, of segregation and fraternity, of life and death, has a sense of hope. Here we want "to give the reason for our hope" (1 Pet. 3:15).

29. The God we believe in is the God of life, of liberty, and of justice. God created "the world and all that is in it" for man and woman so that they might live, communicate life, and transform this world into a home for all their children. The sin of human beings, who take the earth unto themselves and murder their brother, does not destroy God's plan (Gen. 2–4). So God calls Abraham to be the father of a people (Gen. 12ff.) and Moses to free that people from oppression, to make a covenant with it, and to guide it to the promised land (Exod., Deut.).

30. Jesus proclaims the new presence of God's Kingdom to this same people. The Kingdom that Jesus points to with his messianic practice is the efficacious will of the Father who desires life for all his children (Luke 4, 7:18–23). The meaning of Jesus' existence is to give his life so that we all might have life, and abundantly. He did this in solidarity with the poor, becoming poor himself (2 Cor. 8:9; Phil. 2:7) and in that poverty announced the Kingdom of liberation and life. The religious elite and political leaders that controlled Jesus' people rejected this Gospel: they "took from their midst" the Witness to the Father's love, and "they killed the Author of life." Thus the "sin of the world" reached its limit (Acts 2:23; 3:14–15; Rom. 1:18–3:2; John 1:5, 10–11; 3:17–19).

31. But God's love is greater than human sin. The Father carries his work forward, for the Jewish people and for all the peoples of the world, through Jesus' resurrection from the dead. In the risen Christ we have the definitive triumph over death and the first fruits of "the new heaven and the new earth," the city of God among humankind (Rev. 21:1–4).

32. The Kingdom does not have the same kind of tangible presence for us as it did for Jesus' companions (1 John 1), nor can we yet see the fullness of the Kingdom we hope for. Therefore the risen Lord pours out his Spirit on the community of his disciples, so that by its very life the church might be the visible body of Christ among human beings, revealing his liberating activity in history (Acts 2; 1 Cor. 11–12; Eph. 4).

33. The coming of the Kingdom as God's final design for his creation is experienced in the historical processes of human liberation.

On the one hand the Kingdom has a utopian character, for it can never be completely achieved in history; on the other hand, it is foreshadowed and given concrete expression in historical liberations. The kingdom pervades human liberations; it manifests itself *in* them, but it is not identical *with* them. Historical liberations, by the very fact that they are historical, are limited, but are open to something greater. The Kingdom transcends them. Therefore it is the object of our hope and thus we can pray to the Father: "Thy kingdom come." Historical liberations incarnate the Kingdom to the degree that they humanize life and generate social relationships of greater fraternity, participation, and justice.

34. To help us understand the relationship between the Kingdom and historical liberations we might use the analogy of the mystery of the Incarnation. Just as in one and the same Jesus Christ the divine and the human presence each maintain their identities, without being absorbed or confused, so too is the eschatological reality of the Kingdom and historical liberations.

35. The liberation and life offered by God surpass everything that we can achieve in history. But these are not offered outside history nor by bypassing history. It is all too clear, however, that there are other forces in the world, those of oppression and death. These are the forces of sin, personal and social, that reject the Kingdom and, in practice, deny God.

36. All people are called by the word of the Gospel to receive the Kingdom as a gift, to be converted from injustice and from idols to the living and true God, proclaimed by Jesus (Mark 1:15; John 16:3; 1 Thess. 1:9). The Kingdom is grace and must be received as such, but it is also a challenge to new life, to commitment, to liberation and solidarity with the oppressed in the building of a just society. Thus we say that the Kingdom is *of God*; it is grace and God's work. But at the same time it is a demand and a task for human beings.

37. The Kingdom is the horizon and meaning of the church. In the Third World context we must recall that the church does not exist for itself, but to serve human beings in the building of the Kingdom of God, revealing to them the power of the Kingdom present in history, witnessing to the presence of Christ the Liberator and to his Spirit in the events and in the signs of life in the peoples' march.

In fulfillment of its mission the Church seeks to follow Jesus, taking its stand with him on behalf of the poor, "pitching its tent" among them (John 1:14). Thus it can live in an intense and meaningful way the new reality of the Kingdom. From this starting point it can be a credible witness and living sacrament of the Good News of the Kingdom for all human beings.

38. The Kingdom also judges the church. It incites it to conversion, denouncing its contradictions, its personal and structural sins. It makes it confess its historical mistakes, its complicities, and the betrayal of its evangelizing mission. And in this act of humble confession the church encounters the grace of the Lord that purifies it and encourages it on its pilgrimage.

B. Evangelization and the Basic Ecclesial Communities

39. A community is Christian because it evangelizes: this is its task, its reason for being, its life. Evangelizing is a diverse and complex activity. A

Christian community is called to evangelize in all that it does, by word and by works.

40. To evangelize is to announce the true God, the God revealed in Christ, the God who makes a covenant with the oppressed and defends their cause, the God who liberates his people from injustice, from oppression, and from sin.

41. The liberation of the poor is a journey full of grief, marked by both the passion of Christ and by the signs of resurrection. The liberation of the poor is a vast history that embraces all of human history and gives it true meaning. The Gospel proclaims the history of total liberation as it is present in today's events. It shows how, here and now, among the poor masses of Latin America and all marginated peoples, God is freeing his people.

42. Puebla spoke of "the evangelizing potential of the poor" (no. 1147). With this expression, Puebla wanted to recognize the rich and varied experience of many Christian communities. For it was this lived experience that allowed for the rediscovery of an evangelization carried out by the poor. The poor—a believing, oppressed people—announce and demonstrate the presence of God's Kingdom in their own journey, in their struggle: new life, the resurrection manifested in their communities, is living testimony that God is acting in them. Their love of their brothers and sisters, their love of their enemies, and their solidarity, show forth the active presence of the Father's love. The poor can evangelize because the secrets of God's Kingdom have been revealed to them (Matt. 11:25-27).

43. In Latin America evangelization carried out by the poor has its privileged locus in a concrete experience: the basic ecclesial communities. In these communities is incarnated a Church that is, by vocation, continuously born of the people's faith, of "those not invited to the banquet" (Luke 14:15-24). In them a committed life of faith is subjected to evaluation. In them the hope of the poor is celebrated and bread is shared, the bread that so many lack and in which the life of the Risen One is present and acknowledged. They are privileged places in which the people read the Bible and in their own words and with their own expressions make its message their own. These communities allow for moments of fraternal encounter in which God is recognized as Father. The community dimension is joined with the evangelizing task, with the call to make disciples and to form an assembly of disciples, a church of the poor.

44. The purpose of evangelization is not the formation of small elite or privileged groups in the church. It is addressed to the flock without a shepherd, as Jesus says (Matt. 9:35), that is, to the abandoned masses, dispossessed of all their goods. Therefore, the Christian communities are renewed in the movement that leads them to seek out the most exploited of the poor. Evangelization of the masses is carried out within the perspective of the preferential option for the poor.

45. It thus contributes significantly to transforming the masses into a people. On the other hand, human multitudes are not isolated individuals. The poor are downtrodden together, with regard to what brings them together and gives them their identity: their culture, their language, their race, their nationality, and their history; this is doubly true in the case of women.

Evangelization is a concrete activity that is addressed to concrete people, here and now. Thus it undertakes the liberation of the poor through the liberation of their culture, their language, their race, and their sex. The popular Christian communities are the first fruits of the whole people at whose service they are. In them the poor people better discover their identity, their worth, their evangelizing mission within the history of the liberation of the poor. The universality of the gospel proclamation passes through this historical process and through this commitment of the Christian community.

C. Following Christ

46. The crowds who follow Jesus and are amazed at the good he does for all (Acts 10:38) are the first to hear the Good News of the Kingdom. Jesus "gathers around him a few human beings chosen from various social and political strata of the day. Though confused and often unfaithful, they are moved by the love and the power that radiates from him. They are the ones who constituted the foundation of his Church. Drawn by the Father, they start out on the path involving the following of Jesus" (Puebla, no. 192).

The power of the Spirit leads to conversion, to a radical change of life; thus an apostolic community is constituted, the seed and the model of the first ecclesial communities. In God's plan, if the rich and powerful of this world are to receive the Gospel, they must learn it from the people.

47. These first communities witnessed to Jesus Christ and taught the way to follow him: Jesus was poor and lived among the poor and proclaimed hope to them. This was a messianic hope, different from certain erroneous notions of his time, but a faithful fulfillment of the Father's promise. The Messiah announces God's Kingdom, that is, a God who is revealed as such because he reigns by doing justice to the poor and oppressed. To separate God from his Kingdom is to not know the God proclaimed by Jesus, a God who calls together brothers and sisters from among the poorest and most abandoned. Jesus proclaims that they are blessed and that the Kingdom belongs to them as a gratuitous and preferential gift of the Lord. This gift brings with it the demand of a commitment to justice.

48. The good news that announces to the poor the end of oppression, of deceit, of hyprocrisy, and of the abuse of power, is also bad news for those who profit from this abuse and injustice. Thus the powerful persecute Jesus unto death. Jesus "chose to be the decisive victim of the world's injustice and evil" (Puebla, no. 194) and so practice what he had taught: that none have greater love than those who give their lives for others. By such great love we will be recognized as his disciples. Such are "the demands of the justice of God's Kingdom in a radical and obedient discipleship" (Letter to the Christian Churches and Ecumenical Organizations of Latin America, Oaxtepec, Mexico, September 24, 1978).

49. The first communities walked the liberating path of Jesus Christ, proclaiming him as the one Lord. They were martyred for rejecting the idolatrous worship of the powerful of this world. Today many popular Christian communities in the Third World walk the same path in following Jesus. They refuse to accept the mechanisms of domination that enrich the powerful sectors and countries with the poverty of the weak (cf. the Address of Pope John Paul II to the Episcopal Conference at Puebla). For the oppressed and exploited they claim justice and dignity, work and bread, education, shelter, and participation in the building of each people's history. In this liberating struggle these communities experience the Lord as alive and present. They feel the action of the Spirit who both calls them to trial in the desert and sends them to evangelize the poor and the oppressed with the courage of a new Pentecost.

50. In the following of Jesus the spiritual experience is never separated from the liberating struggle. In the heart of this process God is experienced as a Father to whom every effort and every struggle is offered. From him come bravery and courage, truth and justice. Filial trust assures that if the Father raised his Son to demonstrate the truth of his Word, he will also give life to those who, in the path of Jesus, give their lives for others.

51. Those who denounce destitution and oppression have, like Jesus, been persecuted. This denunciation unmasks the illusion of continuous, unlimited progress. Moreover it proclaims that the poor demand justice. These are uncomfortable truths that must not be silenced.

52. Jesus' journey, that of the basic ecclesial communities, is a journey of faith in a God whom we do not see and of a love of our brothers and sisters whom we do see. Those who say they believe, but do not love, or who say that they love but in practice do not, are not on Jesus' path. Thus the martyrs of justice, who give their lives for the freedom of their oppressed brothers and sisters, are also martyrs of faith, for they learn from the Gospel the commandment of fraternal love as a sign of the Lord's disciples.

III. DEMANDS AND QUESTIONS

A. Spirituality and Liberation

53. During our meeting we have dedicated a good deal of time to the common celebration of our faith and our hope.

54. We believe that cultivating spirituality, or life according to the Spirit of Jesus, is a fundamental demand placed on every one of us and on the Christian communities. Many of us, many of our communities, are living the search for Christian spirituality in the new conditions of the church in the Third World.

Because of its crucial importance we think that the theme of spirituality must be taken up again in future meetings, writings, and events.

55. We must help our communities to appropriate the great spiritual tradition of the church that today, as in every age, is incarnated and expressed by taking up the present challenges of history. Thus, we can speak of a "spirituality of liberation." We must revitalize, and even at times recover, Christian spirituality as the original experience that drives Christians and the popular communities into an evangelizing political commitment and theological reflection.

56. This implies continually overcoming dualisms alien to biblical spirituality: faith and life, prayer and action, commitment and daily work, contemplation and struggle, creation and salvation. Spirituality is not merely a distinct moment in the process of the liberation of the poor. It is the mystique of the experience of God within this process. It means the encounter with the living God of Jesus Christ in collective history and in daily personal life. Prayer and commitment are not alternative practices; they require and mutually reinforce one another. Prayer is not an evasion but a fundamental way of following Jesus that makes us ever ready for the encounter with the Father and for the demands of our mission.

57. Spirituality also demands of us today that we enrich ourselves with the great religious and cultural traditions of the Third World. All this will teach us to introduce poetry, music, symbols, festivity, fellowship, and above all the gratuitous dimension into the celebration of our faith.

58. The agents of evangelization are not to celebrate for the people but rather with them. The people evangelize us by passing on to us the mystique of their faith, their solidarity, and their struggles.

59. The spirituality that we today seek to revitalize ought to emphasize the love of God that calls us to follow Jesus and is revealed in the poor. In the struggles, in the commitment, in the martyrdom of the people, Jesus is followed not only to the sacrifice of the cross, but also to his liberating resurrection.

60. In the spirituality that we want to recreate, the option in solidarity with the poor and the oppressed becomes an experience of the God of Jesus Christ. All this demands a continual coming out of self and a change of social and cultural position. It commits us to live the political and economic consequences of the commandment of love.

61. The Eucharist, or the Supper of the Lord, should hold the central place in our communities, together with the sharing of the Word of God. When they are celebrated among the poor and oppressed they are both promise and demand of justice, of the freedom and the fellowship for which the peoples of the Third World are struggling.

62. For the Christian communities, Mary, the mother of Jesus, is seen above all as the poor, free, and committed woman of the Magnificat, as the faithful believer who accompanied her son to the Pasch. For the Catholic communities, the saints of their devotions become family in the Kingdom and companions on the way.

63. Our popular Christian communities should grow in their contemplative dimension. In their prayer, these communities of the Third World must be grateful for nature and life, because of the joy these produce in us. They should also be grateful for the gift of communion with the God who supports all in history. Besides living our prayer, our Christian communities must educate for it. Open to life, they will include in their prayer the cry of the people who demand justice and seek without rest the face of their liberating God.

64. We believe, finally, in the liberating and evangelizing efficacy of prayer—in ourselves and in the people. We believe in its humanizing efficacy in the struggles. We believe that Christian contemplation gives sense to life and to history, even in the failures, and leads us to accept the cross as the way of liberation.

B. Persecution, Repression, and Martyrdom

65. The church that is reborn by the power of the Spirit among the exploited and oppressed classes of our peoples keeps alive the dangerous memory of the martyrs, who laid down their lives as a sign of their great love (John 15:13). With a genuinely Christian feeling this church thus recovers the tradition of the most ancient Christian communities and touches the heart of Christian faith: the recovery from the hands of an impious, unjust, and idolatrous world of the maligned memory of one who was excluded from human society—Jesus of Nazareth.

66. Besides putting an end to his life, the murder of Jesus (Acts 5:30) was intended to malign his reputation and deal a mortal blow to his cause: "He has blasphemed" (Mark 14:64); "if he were not a subversive we would not have brought him to this tribunal" (John 18:30); if they do not put a guard on his grave, "his disciples will come and steal the body and tell the people that he rose from the dead" (Matt. 27:64).

67. The dominant powers of Jesus' time were afraid that the one they had murdered would be remembered. However, the empty tomb and the power of the Spirit that made the risen Jesus present again among his friends stirred up the Easter faith that freed the disciples from a paralyzing fear. Timid people proclaimed vigorously that this man "killed outside the city wall" (Heb. 13:12), this Jesus whom you crucified, was raised by God and made Lord and Christ (Act 2:32,36).

68. The "way of life," or "way," that the disciples proclaimed, that common mind and heart, having all things in common and not allowing the exploitation of anyone, that "effectiveness" in the proclamation of the risen Christ, in a word, that coming of the Kingdom that the early Christian communities embodied (see Acts 4:32–35), was persecuted and repressed by the same people who murdered the Lord. United in the common life, in prayer and the breaking of the bread (Acts 2:42), those who before were silent through terror joined the resistance, full of the Spirit, and proclaimed that "we have to obey God rather than men" (Acts 5:30).

69. Throughout the Third World today the popular classes and oppressed ethnic minorities resist, organize, and struggle to build lands of cooperative, humanizing justice, work, and life. They are thus obeying God, who wills that people should live and dominate the earth as heirs, as children who feel that they are in a home of brothers and sisters. The church, which is reborn of this people, in spontaneous and organized struggles, shares this struggle and often encourages it with its unshakeable faith in the love of God that guarantees the ultimate meaningfulness of this struggle.

70. For this reason the church suffers the same repression that the dominating classes visit on the people. This repression, unleashed out of hatred for justice, hatred for human dignity, is what today we call persecution of the church. We have the right to celebrate as martyrs the tortured, the disappeared, the exiled, the imprisoned, and the murdered of this people. They are workers, peasants, indigenous peoples, and blacks, men and women and innocent children caught up in their parents' political commitment. They are also catechists, ministers of the Word, leaders of Christian communities, priests and pastors, men and women in religious orders, bishops and martyrs, whom we have the right to celebrate as heroes sacrificed from among the poor.

71. When our church does not consent to live a life generously surrendered for the cause of God in the cause of today's exploited and oppressed classes, when it allows itself to be paralyzed with fear and does not remember its martyrs in solidarity with the people, we have the right to ask if it has new eyes to recognize the crucified Lord in the disfigured faces of the impoverished people of the Third World (see Puebla, nos. 31–39).

72. We have the right to ask whether as a church we live out the prayer of agony that Jesus lived out, the prayer of submission to the Father and of resistance to the oppressor, the prayer that gave Jesus the strength to follow the way of the cross, from which God raised him up. We have to ask our church if it recognizes the "greater love" in giving up one's life for one's friends.

73. Nevertheless, we give thanks to God because of the growing number of pastors and communities who proclaim the death of their martyrs and extend it with their own witness.

C. Unity of the Churches Starting from the Poor

74. The greatest division and disunity that the Third World suffers is the sin of injustice, through which "the many have little and the few have much" (Puebla, Message to the Peoples of Latin America). This injustice goes beyond and also divides all our churches and leads them to take diverse and contradictory positions.

75. We affirm with joy that through solidarity with the cause of the poor, through participation in their just struggles, in their sufferings, and in their persecution, the first great barrier that for so long has divided our different churches is being broken down. Many Christians are rediscovering the gift of unity as they encounter the one Christ in the poor of the Third World (Matt. 25). The promotion of total liberation, the common suffering, and the sharing of the hopes and joys of the poor have put in clear relief all that we Christians hold in common.

76. In this option for the poor and in the practice of justice, we have deepened the roots of our faith in the one Lord, the one church, the one God and Father. In the following of Jesus we confess Christ as the Son of God and the brother of all people. In the struggle for a just life for the poor we confess the one God, Father of all. In our ecclesial commitment we confess the church of Jesus Christ as his body in history and as sacrament of liberation.

77. In this faith and practice the various popular Christian communities, Catholic and Protestant, share the same historical and eschatological vision. That faith and practice lead us forward in unity at the levels of evangelization, liturgical celebration, doctrine, and theology. If it is true that the poor evangelize us, it is also true that they open the way toward our unity. They accelerate the fulfillment of the last testament of Jesus, that all may be one; that all, Catholic and Protestant, and even more, all men and women of all races and cultures, may come to form the people of the children of God.

D. Churches and Peoples of the Third World

78. In this Congress, with its profound encounters, we have noted a considerable lack of knowledge of one another and a lack of permanent, effective communion between our peoples and churches of Asia, Africa, America, the Caribbean, and the ethnic minorities of the U.S.A.

79. We cannot fail to recognize in each of the peoples and churches of the Third World their own identities and distinct contributions in the process of liberation: through the sufferings, struggles, and achievements of their respective histories and through the specific richness of their cultures. These are facets of the countenance of a poor, oppressed humanity that is open to contemplation and hope.

80. From today onward we commit ourselves—in order to be faithful to this hour of the Gospel and of the poor—to a greater intercommunication and mutual help, with greater effectiveness and ecumenical spirit, within the liberating process of the churches of the Third World.

81. All these processes have a global frame of reference. The poor of the Third World are making painful efforts to achieve unity in the common struggle against every kind of colonialism, neocolonialism, and imperialism. The churches must be committed to this effort.

E. Conversion and Structures of the Church

82. The church is not invited simply to reform itself, but is rather called to be converted from its personal and structural sins and conformity to the spirit of "this world" (see Rom. 12:2).

83. If the church is not converted in its structures, it loses credibility and prophetic power. A rich, dominating church cannot make an option for the world of the poor and oppressed (see Medellín, "Poverty of the Church"; Puebla, no. 1140).

84. The newness of the Spirit of the risen Christ demands a church constantly renewed in the service of the new world of the Kingdom. In order for the church to be able to liberate itself and to be a sacrament of liberation, we have to imitate in our church structures the new way of living together that Jesus inaugurated (see Phil. 2; Matt. 18:15–35; 20:25–28; 23:1–12).

85. In regard to its ministerial structures, this newness obliges the church to accept as a gift of the Spirit the new ministries that the communities need and are generating. In this new vision, the discrimination that women suffer in the churches cannot be justified biblically, theologically, or pastorally.

86. The liberty of the children of God that Jesus teaches with his word, life, and death clearly must also be exercised within the church itself. This means not passively accepting coercion in the church, and helping Christian people not to regard as rebelliousness what is intended as free gospel loyalty.

F. Specific Struggles and the Global Process of Liberation

87. The church of the Third World must commit itself to those struggles for liberation that take up the specific concerns of ethnic, racial, and sex groups, within the overall framework of the struggle of the poor. Indigenous peoples, blacks, and women of the popular classes will always deserve special attention from our church and a growing concern on the part of our theology.

88. The church should contribute, from its faith and gospel love, to the end that these various struggles become a genuine joining of forces of oppressed people, without power takeovers that in turn become new modes of oppression. We ought to work together so that this grand alliance and this mutual respect become effective now in the global struggle.

89. As its proper mission, the church will proclaim and foster in this process those evangelical values that defend the life and liberty of the human person, that open space for communion with the Father and with our brothers and sisters, and that make an original contribution to forging the new person in the new society.

90. The church, like Jesus, will always be gratuitously present among the weakest and most marginalized, and will always be free and critical before the great and powerful of this world.

G. Clarifications

91. The participation of the entire people of God in the inner life of the Christian churches has been continuously growing. The form that this participation has taken in contemporary church structures has not been an object of our study. But we are happy to see the way our bishops and pastors have on their own initiative taken effective measures to insure that this participation, within the ecclesial community and under their pastoral direction, be ever broader and more effective.

92. The Christian churches, as institutions, should not limit themselves to a particular part of society to the detriment of the universality of Jesus' message. In the carpenter of Nazareth, God made his option for the poor and oppressed. To be poor is the vocation of the entire church. But the ecclesial community is open to all—to the rich young man and to Zaccheus—challenging them to respond to the gospel demand to share the poor's aspirations for freedom (Luke 19:1-10).

93. In our societies in the Third World there is a serious division that negates evangelical fraternity by the existence of different social classes. Still, conversion to the Gospel of Jesus cannot be limited to becoming aware of the need to be at the side of the oppressed. This is doubtlessly a demand made by the Lord, who sends the rich away empty and fills the hungry with good things. Christian conversion implies, above all, an openness to the Word of Jesus, accepted in faith, lived out in a liberating hope, and made concrete in the love that transforms humankind and the world.

94. We should praise the Lord for Christians' participation in the building of just and fraternal societies. Liberation, its socio-political implications, and the analytical categories that define it are not limited to social theories. Before the social sciences spoke of liberation, the people of God had already achieved it in the Egypt of the Pharaohs. Liberation is at the center of the biblical message. Within the perspective of our paschal expectations, liberation is not reducible to one or another political model; rather it transcends all history. And it attains its fullness in the manifestation of the Kingdom assured by the liberating practice of Jesus and the merciful goodness of the Father.

95. We close our Congress and end this document strengthened by the promise of Jesus to his followers: "Do not be afraid; I have overcome the world. I am with you always" (John 16:33; Matt. 28:20).

20

Letter to Christians in Popular Christian Communities in the Poor Countries and Regions of the World

We who write this letter to you are Christians, lay people of the popular Christian communities, pastors, priests, and bishops, men and women, blacks, whites, and indigenous peoples, gathered from various Christian churches in forty-two countries of Latin America, Africa, Asia, the Caribbean, and North America. We have met in the name of Jesus Christ in São Paulo, Brazil, from February 20 to March 2, 1980, in a spirit of great fellowship, to pray, study, and reflect together about the call of God that reaches us through the cry of the poor of the whole world, above all of Latin America.

Our brothers and sisters from Latin America, Asia, Africa, and the black and Hispanic minorities of North America have told us of the situation of the poor, of the blacks, of women, of the indigenous peoples of their countries. And all of us together have seen that the poverty that exists in Latin America and in the rest of the world is not the result of destiny, but the fruit of a great injustice that cries to heaven like the blood of Abel, murdered by Cain (Gen. 4:10). We have also seen that the principal cause of this injustice is to be sought in the capitalist system, which, like a new tower of Babel (Gen. 11:1–8), raises itself over the world and controls the life of the poor, favoring a few who get constantly richer at the expense of the growing poverty of the others. This is why the impoverished peoples of our countries live in real captivity within their own lands.

But we have seen something else that gives us great hope and that we want to share with you: namely, that the living power that comes from God is manifesting itself precisely in those places where life is oppressed, enslaved, and crucified on the Calvary of the world. Indeed, in every part of the poor world, and above all here in Latin America, the poor, Christian and non-Christian alike, are waking up, wanting to shake off the yoke of slavery. And Christians are realizing that, in the name of their faith in Jesus Christ, they can no longer tolerate this situation. So in the midst of this struggle for freedom they are meeting in communities to renew their faith in Jesus Christ and thus to be leaven in the mass that seeks its freedom. Like Abraham and Moses, they are setting out in the quest to create a new people and a new and renewed earth, where the blessing of life that comes from God may be recovered for everyone (Gen. 12:1-4). They are organizing and struggling in the popular movements so that all may have work, bread, shelter, health, education; so that all may have the abundant life that Jesus wishes (John 10:10). They are struggling for conditions in which people may be owners of what they produce (Isa. 65:22), in which they may live in the houses that they themselves have built (Isa. 65:21), and eat the fruit of the land that they themselves have cultivated (Isa. 62:8-9); conditions in which all may live in peace on the hills of their own land (Ps. 71:16). They want a country where power is shared by everyone, where all are authors of their own destinies and can thus praise God, the Creator, for the gift of life. Many have already given their lives for this cause. They were not able to see the coming of this new day, but greeted it as from afar (Heb. 11:13). Others have been imprisoned, tortured, or exiled. But all have struggled and still struggle in the faith that life is stronger than death and in the hope that the blood they have shed will produce the fruit of freedom for their brothers and sisters.

Reflecting on all that is happening today in our countries, we think that you, who are struggling and suffering courageously in the popular movements, and living and celebrating your faith with joy in your communities, are the Good News of God already proclaimed throughout the world. This Good News has already been heard by the pastors of the church, meeting in Puebla and in Oaxtepec. In Puebla they recognized: "Not all of us . . . have committed ourselves sufficiently to the poor. We are not always concerned about them, or in solidarity with them" (no. 1140). And they went on to say: "Commitment to the poor and oppressed and the rise of grassroots communities have helped the Church to discover the evangelizing potential of the poor. For the poor challenge the Church constantly, summoning it to conversion; and many of the poor incarnate in their lives the evangelical virtues of solidarity, service, simplicity, and openness to accepting the gift of God" (no. 1147). In Oaxtepec they affirmed: "We confess that our indifference to the cry of these groups that are the most forgotten, oppressed, and needy in our countries contradicts the demands of the Gospel. We are united in appealing to the Christians of Latin America to respond to the demands of the justice of God's Kingdom in a radical and obedient discipleship."

Thus, through you, the face of Christ is shining once more on the world (2 Cor. 4:6). You are the letter of Christ, recognized and read by everyone, written not with ink, but with the Spirit of the living God, not on tablets of stone, but on the tablets of your living hearts (2 Cor. 3:2-4). Through your witness, Jesus evangelizes the poor, opens the eyes of the blind, sets free the captives (Luke 4:18-19), confronts the powers of domination, and reclaims life for all.

Today, as in the time of the captivity, the God who raised Jesus from the dead is hidden in the midst of history, on the side of the poor, working and liberating his people with the victorious power that overcomes death and creates life anew (Isa. 43:18-19).

We, gathered in this Congress, undertake your struggle as our own and ask the Father to give you the courage and joy necessary to continue the mission you are already carrying out: to proclaim to all the Good News that the Kingdom of God is at hand (Mark 1:15), that the blind see, the lame walk, the lepers are cleansed, the deaf hear, the dead are raised, the poor hear the Gospel (Matt. 11:5)—and they are proclaiming the Gospel! Happy are those who are not offended by this news! The resurrection that comes from God is already at work in the crucified lives of so many of our brothers and sisters!

The signs of this resurrection are visible in the empty tombs of those thousands who have disappeared, in the blood shed by countless martyrs, especially in Guatemala, El Salvador, Argentina, Chile, Paraguay, Haiti, and so many other places; in the struggles of the poor for land and for their rights; in the silent resistance of so many; in the victorious revolutions of Grenada and of Nicaragua, where the people won their freedom to be free; in the people and the communities missing from this Congress, but who are also in the struggle for a more just and fraternal world, such as the Cuban people and others; in a word, in the poor and oppressed people who in so many different ways organize to face up to the dominations that time and again try to crush their efforts.

In all this the Kingdom of God marches forward with its justice and truth, judging the world and denouncing the powerful. Just as in the time of captivity, Christians must rip off their blindfolds and try to perceive this extraordinary Good News from God that today is announced throughout the world by means of the poor (Isa. 42:19-21).

We reflected on all this during these days of study and prayer. We beg of you, and of ourselves, that in this struggle we may never forget those who are poorer than we are and the poor of Asia and Africa. May we remain ever attentive to the outcry of God that comes to us from the millions of the world's poor; and may we always continue celebrating our faith and interpreting our lives in the light of the Word of God. May we never forget that the popular Christian communities are, as it were, a "first attempt of the Kingdom," where the world should be able to see "the people, the land, and the blessing" that God desires for all, and where the churches themselves encounter a motive for their conversion and constant transformation. And finally, may we never close ourselves in on our own interests, dividing ourselves because of internal battles, but may we organize in a common struggle to take away the sin of the world, the great social sin of the capitalist system that snuffs out the life of so many of our brothers and sisters. Let us strive to conquer it by uniting all our forces, Christians from the many churches as well as non-Christians of good will, who like yourselves fight for the victory of life over death, since "whoever is not against us is with us" (Mark 9:40).

The common enemy of us all, this dependent capitalist system, is like the dragon of the Apocalypse. The small and fragile communities are like the woman who groans with the pains of childbirth in order to bring forth the new life that conquers the dragon (Rev. 12).

Do not be afraid! Christ has risen! He is alive! He has assured us: "I have overcome the world. I will be with you always, even to the end of the world" (cf. John 16:33; Matt. 28:20).

PART V

EVALUATION AND INTERPRETATION

21

The Challenge of
the Non-Latin Americans

INTRODUCTORY REMARKS
Preman Niles (Sri Lanka)

There is a total agreement among those of us who are from outside Latin America that the poor should be at the center of theological construction and ecclesial practice in Latin America. On our own continents there is the same emphasis. And we are appreciative of the debate that is going on in Latin America.

However, we detect a certain rigidity in the understanding of who the poor are, a rigidity that leads to exclusivism in spite of some attempts to be open and not overly dogmatic. At this point we can learn a lesson, albeit a negative one, from models of capitalistic development in Asia. When the people ask questions about their participation, they are often told: Wait; first the skilled people must do their job of developing the county; then you will be included. Our experience has been that the people are never included, and they continue to be simply the objects and not the subjects of history.

The basic question is this: Do the poor speak for themselves, or do others speak on behalf of the poor and incorporate them or accommodate them into a given schema? This question applies particularly to the participation of the blacks and the indigenous people in the process of liberation. But there are also other aspects of this issue.

These aspects will be raised from five contexts: that of the North American Hispanics, by Maria Iglesias; the North American blacks, by Cornel West; the Africans, by Ruvimbo Tekere; the Asians, by Tissa Balasuriya; and the West Indians, by Alfred Reid.

The term "challenge" is too strong. Actually the challenge of all of us is to the First and Second Worlds. We offer responses in the context of a dialogue. The concern of the Ecumenical Association of Third World Theologians is that we avoid theological ghettoism, that we be open to each other. Neither should we attempt to export theology and ecclesial practice from one conti-

253

nent to another. We should be open to each other and challenge each other, for we are in a common struggle.

What is said by us is meant to be a contribution to the ongoing historical project in Latin America: theological construction and ecclesial practice in solidarity with movements of your oppressed peoples. May I recommend a Buddhist way of responding. You are not allowed to speak immediately. You have to swallow what you want to say and reflect for a long time in silence. Then, respond. Systems may have to change if responses are to be taken seriously and not simply accommodated into existing schemes and practices.

THE NORTH AMERICAN HISPANICS
Maria Iglesias (U.S.A.)

We represent twenty million Latin Americans living in the United States today. Many say that our people are the future of the Catholic church in the United States; we are already 30 percent of that church. Some of us became part of the United States when the U.S. conquered half of Mexico as well as the island of Puerto Rico in the nineteenth century. Others have immigrated from Latin America—not as tourists, and much less as delegates to ecumenical theology meetings. They came, taking inhuman risks, because they were looking for bread: the very bread being exported from their homelands to far away places.

We are part of your family: we too are mestizos, Europeans, Indians, and blacks from Latin America. We share your language, your culture, your religion, and especially your poverty and oppression. We are your brothers and sisters in the heart of the empire.

Many of you have visited us and have challenged us: Francisco Aguilera, Jesus García, Edgard and Amparo Beltrán, Enrique Dussel, Leonardo Boff, José Marins, Samuel Ruiz, and especially Gustavo Gutiérrez. Together we thought through and clarified our faith and our struggle; many of us in the U.S. still take strength from that sharing.

You are asking us to reciprocate. In solidarity we offer some observations.

The examples of politicization and conscientization in the basic communities, often through the blood of martyrs, causes us both shame and profound pain: shame because we are from the country that has often provided arms and support for the slaughter; pain because we are brothers and sisters of those who died.

This politicization leads us to work much more along class lines. Individualism has appeared more clearly as one of the tools of the oppressors. We feel the lack here of more black and indigenous voices, for racism for us continues to maintain white European domination. We hope to see in the Latin American peoples an authentic pluralism that truly includes all the races on every level of society and that will show forth still more clearly that new human being, the mestizo.

We also question the numbers of missionaries who still go to Latin America from the United States and Europe. How do they fit into the popular church in Latin America, and especially into the indigenous communities?

We might have dealt more with institutionalized poverty as well as suffering in its global dimensions. The poverty of my own people, for example, has dimensions not treated here; to deal with it could be enlightening and could help create greater solidarity.

The situations of the various national groups of Latin Americans in the United States have their roots in the movements towards national unity in their respective homelands. We haven't been able to consider unity among Latin Americans and concrete steps that might be taken in this regard.

Pluralism in the United States creates great divisions and prevents our raising a voice united in support, as in the case of Nicaragua and El Salvador. But we hope that you will be able to support the struggles of the Hispanic people in the U.S.

Following the brilliant ecclesiological exposition of Miguel d'Escoto (see Document 15 above) we were surprised that all the questions were of a sociopolitical nature. The rich ecclesiological theme was not pursued.

When I was young they used to tell me about a revolution in our country. They said that the whole world looked on our revolution with great joy. They even gave us a beautiful statue since we were the symbol of liberation and of a new idea of democracy. Our country was begun in a spirit of sacrifice for the common good—all "under God." But it became the monstrous capitalistic machine that leaves human refuse in its cities and eats all humankind alive. It is a joy for us to live with you the Resurrection of the new and true liberation.

Congratulations!

THE NORTH AMERICAN BLACKS
Cornel West (U.S.A.)

I want to speak of the limitations of Marxist theory often employed by liberation theologians and the political praxis it yields as two sides of the same coin.

Marxist theory easily tends to be dogmatic—not in the sense of refusing to look at itself, but in the sense of refusing to be aware of what others say and see.

This is seen in the very charge of dogmatism: one is dogmatic precisely when one refuses to believe that one is being dogmatic, despite a chorus of charges of dogmatism. The mark of dogmatism is the lack of openness, when one believes that significant revision, modification, or innovation of one's theory or praxis must come from one's *own perspective* rather than from that of others.

For example, surely we all agree that some form of Marxist analysis is indispensable to understand the international economic order, capitalist societies and the perpetuation and preservation of gross inequalities and injustices in those societies. But the Achilles heel of Marxist theory is found in the issues of culture, self-identity, ethnic and racial communities, and existential security. For Marx, writing in an ethnically and racially *homogeneous* society (England) in the nineteenth century, self-identity came from one's position in the productive process, from one's work situation. In ethnically and racially *heterogeneous* societies and for those whose degraded and oppressed culture serves as the principal means of self-preservation and source of self-identity, any analysis for social change that is weak with regard to culture is suspect. And one can understand this suspicion best if one adapts—or better still, listens to—the perspective of those whose cultures and peoples have been subject to genocidal attacks for over four hundred years—by the forebears of the very people who presently seem reluctant to listen. When Marxists are preoccupied with an analysis that downplays or ignores the liberating aspects of degraded and oppressed cultures, it suggests that such Marxists share the ethos—not of the degraded and oppressed minorities—but of the dominant European culture.

Historically, a central feature of this dominant European culture has been its inability to take seriously the culture of colored peoples and its tendency to degrade and oppress the culture of these people. For oppressed colored peoples, the central problem is not only repressive capitalist regimes, but also oppressive European civilizing attitudes. And even Marxists who reject repressive capitalist regimes often display oppressive European civilizing attitudes toward colored peoples. In this sense, such Marxists, though rightly critical of capitalism, remain captives of the worst of European culture.

It is not surprising that the Latin American church and theology seem concerned more with the nonblack urban proletariat than with the Indians or blacks. My point here is not that one should not be concerned with the urban proletariat. Rather, we should openly acknowledge that it is culturally easier for nonblack Latin American theologians—and I use the term "nonblack" since I don't know of any noteworthy black Latin American theologians—to identify with a predominantly nonblack urban proletariat. In such ethnically and racially heterogeneous societies in Latin America, is it more than a coincidence that nonblack Latin American theologians opt for a Marxist analysis so weak on culture?

The gravity, weight, significance, and importance of the Indian and black issue is raised not to point accusing fingers at the Latin American church and theology, but rather to help us all change the world together. The raising of the Indian and black issue forces descendants of Europeans to acknowledge the cultural gap between themselves and the degraded and oppressed cultures of Indians and blacks. In short, it forces European Latin Americans to admit their relative ignorance—and in most instances avoidance—of these degraded and oppressed cultures.

Often it is the sheer admission of this ignorance that is irritating. Yet, it should be obvious that it is quite natural to be ignorant of cultures that one's own ancestors attempted to destroy, dismantle, and debunk. The only alternative in the present is to listen—an extremely difficult activity for those imprisoned by a dominant culture that has thrived by commanding and ruling those people who must speak for themselves. In short, ignorance of the degraded and oppressed cultures of Indian and black peoples demands listening. To refuse to listen is arrogant. Of course, this listening must not lead to uncritical acceptance. But one must have some understanding of the cultures and peoples, before one criticizes them.

The cultural gap between Europeanized Latin Americans on the one hand, and blacks and Indians on the other, holds not only at the level of evangelization in the *comunidades de base* or of the mobilization of political parties, but also at the level of armed struggle. For example, even among rural guerrilla groups—and I use this example because I believe some form of armed struggle is inevitable for revolutionary change in most Latin American countries—the Indian and black question is rarely addressed.

Yet surely no large scale rural guerrilla action is possible in ethnically and racially heterogeneous Latin American countries without at least some participation of the Indian and/or black masses.

Che Guevara noted in his diary two months before his death, "Not one peasant has yet joined the guerrilla group." It seems that it never occurred to his European-trained mind that it may have been his fault more than theirs—stemming from his ignorance of their culture and his reluctance to learn anything about it (contrast this with Hugo Blanco who mobilized Indians in the Valley of La Convención in Peru or the South Vietnamese National Liberation Front, which learned from and lived with peasants in the Mekong Delta). Similarly, I recently heard a prominent Latin American theologian say, "Not too many Indians or blacks have joined our movement." I hope that this presentation on behalf of the black delegation from the United States will contribute to the courageous struggle being waged by the Latin American church and theology by humbly suggesting that there is an alternative set of attitudes toward the degraded and oppressed cultures of Indians and blacks than that adopted by many Latin American theoreticians and practitioners.

THE AFRICANS
Ruvimbo Tekere (Zimbabwe)

We begin by paying tribute to the efforts being done to analyze Latin American realities and to the theological bases being used in reflecting upon these realities.

We are aware of the progress made in the last ten years in the Latin American theology of liberation. We are also aware of the continental and global implications of the practice of such a theology.

However, we are also concerned that the analysis of the struggle to liberate the oppressed and to bring them to full life in Christian communion has so far ignored the realities of cultural oppression of the poor—namely, that of blacks and Indians. This is a cultural oppression that arises mainly from racism.

In this conference we feel the absence of Indians and blacks. We also feel the absence of the same people in the larger Christian church. Where are the blacks? We know that thousands of them came here as slaves many years ago, and millions of them are in Brazil. They are not in government nor employment, nor in the main parts of town, nor in church. Where are they?

The fact that the cultures of the Indians and blacks have been ignored seems to indicate why they are absent from the larger participation in Latin American life. It is a cultural domination in which the church actually participates. The church cannot point a finger at the state, because the church has perpetuated and continues to perpetuate cultural domination and alienation in its educational and religious institutions. And the state continues to enjoy such a sad solidarity with the church. The rich cultural attributes of the Indians and the blacks have been ignored by the church in conformity with the ruling dominant class.

As Latin Americans evolve a new theology or new definition of theology —that of liberation—they cannot afford to overlook one of the greatest obstacles that has kept the poor from the Christian church: the obstacle of cultural oppression.

Evangelization cannot take place with cultural neutrality. Those indigenous and blacks who joined the Christian community had to renounce their traditional religious beliefs. This has not changed. Even liberation theology does not seem to have gone far enough in redressing this wrong.

The blacks and the Indians have a rich religious culture that continues to this day to influence/their religious and cultural values. Further, these values continue to influence even those who conform to Christian authority. So many Indians and blacks superficially practice Christianity but are more deeply influenced by their own native beliefs.

A marriage of these cultures, traditional and Christian, is critical for Latin American liberation theology. Traditional or native culture is not opposed to the gospel. Only in such a marriage, when the oppressed and dominated feel they have a heritage that contributes positively to the present will they participate fully in the Christian church without a schizophrenic identity of "Christian" and "heathen."

The affirmation that the Bible must be read in the context of the community—the poor—must be interpreted in a very radical manner: seeing Christ in the vision that is most real to the Indian and black cultures. This is a big challenge.

We say this because we believe culture is a gift of God to be returned in worship to God. To deny people enjoyment and utilization of this gift must be considered as oppression and domination: a sin.

In conclusion, I would like to say very strongly that those in free Africa shall not rest until all our brothers and sisters in diaspora and all oppressed minorities in the world have been culturally liberated. We shall insist that those countries we share with economically, politically, culturally, and religiously are cognizant of such a demand.

THE ASIANS
Tissa Balasuriya (Sri Lanka)

We are very happy that the Latin American theologians of liberation have contributed significantly to Christian thinking as well as to the radical commitment of Christians to the revolutionary process in Latin America. Personally, I think that this is the most important theological innovation since the Protestant Reformation of the sixteenth century. It is the first time that Christians as a body have made an active commitment on the side of the poor and the oppressed since the late Middle Ages.

While appreciating these contributions and the great personal suffering that so many of our fellow Christians are facing in these lands, we wish to present some further aspects of the overall world situation for your theological reflection and practical action, so we will be participants together in the struggles of the people of the world.

Beginning with your own analysis and reflection we would like to ask you to reconsider more deeply some of your categories, tools of analysis, and your whole mindset.

What is the "reality" at the world level? How does Asia find itself in this reality?

Who are the "oppressed peoples" of the world? What has been the nature and historical length of "repression"? Twenty or thirty years? Four or five hundred years? Who are the world's poor?

The Amerindians of Bolivia spoke to us of their situation of extreme poverty with very poor incomes. No clothes. No means of transportation and communication. They live in fear, lack self-confidence, and suffer in sorrow and silence.   When you meditate on the map of the world you can see that this is the plight of the vast majority in Asia, especially South Asia. Asia is over 50 percent of the human race. Asians live in poverty much worse than that of the average Latin American—especially if we leave out the indigenous and black population here.

The Asians are the poor of the world. They have been exploited for thousands of years—five hundred of those years by Europeans. Asia is the continent of the hungry masses of humanity.

You rightly regard international capitalism as the main mechanism of domination in the world today. We would like to remind you that we have experienced a much longer and more deep-rooted domination by the expansion of the European peoples into the rest of the world.

From about the year 1500 the peoples of Europe, in a most dynamic period of their history, spread out into all the continents of the world. From Western Europe they went to the Americas, to Africa, Asia, and Oceania. From Eastern Europe the Russians under the Czar spread their empire from the Urals to the Pacific shores, occupying a vast land mass of Asia.

The political configuration of the map of the world today is the product of this expansion. The European peoples carved out the world for themselves. Everywhere they went about annexing lands, annihilating peoples, and destroying cultures. From our point of view this stands as the most terrible wave of genocide in human history. For us these were barbarian invasions more widespread and devastating than anything history has ever seen, including the barbarian invasions of Attila.

We are not merely harking back to the past, for the present world system is a solidification of the past. The nation-states are a result of this European expansion. The big multinational corporations are a development from this worldwide takeover of the lands, resources, and markets of the weak, impoverished peoples of the world.

We question the main categories of thinking of your socio-economic analysis. The principal obstacle to economic development is not merely lack of capital, technology, or organizational ability. Rather it is the relationship between people and land. Land is the main resource base for human living. The present national frontiers, set up by the European takeover of the earth, are the main impediment to human beings going to the vast land spaces of this planet. Land hunger or land acquisition is the main cause of international wars, such as the colonial wars and the two world wars.

There are inequalities of incomes, capital, technology, and resources—but principally of land. The people of Asia are confined by the vast Soviet empire, which the USSR gladly inherited from the imperialist Czars. Socialism in the USSR has made no difference to this land grab. In the South are "white" Australia and New Zealand. The Americas are also reserved for white immigration. These are the large uncultivated land masses of the world, to which Asia's farmers may not move.

The Latin American countries, along with the United States, the USSR, Canada, Australia, and New Zealand, are the world's landlords, keeping out the land-hungry Asians. Are not these countries, the world's breadbasket or rice bowl, meant for the whole of humanity?

Take Brazil where we are now. You have 8.5 million square kilometers for about 120 million people. This is about the size of China, which has some 900 million people. You have an enormous land mass that is extremely fertile and very scarcely populated. In the north region of the Amazon you have 3.6 million square kilometers with only about one or two persons per square kilometer.

Argentina is as big as India. Argentina has 27 million people and India about 620 million. Bangladesh has 80 million on land that is about 3 percent the size of Brazil.

Do not all the Latin American countries have anti-Asian legislation in their immigration policies? I am told Brazil was prepared to take all the white population from Rhodesia—about 250,000. But when the Vietnamese boat people knock at your doors you have "no room in the inn." All types of legitimizations are trotted out when it is a question of sharing your lands with the Asians: your unemployment, climate, and culture. Of course, what is required is not mere tokenism but a genuine response to this large scale, worldwide inequality and injustice.

We need a fundamental restructuring of the entire world distribution of land and resources. It is not enough to have socialism within countries. Today the rich socialist and capitalist countries are together in sharing the world's wealth. The animals of the USSR are more sure of their food than the poor of Asia; world trade ensures this. The grain from the fields of North and South America are fed to cattle rather than to the hungry children of Asia. Armaments are amassed to prevent any disturbance of the present world system, or rather to continue the land and resource grab by the rich, who are mainly the Europeans.

What is the responsibility of Christians for and in this situation? Do we really believe that we are all children of the same Father: "Our Father." What do we mean when we pray, "Give us this day our daily bread."

Do we genuinely accept each other as brothers and sisters, companions in a common struggle?

Our people have no food, no land. You are the world's landlords. You control the resources that can make human life possible for our people. But do you even consider sharing them?

What is the meaning of the Eucharist—of sharing bread? Is it only "spiritual" sharing?

Do you consider how much your thought patterns and analyses fail to see the human problem today in its historical and global dimension? Are not your categories those which permit you to challenge radically the dominant capitalism of North America, Europe, and Japan without having to consider sharing your own wealth? Is not the lack of population the main reason why the immense territories of Brazil, Argentina, Colombia, and Bolivia are not being utilized to maintain human life in a world of hunger? Are not these lands undeveloped, virgin forests that can sustain millions of human lives without any damage to your economy or ecology?

Does Latin American theology, while basing itself on social analysis, consider seriously the causes and effects of present-day problems as in Iran, Afghanistan, Vietnam, Kampuchea, South Africa, etc.? How do your analyses of capitalist and socialist societies understand these global conflicts? What support do you bring to our peoples as they are devastated by the big powers? We would like to see your theology develop in the direction of more practical international cooperation with the efforts of the people in the Third World to restructure the world economic system, e.g., through UNCTAD and the other U.N. agencies—even though these are not radical enough.

We would like to invite Latin American theology and Christian praxis to relate themselves to this global aspect of our problems. You cannot relate to Asia except by a global consideration, as Asia is over half of humanity. Gustavo Gutiérrez spoke of the irruption of the poor of Latin America. The poor masses of Asia are also in a process of a historic transformation. Whether we like it or not, with or without us or you, the poor of Asia will irrupt and take their destiny into their hands in the coming decades.

The great challenge to humanity is whether this vast elemental change in the world system can be brought about rationally and peacefully, or will it mean war and destruction? It is important that we understand the global nature of the struggle and do all we can to meet human needs and aspirations through international cooperation for a revolutionary restructuring of the world. Otherwise it will be chaos and continuing human misery of the millions of Asia.

What is the ecclesiology related to this situation. Are not our Asian masses the "uninvited" to the banquet of the kingdom to which Gustavo Gutiérrez refers? What is the church? How Christian are our communities if they do not open up to these issues? Who are the true believers in the gospel of Christ—the gospel of love and sharing? What is the meaning of the universality of the church in this context? We need a global vision as well as local action. Can the basic Christian communities here take up these challenges?

If we can genuinely share these anxieties and hopes, we can work together for integral human liberation. We should not be merely allies of convenience in the fight against capitalism; we must rather be friends in the large human struggle to build a new world order based on new persons who accept each other as brothers and sisters. It is only on this basis that we can think of the millions of our people in Asia being accepted as human beings equal in dignity, rights, and responsibility to all others. It is only then that they will be able to walk the face of this earth as children of the same Father—brothers and sisters of all.

THE WEST INDIANS
Alfred Reid (Jamaica)

I present these remarks on behalf of the delegation from the West Indies, otherwise called the non-Latin Caribbean. We are a community of several countries and nations, mostly islands, but also including countries on the mainland of South America such as Guyana and Belize.

The most outstanding feature of this community is its diversity: its many cultures, religions, and political systems; its openness to many influences; its affirmation of the contributions of many civilizations—African, European, Asian, and American—that have gone into the rich texture of the Caribbean personality.

It is from this point of view that we look at the Latin American church and at liberation theology. We ask ourselves and we ask you: Can your church and its theology really accommodate the fullness of the human reality as we have experienced it and as it exists here in Latin America? Where is the contribution of the 40 million blacks of Brazil? What mark have they made on the life and thought of the Christian community? What about the blacks of Nicaragua? What fellowship is there with the Caribbean, with Guyana and Belize, which are part of this continent? As we witness the vitality and color of the Carnival in Rio we get a picture of the exciting possibility effective black participation could have on the life of this church.

These remarks are not mere reactions from the black nations of the hemisphere. They are implicit in the theology of liberation itself. For this theology is unique among modern theologies in that it claims to arise out of the life, the experience, and the struggles of the poor, just as genuine liturgy is always the celebration of the victories the people experience in the struggle to bring the kingdom into being.

We have used the words "people" and "the poor" over and over, but what do we mean? Whom do we mean by "the people" and "the poor?" Do we mean the blacks, the Indians, the women? The cultures of the Indian nations are absolutely fundamental in the hemisphere. Are we satisfied that they speak in our liturgy and theology? *Not*—please note—*not* that they are spoken for, or spoken about, but that they speak for themselves and speak to all of us even as we speak to them: 70 percent of the population of Bolivia, almost 50 percent of Peru, significant proportions of Ecuador, of Guatemala, of Mexico. These are the people. And no doubt they have made their mark. But are you convinced that the church has really learned from them? Have you in your very impressive pastoral strategy and in your basic Christian communities made absolutely sure that manipulation of the people, imposition, and alienating ideologies are brought under the rule of justice, respect, and human liberation? Are the people the real subjects of their history? Or are they once more the objects of history?

This is crucial, because we believe that no theology can be separated from anthropology, as you also believe. What a people believe about people is the most accurate test of what they really believe about God and God's commitment to people (not people in the abstract but the actual people with whom God is in contact). This is the index of commitment to God. It is our belief that "the people" and "the poor" need to be defined more concretely and specifically. They have a contribution to make that no one else can make. They make this contribution not by conversion to white middle-class culture, but by the liberation of their own unique personality and the precise culture with which God has endowed them.

In faithfulness to the pluralistic tradition of the West Indies we go even further. We place a positive value not only on diversity in culture as such but also on religion as well. After all, behind every great culture there is a great religion. The God who is really God is always bigger than the particular systems that claim to describe God. God is revealed in many ways, by many names, in many colors, and there is no one who cannot teach us something about God. What the situation calls for is a radical ecumenism, not just talking with other Christians of our own class and culture, but an ecumenical oneness that liberates us to see dignity, beauty, and rationality in symbol systems that in our arrogant parochialism we have in the past described as primitive and pagan. Both Marxism and modern Christianity, as products of white western rationalism, need at this time a humanizing exposure, an enriching relationship of sharing and religious adventure.

We realize that in the diversity, pluralism, and openness of which I have spoken we West Indians have not succeeded in finding that unity among ourselves that would give us greater strength. But we hope that whatever unity we forge in the future will leave behind no forgotten peoples, cultures, or faiths.

Finally, let me say that we do not presume to impose an alien idea on this congress. Rather we challenge you to take your own theological task to its logical conclusion. For what else can it mean to have a church not only for the poor but of the poor, and a theology not of the people but from the people.

22

From Geneva to São Paulo:
A Dialogue between Black Theology
and Latin American Liberation Theology

James H. Cone (United States)

What is the relation between class and race oppression? This is the primary question that has defined the focus of the dialogue between North American black theologians and Latin American liberation theologians. The dialogue has been characterized by the attitudes of indifference, hostility, and mutual support. Although these three attitudes have been present among some Latin and black theologians during the entire period of our dialogue, there have been occasions in which one of the three has dominated the consciousness of most of the participants. In this essay, my purpose is to evaluate the development of this dialogue (from Geneva, 1973, to São Paulo, 1980) in the light of my participation in it and also with the hope of the deepening our understanding of each other.[1]

Before Geneva, May 1973, black and Latin theologians had had almost no contact with each other, and thus knew very little about each other's historical projects and the theologies arising from them. Since most black theologians do not speak or read Spanish, and since Latin American theologians are under European influence and consequently not trained to look for theological ideas among people of color, the theological works of both blacks and Latin Americans were virtually unknown to each other. Of course, black theologians had heard about Camilo Torres, Archbishop Dom Helder Camara, and the 1968 Latin American Episcopal Conference at Medellín. We had also read Paulo Freire's *Pedagogy of the Oppressed*[2] and Rubem Alves's *Theology of Human Hope*.[3] But it was not until Gustavo Gutiérrez's *A Theology of Liberation* was published by Orbis Books in 1973 that black theologians began to take seriously Latin American liberation theology as a distinct perspective, completely different from the theologies of freedom from Europe and North America.

Latin American theologians, of course, had heard about the black Civil Rights movement and Martin Luther King, Jr. They also knew about Black Power and the black unrest in the urban cities during the 1960s. Some had heard also about a black theology emerging from the black struggle of the sixties. However, it was not until the publication of the Spanish translation of my book *A Black Theology of Liberation*[4] in 1973 that a significant number of Latin American theologians were presented with the opportunity of dialoguing with black theology.

Since the origin of black and Latin American theologies happened independently of each other,[5] it is revealing that both chose the term *liberation* to describe the major emphasis of their theological perspectives. One might expect that their mutual focus on liberation would also make them natural partners for dialogue in the struggles of freedom, but that has not always been the case. The Latin American theologians' emphasis upon the class struggle, with almost no mention of race oppression, made black theologians suspicious of their white, European identity. Black theologians' focus on race oppression, with almost no mention of class, made Latin American theologians suspicious of our capitalist, bourgeois identity. However, because both groups were speaking and writing about theology from the perspective of the poor, neither group said much about the theological enterprise of the other. Each acquired an attitude of indifference, speaking about the other's theological viewpoint only when questioned about it by their mutual enemy, namely, white European and North American theologians and churchpeople.

GENEVA 1973

The first major encounter between Latin and black theologians occurred in Geneva, May 1973, at the World Council of Churches.[6] The occasion was a symposium on black theology and Latin American liberation theology. The title of this symposium suggests that its major concern was to initiate a dialogue between these theologies, but that was not the case. The chief concern of this symposium was to introduce Latin and black theologies on the agenda of the WCC. That was why more than sixty Europeans and North American theologians were invited to participate in the discussions, along with a much smaller number of blacks and Latin Americans. However, during the course of our debate with Europeans about the nature and significance of black and Latin American theologies of liberation, each of the black and Latin American participants realized that we should be talking to each other and not to Europeans. Hugo Assmann, one of the Latin American presentors, expressed this concern sharply.

> My biggest mistake in the first days of the symposium was that I was speaking to the participants [Europeans] and not to my friends who represent Black Theology. In my group . . . it was a dialogue between Latin American Theology of Liberation and European questions and

problems. I would like to enter into dialogue with Black Theology.
. . . It would be terrible to remain in 'incommunication' with Black
Theology.[7]

Assmann expressed a concern that was deeply felt by all Latin American
and black participants. But we did not know what to do about it. For both
blacks and Latin Americans knew that creative dialogue would not be easy to
accomplish. No one at the symposium expressed the problems of dialogue
between blacks and Latin Americans any clearer than Assmann. He referred
to the western and European character of Latin American theology of liberation and the difficulty it has in being understood by the non-western part of
Latin America, that is, "the Brazilian Africans, the people of the Caribbean
Islands, the mysterious Mexicans. . . . Traveling in Latin America, I have
had the experience of terrible 'incommunication' with these people."[8] Assmann rightly anticipated that a similar problem would emerge in his attempt
to talk with black people in the United States.

Until now I have had very little communication with Black people in the
United States because when as a Westernized Latin American I read
books and articles about the problem of black people, . . . I am
tempted to introduce Western Marxism. What must I do in order to
have a better dialogue with you?
  I don't know how this dialogue with you can be improved, but it is
more important than European theology for us Latin Americans. I
don't want to destroy the connection with you. But I do want to reach a
state of tension with you—a third kind of tension which is found more
and more in the Third World.[9]

Other black and Latin American participants in the symposium also expressed the need for dialogue with each other. But unfortunately the limitation of time and the European context prevented a deeper encounter with
each other. Despite these difficulties, however, the fact that both Assmann
and Freire spoke of North American blacks as Third World people meant
that an openness was created from the Latin American side,[10] while several
blacks made similar gestures from our side.
  Blacks left the Geneva symposium feeling that the dialogue between Latin
American theologians and us had already begun to move from indifference
(created largely by a lack of knowledge) to mutual support. But the preparation for and the event of the 1975 Detroit conference proved us wrong.

DETROIT 1975

The August 1975 Detroit conference of the Theology in the Americas was
organized by Father Sergio Torres with the expressed purpose of initiating a
dialogue between Latin American theologians of liberation and North

American white theologians. An announced statement of the conference read:

> The intention of the planners of the "Theology in the Americas: 1975" conference is to invite a group of Latin American theologians, representing the theology of liberation, to dialogue with North American theologians concerning the context and methodology of this new theological current. It is hoped that such a dialogue would help both groups: the Latin Americans to understand the complex reality of the U.S.; the North American theologians to initiate a process of evaluation of the American reality from the viewpoint of the poor and the oppressed.

Black theologians were surprised and angry when they were confronted with the plan of the conference, and we protested vigorously. Several blacks had heated discussions about this matter with Sergio Torres, but he seemed incapable of understanding our concern. I reminded him of the Geneva symposium and Hugo Assmann's comment that Latin American theologians' dialogue with black theology was more important than their conversations with European theology. If Assmann is right, then why are Latin Americans being invited to the United States for dialogue primarily with white North American theologians and not with blacks and other racial minorities? Indeed the manner in which the conference was being organized seemed to disregard completely black theology's presence in North America as a theology from the perspective of the oppressed.

The structure of the conference was designed according to the stated intentions of the brochure. About fifteen Latin American theologians were given the opportunity to state their theological and political perspectives to about two hundred North American white theologians and church people. The small number of oppressed racial minorities of the United States were given a secondary role in the conference, and their minor status was based apparently on the assumption that they did not have much to contribute to the discussions. It was also assumed by most Latin Americans and white North Americans that race oppression can best be understood in the context of class analysis. These assumptions did not go over well with black and other minority participants from the United States. The reason for our resistance to the Latin American emphasis on class analysis was our deep distrust of the white religious left in North America whose past and present behavior in our communities contradicted the public affirmations of their solidarity with the struggles of poor people for freedom. For minority people at the Detroit 1975 conference, class analysis appeared to be used by whites as a camouflage for evading the fact of racial oppression in the world, the United States, and also in the conference itself. In protest to the white takeover of the conference, minorities formed a caucus and issued a joint statement expressing our concerns. To my knowledge, this was the first occasion for such strong expressions of unity among U.S. minorities in a theological and church context.[11]

In addition to our distrust of the white religious left, we were also concerned about the failure of most Latin Americans to be open to the suggestion that they might have something to learn from our struggles for justice in the U.S. and from the theologies emerging from those struggles. How can Latin Americans claim that Christian theology must come from poor people's struggles when they seemed more interested in dialoguing with dominant white theologies than with theologies arising from the poor in North America? Also, if Latin American theologians really wanted to talk with black theologians about class and race, why do they invite white Americans to be the dominant participants in the dialogue?

In an attempt to move beyond the hostility in the conference sessions, black and Latin American theologians called for a dialogue (in the late evening) between Latin Americans and other racial minorities in the United States. On the Latin American side, Hugo Assmann, Enrique Dussel, José Míguez Bonino, and others were present. On the black side, J. Deotis Roberts, Preston Williams, and I, along with others, were present. There were approximately twenty persons present. The discussion began on a hostile note, with blacks emphasizing the importance of race oppression and Latin Americans stressing class. I was very disappointed that we began by pointing to a weakness in the other's perspective rather than its strength. Apparently a negative atmosphere had already been set by our earlier conversations in the conference itself. Whatever the case, most blacks felt that Latin Americans suggested this late night discussion in order to set us straight regarding the primacy of the class struggle. Latin Americans probably had a similar feeling about blacks regarding the race struggle. It does not really matter who started our heated exchange. We were all responsible for the alienation, and most persons on both sides participated in it. Blacks came close to saying that the Latin Americans were white racists, and the Latin Americans accused blacks of being North American capitalists. I felt deeply frustrated as we hurled accusations at each other. It was as if the Geneva symposium had not taken place. What had happened to our concern to learn from each other, stated so clearly by Assmann in Geneva? This late night discussion did more to alienate blacks and Latin Americans than any other encounter during our eight years of dialogue.[12]

Fortunately, Hispanic Americans from Texas and California played an important role in minimizing our tensions; but the words between blacks and Latin Americans were too harsh for reconciliation to take place during the evening. Black theologians left the meeting thinking that Latin Americans were hopelessly European and racist. And it was natural for Latin Americans

to leave thinking that we were too North American to see the global significance of the class struggle.

MEXICO CITY 1977

Between the Detroit conference of August 1975 and the Encounter of
Theologians in Mexico City in October 1977, the hostility between blacks and
Latin American theologians was greatly reduced by Sergio Torres and Gustavo Gutiérrez. Sergio Torres eventually heard the concerns of the racial
minorities at the Detroit conference. Through his influence Theology in the
Americas was completely reorganized with an emphasis on the theology projects of black, native, Hispanic, and Asian Americans. Because minority projects did not have many resources for financial support, Torres spent some
time generating help from other sources. At the second Detroit conference of
Theology in the Americas (August 1980), racial minorities, with the help of
some whites, continued their reorganization of TIA for the purpose of developing a unique North American theology of liberation as based on the struggles of racial minorities in this country. This reorganization of TIA by racial
minorities could not have happened without the support and encouragement
of Sergio Torres.

A similar role has been played by Gustavo Gutiérrez. He arrived late at the
1975 Detroit conference and was not a part of the hostile dialogue between
Latin Amerians and blacks. But even during his brief stay at the Detroit
conference and in the midst of a hostile atmosphere, most blacks recognized
that Gutiérrez had a more open attitude toward black theology. We blacks
speculated as to whether his openness to black theology was due to his Indian
origin.

In 1976, Guttiérrez was invited to Union Theological Seminary as the
Henry Luce Visiting Professor. During his stay at Union, we spent much time
together talking about the similarities and differences between black and
Latin American liberation theologies. We also taught a course together, fo-
cusing primarily on black, Asian, Latin American, and African theologies.
Black theologians' encounter with Gutiérrez has been entirely different from
that with any other Latin American theologian. The chief reason for this is
our feeling that he has really learned from us, and we have learned much
from him in particular and Latin American liberation theology generally.
Without exception, every black person that I know who has met Gutiérrez
speaks of his openness to listen to black people and to be taught by our culture and history. I have heard similar comments from Africans, Asians,
women, and other racial minorities in the United States.

An indication of the widespread appreciation among blacks for Gutiérrez's
openness to learn from their culture and history was shown in the black response to his presentation at the recent Theology in the Americas conference
in Detroit (August 1980). His analysis of the role of joy in poor people's
struggle and his use of black music as an illustration of his point was so

illuminating that even blacks were amazed by the profoundity of his interpretation. Their response to Gutiérrez was similar to their response to one of their own. One could hear blacks saying "Amen," "Speak, sir," "Tell it like it is," and other responses of agreement. We could hardly believe what we heard. "How could a non-black be so accurate in his interpretation of our experience?" we asked ourselves. It was at this point that we reminded ourselves that such insight comes from not mere academic reflection but from the gift of the Spirit. God's Spirit transcends racial and national boundaries and joins poor people together in the one struggle of freedom.

Through the influences of Gutiérrez, Torres, and others, the impact of the Latin American liberation theology upon black theology began to happen in a visible manner at the Black Theology Project Conference in Atlanta, Georgia, August 1977.[13] Several black theologians had come to realize that, regardless of our personal feelings about the racism of some Latin Americans, we cannot continue to avoid saying something about the issue of socialism versus capitalism. Neither can we ignore the global context of our struggle for freedom. We must seek ways of expressing our solidarity with the poor throughout the world. Indeed we can no longer speak of racism as if it is the only problem in the United States and the world. For if the black poor in the United States are to achieve freedom, the achievement will take place only in solidarity with other poor people in the U.S. and the world context.

In recognizing that race analysis must be combined with class and sex oppression, we also realized that an analysis of imperialism reveals the importance of Marxism as one of the primary tools of social analysis. In my address "Black Theology and the Black Church: Where Do We Go From Here?" I raised the issue of Marxism and socialism, inviting black theologians, church people, and others to move beyond our exclusive preoccupation with race oppression to an inclusion of class and sex oppression.[14] The response was much more positive than I expected, and it is reflected in the "Message to the Black Church and Community" drafted and adopted by the conference. This message not only condemned racism but also capitalism, sexism, and imperialism. There was also a concern to find ways to support our brothers and sisters engaged in the struggle for freedom.

> The Black Church must be one with and inseparable from our brothers and sisters around the world who fight for liberation in a variety of ways, including armed struggle. We affirm whatever methods they decide best in their particular situations and make no pious and hypocritical judgments which condemn those efforts to bring an end to their oppression, recognizing we in this country have ourselves been compelled to make similar choices and may be so compelled again.[15]

The Atlanta conference was the first major public declaration by a group of black theologians and church people to express the intention to enter into dialogue with Marxism and the expectation to learn from it. Therefore when

I was invited to Mexico City (October 1977) to participate in the Encounter of Theologians, I went prepared to communicate a black openness to dialogue with Latin Americans about class oppression and the global context of our struggle against it.[16] Even though the Encounter of Theologians appeared to be designed primarily to chastise Jurgen Moltmann for his "Open Letter to José Míguez Bonino,"[17] there was time for dialogue about the relation of Latin American and black theologies on the issue of race and class immediately following my presentation on "Christian Theology and Political Praxis."[18] In this dialogue, our differences in emphasis emerged but not with the hostile overtones found at the 1975 Detroit conference. There was unquestionably much more of an openness to each on both sides.

The presence of Sergio Arce Martínez of Cuba at the encounter helped our conversations. No one could question his commitment to Marxism, and unlike most Latin American liberation theologians, he was doing theology in the context of socio-political structures more conducive to the implementation of his theological project. His public display of his willingness to learn from black theology helped other Latin Americans to do the same. I would point to the Mexico City conference as the turning point in the attitude of many Latin American theologians toward black theology. At this meeting, the indifference and hostile attitudes began to be transformed into a creative openness to learn and share in a common struggle of freedom. For the first time since the 1973 Geneva symposium, most Latin Americans referred to black people in the United States as their oppressed brothers and sisters in the First World.

EATWOT: DAR ES SALAAM, ACCRA, WENNAPPUWA

The Ecumenical Association of Third World Theologians (EATWOT) has been the most creative force in removing the attitudes of indifference and hostility from our conversations. The first major meeting of EATWOT was held in Dar es Salaam, Tanzania, August 1976.[19] Only one black North American was present at that historic meeting. The reason for our absence was the ambiguity in some people's mind regarding the meaning of the term "Third World." Perhaps remembering our previous unpleasant encounters in the 1975 Detroit conference, and forgetting their earlier more inclusive definition of the Third World, Latin Americans were vehement in their rejection of North American blacks as members of an association of Third World theologians. They wanted to limit its meaning to geography, that is, to persons born and presently living in Asia, Africa, and Latin America. But Africans (and some Asians) were even more vehement in their insistence on the inclusion of North American blacks, because Africans said that the Black World is one. They contended that the Third World referred to the condition of dependence, a situation of exploitation and oppression.[20]

No final decision was made in Tanzania regarding the inclusion of North American blacks as members. But Africans and Asians were sensitive to the attempts of some Latin Americans to dominate EATWOT by insisting on the dominance of Marxian analysis to the exclusion of other concerns. As one Asian reported:

> The Latin Americans were the whole time harping on socio-economic-political dimensions as the major or only reality, and applied rigorously the Marxian tool of analysis. All the other realities were so insignificant for them that they could be integrated into the economic-political domination or its consequences. This was questioned strongly by Asians and Africans though they agreed with the analysis and results of socio-economic-political reality.[21]

It was interesting to find out that the same issue that alienated blacks and Latin Americans also produced a similar relation between Latin Americans and other Third World peoples in Africa and Asia.

In an attempt to counter the Latin American endeavor to exclude North American blacks, Africans invited eight black theologians to the second EATWOT conference, which was held in Accra, Ghana, December 1977.[22] The major emphasis of the conference focused on African theology. Among the black theologians present were Gayraud S. Wilmore, Jacquelyn Grant, George Thomas, and I. Among the Latin Americans present were Sergio Torres, Gustavo Gutiérrez, Enrique Dussel, and José Míguez Bonino. To my surprise, Latin Americans, Asians, and North American blacks worked together with Africans for the purpose of developing an African theology for that continent. There were no obvious tensions among Latin Americans and blacks at Accra.

The absence of tensions at Accra does not mean that the issue of race and class had been solved to the satisfaction of both sides. The lack of tension between Latin Americans and blacks can be accounted for in several ways: (1) There was indeed a new openness on both sides, as indicated in our discussion of the Mexico City conference. (2) The focus of the Accra conference on African theology rather than the issue of race and class meant that the second EATWOT meeting did not provide an appropriate context for a discussion of problems relating primarily to Latin Americans and blacks. (3) Sergio Torres and Gustavo Gutiérrez were the most active Latin Americans at Accra, and blacks found both very open to their concerns. (4) The question of the meaning of the term "Third World" and black North Americans' eligibility for membership in EATWOT was postponed until a later time.

The third EATWOT conference was held in Wennappuwa, Sri Lanka, January 1979.[23] Although the focus was on Asian theology, some Latin American, black, and African theologians were invited as fraternal delegates. Our status as fraternal delegates proved to be very revealing. I found out that the Asians resented the dominant and seemingly dogmatic attitude of Latin Americans at least as much as blacks did. When the status of "fraternal" delegates was seriously questioned by some Latin Americans and others,

Asians said in a gentle but firm way that they were not going to allow out-
siders, who know so little about Asian reality, to come to their conference and
tell them how to do theology. Although I was among the fraternal delegates, I
found myself agreeing with the Asian position.

I found out later that there had been some discussion among Asians as to
whether EATWOT was really a Third World association or merely Latin
American. The Christian Conference of Asia (CCA) refused to sponsor the
EATWOT meeting because of the dominance of the association by Latin
Americans. Preman Niles, Secretary for Theological Concerns, expressed it
sharply:

> Asian theologians have usually been co-opted into theological agendas
> and theological positions which originate elsewhere. This is a constant
> danger, and is in many ways why clear Asian theological positions are
> either slow to emerge or do not emerge at all. The danger of co-option is
> particularly evident when an organization [EATWOT] seeks to speak
> for the whole of the Third World while taking its basic theological impe-
> tus from one section of the Third World, namely, Latin America. This is
> not to say that insights from Latin American theologies have no signifi-
> cance for Asia. They do; and many Asian theologians owe much to the
> breakthroughs accomplished on that continent. Also, many of these
> themes were already being explored in Asia before the so-called Latin
> American Liberation Theology hit the theological market. Taking this
> whole rather complex situation into account the CTC Commission on
> Theological Concerns of the CCA felt that it should support [not spon-
> sor] this consultation in a discriminating and critical way so that the
> motif of liberation is explored in relation to Asian contexts and situa-
> tions.[24]

When Asians found out that many blacks had similar feelings about Latin
Americans, we found ourselves supporting each other's concerns. Since Africans and blacks have always supported each other, and since only two Latin
Americans were present at the Sri Lanka meeting, I was invited to become a
member of EATWOT without controversy.

MATANZAS 1979

Immediately following the EATWOT meeting in Sri Lanka, several blacks
were invited to a conference on "Evangelization and Politics" in Matanzas,
Cuba, February–March, 1979.[25] This conference marked another significant
movement in our dialogue, similar to the Mexico City meeting. Until this
time, most Latin Americans had limited their openness to black theology to
oral conversation. Very few references to black theology are found in their
written works. Although Juan Luis Segundo's *The Liberation of Theology* is
a significant exception,[26] this single exception is not enough to remove the

suspicion that Latin Americans still regard black theology as being hopelessly limited by its concern with race oppression.

At the Cuba conference, I decided that I would be more direct in my challenge to Latin Americans in regard to their silence on racism. Is it because they are *white* Latin Americans and thus blind to their own racism? Why are there no black theologians among the large number of Latin American liberation theologians, especially since there are more blacks in Latin America than in North America? Even if class analysis is primary, this fact does not give Latin Americans the right to remain silent on race. Furthermore, no white person, not even a Latin American, has the right to say to blacks that race is secondary, especially since white people are responsible for our racial oppression.

These comments and questions generated heated debates in the plenary sessions and small discussion groups. Because of the vigor with which I pressed my position, I was invited to serve on the writing committee for the "Final Document" so that race oppression could be made an integral part of it.[27] But I declined on the grounds that Latin Americans should struggle to come to terms with the inclusion of race analysis as we blacks are trying to do with class. I did not want Latin Americans to include race in their document merely because of pressure from me. I think the "Final Document" of the Cuba conference represents a significant step forward, and it shows that some Latin Americans have been trying to listen to black theologians.

One major reason for the Latin Americans' openness to black theology was the dominant presence of Cuban theologians. Since my first contact with Cuban theologians in Mexico City, 1977, I have been impressed by the willingness of Cubans to learn from black theology. And since the "Evangelization and Politics" conference was held on their soil and because they have a strong influence among Latin American liberation theologians, the Cubans' open attitude toward black theology caused others to be open as well.

SÃO PAULO 1980

Because of black theologians' dialogue with Latin Americans, we have become much more aware of the importance of class analysis and the global context of theology. This awareness is found not only in my recent writings but also in the writings of Gayraud Wilmore[28] and Cornel West.[29] It is also found in the Black Theology Project (BTP) of Theology in the Americas. At the Ventnor, New Jersey, meeting of the BTP, December 1979, Cornel West made a provocative presentation on the relation of class and race analysis. At that meeting, the BTP affirmed the importance of class analysis and also of socialism. Recently BTP participated with the Democratic Socialist Organizing Committee (DSOC) in a joint publication of my essay "The Black Church and Marxism: What Do They Have to Say to Each Other?" This essay was written for the purpose of initiating a dialogue of black theologians and Marxist-socialist groups. With Cornel West as its director, BTP has made its dialogue with labor and Marxian socialism one of its major concerns for the future.

As black theologians have become more aware of class oppression, Latin American theologians have shown that they are aware of race oppression in their own context and in the world. An awareness of the importance of race and its conspicuous absence from their theology motivated the Latin Americans of EATWOT to hold a conference on "Race, Class, and Liberation Theology" in Mandeville, Jamaica, December 1979. The purpose of this dialogue was to prepare Latin Americans for a serious discussion of race at the then forthcoming fourth EATWOT conference in São Paulo, Brazil. Cornel West and I were invited to attend. Also present were several Caribbean theologians, including Robert Cuthbert and Ashley Smith. Among the Latin Americans were Sergio Torres and Pablo Richards, and a black priest from Costa Rica, Lloyd Stennette.

Enrique Dussel could not be present, but he sent a paper on "Black People in the History of Latin America Social Formation," which served as one focal point of our heated debates. Blacks from the Caribbean and the United States were vehement in their unanimous rejection of Dussel's analysis of racism. Black theologians contended that it was an analysis too much dependent on the conceptual tools derived from the European culture responsible for black people's oppression. Such an analysis is typical among white intellectuals who claim to be in solidarity with our struggle to eliminate racism but fail to turn to the history and culture of the victims for intellectual resources in order to understand the nature of the problem, and what must be done to combat it. It appeared to black theologians that Dussel assumed that black victims had nothing to contribute to our analysis of and the struggle against racial oppression. For the resources he used were exclusively European, with Sigmund Freud's *Civilization and its Discontents* occupying a central place in his analysis. I only regret that Dussel was not present to hear our critique because the issue at stake is very important for our future dialogue.

The central question for most blacks regarding Dussel's paper was this: Can we assume that the culture that enslaves people will also be the one that will provide the resources for their liberation? Almost without exception blacks said an emphatic no! Dussel's paper was strongly rejected because blacks said that it showed no knowledge of or concern for the genuine voices of the victims of racism. We blacks are accustomed to reading essays and books on racism by white university people who think that they know everything about black oppression without even having to consult what black people think regarding their victimization. Unfortunately Dussel's approach to the theme of racism reminded us very much of that white intellectual blindness. Our discussion of this matter with Pablo Richards, whom we blacks were meeting for the first time, did more to reinforce what we felt about Dussel's paper than to eliminate it.[30]

Most blacks left Jamaica having grave doubts about the possibility of Latin American liberation theologians taking racism seriously at the forthcoming São Paulo conference (February–March 1980). The fourth major meeting of EATWOT was called an International Ecumenical Congress of Theology with a major focus on the "Ecclesiology of Popular Christian Communities." Several blacks who attended the São Paulo conference said that the meeting merely confirmed their doubts experienced in Jamaica. While I had a similar feeling, I think that there is a broader context in which to evaluate the question of racism and Latin American theology. We must not minimize the major importance of the São Paulo conference for Latin American Christians struggling for freedom, and what their struggle symbolizes for Christians everywhere. Neither should we underplay the growth that Latin American theologians have made on the issues of racism and sexism. In addition to the Jamaica Conference, Latin American theologians of EATWOT also held conferences on "Women, Praxis and Liberation Theology" (Tepeyac, Mexico, October 1979) and "Indigenous Mobilization and the Theology of Liberation" (San Cristobal de las Casas, Mexico, September 1979). The fact that these three conferences were held shows an openness among Latin American liberation theologians not previously present among them. Unlike the conference on racism, the conferences on sexism and indigenous people were well organized with excellent reports being presented at São Paulo to the EATWOT assembly. In addition there was time spent in the plenary sessions that focused on blacks, women, and the indigenous population with excellent spokespersons for each group. I can therefore say with much confidence that Latin American liberation theologians have come a long way since Geneva 1973. This growth could be seen not only in the São Paulo conference itself but partly in the "Final Document" of the conference. It is within the wider context of our eight years of dialogue that I offer my appreciative comments regarding Latin Americans and the question of racism.

However I do not want my positive comments to lead to a misunderstanding. I am not saying that the São Paulo conference showed that Latin Americans are now dealing with the racism issue to my satisfaction or to the satisfaction of other blacks. For I must say that despite their advances on racism and sexism at São Paulo, there was little evidence that blacks, women, and the indigenous population made any significant impact on the nature of Latin American liberation theology. Indeed Miguel Concha's presentation, "Interpreting Situations of Domination: The Poor, Ethnic Groups, and Classes Made up of the Common People" (see above Document 6) had the same kinds of problems found in Enrique Dussel's essay discussed in Jamaica. There was no evidence of any investigation of the perspectives of the victims about whom they speak. It seemed that the concerns of blacks, women, and the indigenous people were peripheral for most Latin Americans, and their conspicuous absence from the plenary sessions during the discussion of these issues confirmed this suspicion for many non-Latin American participants.

It should be revealing to the Latin Americans that the non-participants at

São Paulo offered a similar critique of the Latin Americans' failure to take seriously the culture of the poor. In our view, this failure conflicted sharply with the Latin Americans' claim to be in solidarity with the liberation of the poor. What *kind* of liberation are Latin American liberation theologians offering the poor blacks and Indians (both men and women), if the cultures of these people are not to be taken seriously in the liberation process? As early as the Geneva 1973 symposium, it appeared that Hugo Assmann recognized precisely this problem when he said:

> Until now the Latin American Theology of Liberation has used mostly Western and European theories and this poses a great question. We are trying now in Christian revolutionary groups to find a new communicative language. The Christians for Socialism movement in Chile is attempting to reinterpret in Marxist popular language the history, the revolution, the struggles and the processes of the proletarian movement in Chile. This strikes a somewhat false note, I must say, in an effort to communicate with Black Theology. It is false, because *who* is making this effort of communication in a popular language, a popular translation? Western people—Latin Americans, but Western people. There is another language—a grassroots language. They have a language; we don't want to give them one. . . . It is necessary to have a dialectic relationship between our Western, colonized, dependent language and their language.[31]

Assmann's comment in 1973 summarizes well the concerns of non-Latin Americans at the São Paulo conference. I only wish he could have expressed similar remarks there as well. Of course, some Latin Americans did recognize the culture and history of the poor and spoke to it. Gustavo Gutiérrez's lecture on the "Irruption of the Poor" was a case in point. But such exceptions did not change the fact that most non-Latins felt that the culture of the non-European poor remained invisible in Latin American liberation theology. Preman Niles summarized the feelings of most non-Latin Americans. After expressing his appreciation for the presence of the poor "at the center of theological construction and ecclesial practice in Latin America," he said:

> We detect a certain rigidity in the understanding of who the poor are, a rigidity that leads to exclusivism in spite of some attempts to be open and not albeit overly dogmatic. At this point we can learn a lesson, a negative one, from models of capitalistic development in Asia. When the people ask questions about their participation, they are often told: Wait; first the skilled people must do their job of developing the country; then you will be included. Our experience has been that the people are never included, and they continue to be simply the objects and not the subjects of history.

The basic question is this: Do the poor speak for themselves, or do others speak on behalf of the poor and incorporate them or accommodate them into a given schema? This question applies particularly to the participation of the blacks and the indigenous people in the process of liberation [see above, Document 21].

Preman Niles's comments were reinforced by other non-Latin participants from Asia, Africa, the Caribbean, and the United States. I was disappointed that many Latin Americans seemed unable or unwilling to hear the critique of the non-Latin American panel. But some Latin Americans did hear it, and their hearing is already being implemented in their theological work.

In addition to the dialogue of black North American theologians with white Latin Americans, the São Paulo conference enabled black North Americans to meet a significant number of black Latin Americans, and we began the discussion of the possibility of organizing a theological conference for blacks in the United States, the Caribbean, and Latin America. Such a conference was expected to take place in July of 1980 in Costa Rica, but the shortness of time prevented it. I do hope that the Black Theology Project and the Caribbean Conference of Churches will be able to realize this event. There is little doubt that such a conference will be helpful in black theology's dialogue with Latin American liberation theology.

THE FUTURE

Where do we go from here in the dialogue with Latin American liberation theology and black theology? I would like to make four concluding comments about our future.

1. It is important to recognize that we have moved from indifference and hostility to serious dialogue on race and class with the expressed purpose of supporting each other's theological projects. I hope that we can keep sharply before us the history of our eight years of dialogue so that we will not be tempted to make the mistakes of the past and thereby create hostile and indifferent attitudes toward each other.

2. There is no need to decide which is primary, race or class, before dialogue begins. There will undoubtedly be persons on both sides of the issue in both groups. What is needed is an openness to reality on both sides. This openness can be created best by persons who come from the same contexts and are committed to the same struggle but who represent different perspectives on race and class. This means that it would be helpful, for black theology's dialogue with Latin American liberation theology, if the former included in its group black Marxists. The same is true for white Latin Americans in regard to the race issue. They need black-consciousness theologians in their group so that they can learn how to face squarely the issue of racism.

3. Both black North American and Latin American theologians need to plan a conference in which the issue of race and class is the central theme. In

this conference, we need people who represent both sides of the issue in both of our contexts. I believe that such a conference is needed so that we can begin to work more creatively with each other.

4. If Latin Americans and black North Americans expect to deepen their dialogue, then our mutual encounter must move beyond the context of international conferences. Neither black theology nor Latin American liberation theology is made in international meetings. Rather the origin and meaning of both theologies are defined by the concrete struggles of the people that they seek to represent. To understand each other's focus on class and race, therefore, we need to live among the people for whom these contradictions are everyday realities. Black theologians need to spend some time with the poor people of Latin America so they can experience for themselves the class contradictions in that country. And Latin Americans need to spend some time in the ghettoes of the United States so they can experience what it means to be black in this society. This mutual participation in each other's communities will unquestionably deepen our dialogue. For much of our disagreement on the issue of race and class arises from the lack of knowledge of each other's praxis.

5. Whatever our future together might be, we must now know that nothing is more important than the fact that we are committed to the one faith that also requires a political commitment in the same struggle of freedom. Our disagreements must not be allowed to blind us to the knowledge that we are fighting a common enemy and our victory is certain only to the degree that we struggle for it together.

NOTES

1. For an earlier report on the dialogue between Latin American liberation theologians and black theologians, see my "Black Theology and Third World Theologies" in Gayraud Wilmore and James Cone, eds., *Black Theology: A Documentary History, 1966-1979* (Maryknoll, N.Y.: Orbis Books, 1979), pp. 445-62.

2. New York: Herder and Herder, 1970.

3. Washington: Corpus Books, 1969.

4. *A Black Theology of Liberation* was translated by Manuel Mercader and published by Carlos Lohlé, Calle Tacuari 1516, Buenos Aires, Argentina.

5. For an account of the origin of both theologies, see Wilmore and Cone, *Black Theology*, and José Míguez Bonino, *Doing Theology in a Revolutionary Situation* (Philadelphia: Fortress, 1975).

6. An account of this dialogue is found in *Risk*, vol. 9, no. 2 (1973). The major participants in the dialogue were Paulo Freire, Hugo Assmann, Eduardo Bodipo-Malumba, and myself.

7. Ibid., p. 59.

8. Ibid.

9. Ibid., pp. 59, 62.

10. Paulo Freire said: "I look at my friend James Cone . . . as a Third World man—it does not matter that he was born in the United States—it's an accident. He is in a world of dependence—of exploitation—within the First World" (p. 58). Assmann also referred to a Third World in the First World: "In the United States and Europe, there are people of the Third World—the poor and oppressed world" (p. 62).

11. This statement can be found in a book on the conference by Sergio Torres and John

Eagleson, eds., *Theology in the Americas* (Maryknoll, N.Y.: Orbis Books, 1976), pp. 359-60. It is also found in Wilmore and Cone, *Black Theology*, pp. 529-30.

12. Enrique Dussel, who was present at the Detroit 1975 conference but absent from the Geneva symposium, has a different interpretation of both events. He says: "This meeting, held August 18-25, 1975, began to overcome the incommunication with black theology (as could be seen in Freire-Assmann-Bodipo-Cone . . .). At Detroit there was a fruitful dialogue between black and Latin American theologians. . . ." (see his "The Political and Ecclesial Context of Liberation Theology in Latin America" in Sergio Torres and Virginia Fabella, eds., *The Emergent Gospel* [Maryknoll, N.Y.: Orbis Books, 1978], p. 192, note 45). I think Dussel gives an unfavorable representation of the Geneva symposium because he was not present and thus misread the emphasis on "incommunication." The "incommunication" at Geneva was not primarily referring to the dialogue between black and Latin American theologies but rather between both theologies *and* the theologies of Europe. I just do not understand how he can say that we left Detroit with a deeper understanding of each other.

13. For Gayraud Wilmore's account of this impact, see his "The New Context of Black Theology in the United States" in Wilmore and Cone, *Black Theology*, pp. 602-8.

14. This essay is included in ibid., pp. 350-59.

15. This document is found in ibid., pp. 345-49. This quotation is found on page 349.

16. For an account of this conference, see Jorge V. Pixley and Jean-Pierre Bastian, *Praxis cristiana y producción teológica* (Salamanca: Ediciones Sígueme, 1979).

17. Jurgen Moltmann, "On Latin American Liberation Theology: An Open Letter to José Miguez Bonino," *Christianity and Crisis*, vol. 36, no. 5 (March 29, 1976).

18. This essay is included in *Praxis cristiana y producción teológica* under the heading "Fe cristiana y praxis política," pp. 75-88.

19. An account of the meeting is found in *The Emergent Gospel*.

20. For two discussions of this matter, see my "Black Theology and Third World Theologies," in Wilmore and Cone, *Black Theology*, p. 461, note 13; and Sergio Torres's "Introduction" in *The Emergent Gospel*, pp. ix-x.

21. D. S. Amalorpavadass, "News and Comments: Ecumenical Dialogue of Third World Theologians," *Indian Theological Studies*, vol. 14, no. 4, (December 1977).

22. An account of this meeting is found in Kofi Appiah-Kubi and Sergio Torres, eds., *African Theology en Route* (Maryknoll, N.Y.: Orbis Books, 1979).

23. An account of this meeting is found in Virginia Fabella, ed., *Asia's Struggle for Full Humanity* (Maryknoll, N.Y.: Orbis Books, 1980).

24. See *HAYYIM*, vol. 1, no. 1 (January 1979), p. 5. For a fuller discussion of this matter, see my " 'Asia's Struggle for Full Humanity: Toward a Relevant Theology' (An Asian Theological Conference)" in Wilmore and Cone, *Black Theology*, pp. 593-601; see also my "A Black Perspective on the Asian Search for a Full Humanity" in Fabella, ed., *Asia's Struggle for Full Humanity*, pp. 182ff.

25. For an account of this conference, see my "Black Theology and Third World Theologies" in Wilmore and Cone, *Black Theology*, pp. 452f. Although several blacks were invited, I was the only black from the U.S. who attended this meeting.

26. Maryknoll, N.Y.: Orbis Books, 1976. See also Paulo Freire's "Prólogo a la edición española" in the Spanish edition of *A Black Theology of Liberation*.

27. This document is found in Wilmore and Cone, *Black Theology*, pp. 543-51.

28. See his "The New Context of Black Theology" in ibid., pp. 602f.

29. See his "Black Theology and Marxist Thought" in ibid., pp. 552-67; "Socialism and the Black Church," *New York Circus: A Center for Social Justice and International Awareness,* vol. 3, no. 5, October-November 1979, pp. 5-8; and "Black Theology and Socialist Thought," *The Witness*, vol. 63, no. 4 (April 1980), pp. 16-19.

30. Since the Jamaica meeting, Pablo Richards and blacks have overcome the tensions we experienced in Jamaica. We have come to realize that most of the difficulties we experienced in Jamaica had more to do with language than with the issue of race and class. Blacks spoke almost no Spanish (with the exception of Lloyd Stennette, a black priest from Costa Rica) and Richards could speak only a little English.

31. See *Risk*, p. 59.

Contributors

Alvarez, Carmelo E.: director of the Seminario Bíblico Latinoamericano, San José, Costa Rica.

Amboya, Manuel: member of the indigenous movement of the diocese of Riobamba, Ecuador.

Arns, Cardinal Paulo Evaristo: archbishop of São Paulo, Brazil, and honorary president of the International Ecumenical Congress of Theology.

Balasuriya, Tissa: Catholic priest and director of the Centre for the Study of Society and Religion, Sri Lanka.

Batista, Mauro: Catholic priest from São Paulo and pastor of a slum parish.

Boff, Leonardo: Brazilian Franciscan priest and director of the *Revista Eclesiástica Brasileira*.

Castro, Emilio: director of the Commission for World Mission and Evangelism of the World Council of Churches.

Chandran, J. Russell: president of the Protestant seminary of Bangalore, India, and president of the Ecumenical Association of Third World Theologians.

Chavannes, Barry: lecturer at the University of the West Indies, Kingston, Jamaica.

Concha, Miguel: theologian, author, and director of the Antonio Montesinos Center in Mexico.

Cone, James: Charles A. Briggs Professor of Systematic Theology at Union Theological Seminary, New York.

d'Escoto, Miguel: Maryknoll priest and secretary of state of Nicaragua.

Dussel, Enrique: professor in Mexico City and director of the Centro para el Estudio de la Historia de la Iglesia en América Latina (CEHILA).

Ferro, Cora: professor at the Universidad de San José, Costa Rica, and coordinator of "Mujeres para el Dialago."

Gómez de Souza, Luis A.: sociologist and member of the Instituto Joáo XXIII, Rio de Janeiro, Brazil.

Gutiérrez, Gustavo: Peruvian priest and author of *A Theology of Liberation*.

Hernández, Guillermina: leader of a popular women's group in Santander, Colombia.

Hernández Pico, Juan: Jesuit priest and member of the Instituto Histórico Centroamericano of Managua, Nicaragua.

Iglesias, María: religious sister from New York and co-director of the Hispanic project of Theology in the Americas.

Lara-Braud, Jorge: director, Council on Theology and Culture, Presbyterian Church in the U.S.

Melano Couch, Beatriz: professor of theology in the Protestant seminary of Buenos Aires, Argentina.

Mesters, Carlos: Carmelite missioner, author, and Scripture scholar working in Brazil.

Míguez Bonino, José: professor of theology in ISEDET seminary in Buenos Aires and vice-president of the World Council of Churches.

Muñoz, Ronaldo: Chilean pastoral theologian and professor at the Catholic University in Santiago, Chile.

Niles, Preman: Sri Lankan secretary for theological concerns of the Christian Conference of Asia.

Peloso da Silva, Ranulfo: labor organizer from Brazil active in basic Christian communities.

Rayan, Samuel: Jesuit priest and professor of theology in Delhi, India.

Reid, Alfred: Episcopal priest from Kingston, Jamaica, and professor of theology at the Episcopal Theological Seminary.

Sobrino, Jon: Jesuit priest from El Salvador and author of *Christology at the Crossroads*.

Stennette, Lloyd: Episcopal priest from Costa Rica and pastor of a parish in Limón.

Tekere, Ruvimbo: Zimbabwean student in social sciences at the University of Dar es Salaam, Tanzania.

Torres, Sergio: Catholic priest from Chile and executive secretary of the Ecumenical Association of Third World Theologians.

Vásquez, Gregorio: indigenous leader from Chiapas, Mexico, and participant in the pre-conference seminar in Chiapas.

Vásquez, Juanita: indigenous religious sister from Guatemala.

West, Cornel: professor at Union Theological Seminary, New York, and director of the Black Theology Project of Theology in the Americas.

Willebrands, Cardinal Johannes: Archbishop of Utrecht, Holland, and president of the Secretariat for Christian unity.